A
YANKEE WAY
WITH
WOOD

BERKSHIRE HOUSE PUBLISHERS
STOCKBRIDGE
MASSACHUSETTS

A YANKEE WAY WITH WOOD

by Phyllis Méras

For Tom

Crafts books from Berkshire House
A YANKEE WAY WITH WOOD by Phyllis Méras
By Ejner Handberg:
SHOP DRAWINGS OF SHAKER WOODENWARE, Vols. 1, 2, 3
SHOP DRAWINGS OF SHAKER IRON AND TINWARE
MEASURED DRAWINGS OF SHAKER FURNITURE AND WOODENWARE
MEASURED DRAWINGS OF EIGHTEENTH CENTURY FURNITURE

All the drawings in *A Yankee Way With Wood* are by Robert Pelletier
except those in Chapter 3, which were drawn by Mark Mulhall.

Cover and front matter design by Dianne Cooper Bridges
based on the original book by Houghton Mifflin.

This book was first published in 1975 by Houghton Mifflin Company.
A portion of the book appeared originally in *Americana*.

Library of Congress Cataloging-in-Publication Data

Méras, Phyllis.
A yankee way with wood / by Phyllis Méras - Rev. & updated
    p.   cm.
      ISBN 0-936399-49-X: $18.95
      1. Woodwork – New England. 2. Wood-carving –
New England. 3. Artisans – New England. I. Title.
TT180.M44   1993
674'8 – dc20   93-14589
            CIP

Printed in the United States of America
10 9 8 7 6 5 4 3 2 1

■ I am grateful to many for their help in the preparation of this book, especially Dr. John E. Wallace for his discerning examination — from the woodcraftsman's standpoint — of the directions in each chapter. Similarly helpful in technical aspects of the work were Joseph Chase Allen, Leighton Authier, Ed Benfield of Stanley Tools, Robert Berkvist, Douglas Cabral, William A. Caldwell, Charles Dudley, John M. Leavens, John W. Mayhew, Jr., John E. Méras, Helen Mills, Robert Mussey, Stanley and Polly Murphy, John R. Painter, Charles H. Spilman, Grace and Marie Turner, and Robert Wood.

And I am indebted to Donal MacPhee, who offered the title *A Yankee Way with Wood*, Thomas D. Stevens for his photographs, printing of photographs, and instruction in photography; Charles R. Brown, C. D. B. Bryan, Richard Nash, John Upton, Alan Perlman, and Peter Vandermark for their photographs; Shirley Mayhew and Robert G. Tobey for darkroom work, Florence Brown for varied secretarial tasks, and Stanley M. Carr for his suggestion on illustrations.

Helpful in the selection of craftsmen have been Linda Barrett, P. J. Kelly, Nelson W. Bryant, Jr., George Carlson; Mason Cocroft, Bill Holt, Rixford Jennings, Archie Post, Dr. George Starr, Frances Tenenbaum, Audrey Tichnor, Deborah Tobin, the Enchanted Doll House in Manchester Center, Vermont; the Fantastic Umbrella Factory in Charlestown, Rhode Island; the Massachusetts Audubon Society, the League of New Hampshire Craftsmen, the Vermont Council on the Arts, and the Victorian Barn in Damariscotta, Maine.

Providing hospitality during six months of travels were Paul and Molly Birdsall, Ned and Marylin Chou, Bridget Cooke, Nick and Ruth Daniloff, Yvette Eastman, Alan and Karen Fortney, Richard and Helen Freedman, Eric and Mary Pat Johnson, Elise and Otto Kreuser, Edmond and Cele Méras, John and Bonnie Méras, Sy and Mickey Pearlman, Michael Pollan, Tom and Dottie Stevens, Jack and Eleanor Upton, Ron and Susan Voake, Tom and Chris Wallace, Margaret Walton and Ray and Inge Weymouth of the Starlight Motel in Brunswick, Maine.

Finally, my thanks belong to my husband, Tom Cocroft, who did the original rough drawings of craftsmen's designs; to the late Hiram Haydn, and Stanley Burnshaw for his guidance in seeing a manuscript through publication, and to James and Sally Reston, Henry Beetle Hough, and the staff of the Vineyard *Gazette*, without whose generosity and encouragement there would have been no *Yankee Way with Wood*.

acknowledgments

■ In the evergreen forests of Maine and the hills of Vermont, where the Connecticut River meanders, where surf nudges the shores of Rhode Island and Massachusetts, where snow falls on New Hampshire mountains, craftsmen in wood have, for generations, whittled and carved and hammered and pegged. They have used the woods of the New England landscape — oak, ash, birch, white pine, sugar pine, black walnut, and basswood — to fashion their decorations, their boats, their boating and fishing and hunting gear.

Nearly two decades ago, at a time when there was a renewed interest in a return to a simpler life and a dissatisfaction with much that was being commercially produced, I first went looking for those perfectionist New Englanders, and New Englanders by adoption, who had no use for fiberglass and plastic. I found that there were many who had steadfastly stayed with, or valiantly gone into, work with wood.

The quality of their work, of course, varied. Some were artists, others artisans; some were primitives, some hopeful hobbyists. I looked for a cross-section of the best of them with the help of crafts societies and museum directors, fellow craftsmen, and crafts buyers.

Then I visited with them through a winter and early spring in their cellars and attic workshops,
by potbelly stoves in barns and sheds. I asked if they would provide directions and plans and drawings for some of the articles that they made — lobster pots, ladders and pitchforks, weathervanes, decoys and cigar-store Indians, even canoes and small boats.

I found the men and women whom I interviewed unfailingly generous in their willingness to tell others how to do what they do. Some were clearer than others in their way of giving directions. Some had philosophies of craftsmanship; others simply crafted because their forebears had.

I could not help wondering, though, how many of the younger generations of craftsmen — the philosophical college graduates of the sixties and seventies who had chosen not to embark on high-powered city careers, but had turned to a simpler country life — would tire of it after a while.

I felt fairly certain that the old-timers would stay with their craft, but I thought it likely that, before long, the young would give up work with their hands for the more cerebral pursuits for which they had been trained.

I was mistaken.

In the spring of 1993, I again sought the craftsmen of *A Yankee Way With Wood*. This time, to help me to find those of whom I had lost track, I enlisted the help of town clerks, police chiefs and postmen, close and distant relatives, town historians, friends and neighbors. As the craftsmen about whom I was asking had been generous of their time nineteen years ago, so their friends and
neighbors were generous this time in telling me what they could of the whereabouts of those I sought. With their help, I have renewed my craftsman acquaintances when I could and learned with sorrow of those whom death has taken.

In this new edition of *A Yankee Way With Wood*, there has been no updating of the original interviews, but in the few pages of this introduction, I bring news of where those craftsmen are today.

Though some have turned to more profitable pursuits, many have remained woodworkers. Others have written books about their craft. Of those who, in 1974, were the younger generations of woodworkers with whom I talked, about half still are working in wood.

Henri Vaillancourt continues to make birchbark canoes and snowshoes in Greenville, New Hampshire. Jan and John Newton still build dollhouses in South Chatham, Massachusetts. Ron Voake, though he has moved from Thetford Center, Vermont, to neighboring Norwich, works "just the way I always did, making wooden trains and trucks and rocking horses, Noah's arks and pull toys." He has, however, expanded his toy line from a handful to some one hundred items.

Andrew Marks, whose specialty was pipes in 1974, is now a sculptor in wood in Cornwall, Vermont.

Enterprising Scots-born John McLeod operates a woodworking plant, John McLeod, Ltd., selling cutting boards and Lazy Susans, clocks, and ready-to-assemble furniture to retail stores across the country and to the Williams-Sonoma and Crate and Barrel national chains. He also sells through a twenty-four-page mail order catalogue. Though he has given up doing the actual woodworking himself, he is the designer of his company's stock.

foreword
by Phyllis Méras

He admits, nowadays, to using "computerized routers and diamond cutters as well as the time-tested processes," but he insists that it is the skills and discipline he acquired in his early years of woodworking that have enabled him to go on.

David Sawyer, who took the art of wooden pitchfork-making he had learned in Pennsylvania-Dutch country to Vermont, now fashions Windsor chairs in Woodbury, Vermont. "It's interesting. Making them involves bending green wood the same way you bend wood to make a pitchfork."

Though George Havell, one of those to whom David Sawyer taught the art of pitchfork-making, today produces only a dozen or so pitchforks a year, he *uses* most of those he makes on the little farm that he now has.

His friend Stanley McCumber, a ladder-maker nineteen years ago, now lives in Charletown, New Hampshire. Similarly, he makes ladders only when he needs them nowadays to pick the pears and apples and peaches on his own fruit trees. "The New England orchards to which I used to sell my ladders are operating more marginally now," he says. He adds, however, that he believes the ladders he makes today are considerably superior to those he used to make. "I've learned that sawn Douglas fir or Sitka spruce makes the best rails and sawn ash or basswood the best rungs. Sawn wood is more durable than what I was using before and has fewer knots in it."

The combination of the cheaper carvings from the Orient now on the market and the need to pay college tuition for his children has forced second-generation carver Duncan Hannah to give up the full-time making of corner cupboard figures of sea captains and Scotsmen in kilts in favor of work as a right-of-way agent for the Central Vermont Public Service Company in Rutland. He still carves to order, however, and has some work in souvenir shops around the country.

Heirloom puzzle-maker Jeremy Guiles has now retired to Sarasota, Florida, and puzzle-making has become largely a hobby for him.

Still making miniature objects full time, however, is Harry Smith of Camden, Maine, though what he makes these days is usually for art museums or art galleries. "When I began in business," he recalls, "miniatures were toys. They've come a long way since then."

Not only is he still working in wood, but also he has learned to cast elaborate miniature tea and coffee sets in silver or gold, and is one of those who has written a book about his craft, *The Art of Making Furniture in Miniature*.

Stewart T. Coffin of Lincoln, Massachusetts is also showing others how to make the puzzles he used to create. He has written two crafts books, *The Puzzling World of Polyhedral Dissections* and *Puzzle Craft*.

Among those woodworkers who were in middle age when I last saw them, Edward G. Norton of Westbrook, Connecticut, has slowed down a little, but he continues to make and sell his miniature furniture across the country. Woodcarver Edward G. Boggis chisels and gouges cigar-store Indians in Claremont, New Hampshire, but he has also added carousel horses that he will make on order to his repertoire. "I guess I'm doing about what I always did, but maybe now it's a little nicer."

In the older generation of woodworkers, George Soule of Freeport, Maine, has reduced his carving to doing only limited editions of his decoys. William Godsoe of Bangor, Maine, who is seventy-eight, in the same way, will carve an occasional yellowlegs or a pair of chickadees to order, but he finds that his eyes tire quickly.

Only a few of the wood-workers with whom I visited those nineteen years ago have given up the woodworking craft entirely.

Maine resident Dick Gardner of Lincolnville let the making of toy sailboats "fall by the wayside" a few years ago in favor of developing a machine shop business specializing in making hardware for boat builders. Then he sold that business and retired.

Irene Taylor of Damariscotta, Maine, gave up doll-making when her husband became ill, but dreams, one day, of getting back to it.

In Winchester, New Hampshire, Jeremiah Thibault built his last birdhouse more than a dozen years ago and decided to become a traveler and see America. He has visited every state and much of Canada. He always tries to be home in spring, however, when the bluebirds nest in the houses he built for them in his yard. "Some of my houses are as much as twenty-five years old, I expect, but they're still standing," he says with pride.

Lobster-pot maker Vincent Clark is in a convalescent home in

Branford, Connecticut, these days, but nothing pleases him more than reminiscing about his lobster-pot-making days.

In Wakefield, Rhode Island, Stephen A. Tucker was forced to give up the making of veneered boxes after heart surgery. These days he displays his artistic talent instead in his effulgent garden.

Winthrop, Maine, fish-carver Lawrence C. Irvine has, similarly, transferred his enthusiasm for fish carving to gardening, although he says he would still like to carve again some day.

Leslie Randall of North Dartmouth, Massachusetts, who made the wheel for the yacht *America II*, replica of the famous America's Cup winner, is ninety now, and has slowed down over the last two years, but he has managed to make a rolltop oak desk for his son-in-law and a cherry table for his daughter.

Eight of the craftsmen in whose shops I spent many satisfying hours, those years ago, have died. Two, however — bird-carver Wendell Gilley of Southwest Harbor, Maine, and hope-chest and eagle-carver John Upton of Damariscotta, Maine — are remembered in museums.

Two years before his death in 1983, Wendell Gilley, in his late seventies then, proudly attended the ribbon-cutting for a museum in his honor in his home town. In it are all the birds he carved for his wife, as well as many that other owners of his handicraft have donated. And his old studio, moved to the museum, is now used as a classroom for the teaching of carving in the Gilley tradition.

John Upton's carvings, drawings, and notebooks, as well as some of his eagles, are now in the decorative arts department of the Maine State Museum in Augusta. And his consummate carving skill has been passed on, as well, to his grandson, Jonathan Whitney, a furniture-maker and finisher in Browenfield, Maine.

Boat-builder and designer, R. D. (Pete) Culler of Hyannis, Massachusetts, died in 1978, but his memory — and his boatbuilding — are kept alive in the three books he wrote, *Boats, Oars and Rowing*, *The Spray*, and *Skiffs and Schooners*, as well as in *Pete Culler's Boats* written after his death by John Burke.

Before ox-yoke maker Lauristan Vinal died at the age of eighty-nine in Jefferson, Maine, in 1987, he passed on his patterns to retired rural letter-carrier and shipyard-worker Ralph R. Bond, who had grown up watching him

at his work. Today, farmers showing oxen at fairs come from all across the state to get a Ralph Bond version of a Vinal bow and yoke.

Wind-machine designer Wilson Hutchins was seventy-nine when he died in 1984 surrounded, as always, by his whimsical wooden ducks and hunting dogs, wood-sawyers and butter-churners. Sadly, his old shop in Nobleboro, Maine, has been sold, and its colorful contents are gone.

Weathervane-designers J. Warren Raynes of Yarmouth, Maine, and Lawrence Winterbottom of Vineyard Haven, Massachusetts, are also gone now — the former in 1984, the latter in 1980. One day, Warren Raynes's son, Joseph, now an engineer with New England Telephone, would like to finish the hulls of ship weathervanes his father cut out. Winterbottom weathervanes, meanwhile, sit on many a Martha's Vineyard rooftop and mantelpiece.

Vermont tub-maker William Trieb died at age eighty-one in 1976, and Walter E. Johnson, whose wife grew up just across the road from the old Trieb shop, bought the property. One day he hopes to get back to making milking stools and tubs again in the Trieb manner in Jericho, Vermont.

I have enjoyed finding these master craftsmen again and talking with them of the satisfactions of creation. It is good to know that there continues, all across New England, to be a tradition of *A Yankee Way With Wood*.

A YANKEE WAY WITH WOOD

Halfway up the hill at Jericho Corners, Vermont, just next to the general store, not yet tumble-down, but not far from it, is the old white garage where, for sixty years, William Trieb has been making wooden tubs.

Out in front, as a symbol of his trade, there is likely to be a giant tub — as much as ten feet in diameter — resting up against the garage doors and yawning out toward State Route 15. Jericho used to be farm country. A decade ago, eighty dairy farms were scattered across its hills and black and white Holsteins speckled the green yellow pastures. And from its sugar bush came maple sap that made sugaring-off a part-time job for Jericho youngsters every year.

In those days, there were more than a dozen maple orchards of sturdy trees in the town. Only two of them still remain, but it was the maple orchards and the farms that made William Trieb a tub-maker. Today, at eighty, he is, as far as he knows, the last of his trade in the Green Mountain state.

Bill Trieb isn't loquacious, and he doesn't think much of publicity. "Nonsense," he is inclined to call it. But he does preen a little as he makes it known to curious passersby that there's nobody else in Vermont in his line of work. And if a visitor to his garage, unapprised of his age, asks him about it, he will teasingly respond with "How old would you guess?" before he proudly admits to being an octogenarian. "Funny thing," says Mr. Trieb, "I've had a lot of operations, but I've always come right back. Just healthy, I guess."

After a childhood in neighboring Essex, schooling in Wisconsin where an uncle and aunt lived, and service in World War I in the army in France, England, and Germany, he went to work in Jericho as an all-around carpenter. If you join him inside the garage, where he is likely to be stamping his feet in his rubbers, keeping his hands warm in woolen gloves, and wearing a quilted jacket and a wool cap, he will tell you how he came to be a tub maker. A wood stove heats his garage and the workshop piled high with barrel bottoms and staves, but, in Vermont tradition, Bill Trieb is no spendthrift. As afternoon comes, even in midwinter, even with guests on the premises, it's unlikely that he'll put extra wood on the fire.

Bill Trieb turned to tub making when the general store next door was called Steigel's and Carl Steigel went sugaring off. "He had

· 1 ·

SIXTY YEARS
A TUB-MAKER

a gathering tub that was six feet long by thirty-eight or forty inches across, and its bottom got rotten, and he asked me if I would fix it. I said I guessed I could and I did. He used it for years afterward to empty his buckets into," Mr. Trieb adds with satisfaction. "Secret of a good tub is using the right stock. You've got to know the moisture content of your wood. I buy native pine from Jonesville, Vermont. They let me pick out good quality. That doesn't mean without knots though. In tub making, knots don't hurt a thing — except black knots because they'll work their way out."

Mr. Trieb sighs as he talks and looks around at his lumber and staves and planters and troughs. "There's enough junk in here so it's hard not to break your neck," he says as he clambers over the planters after another item he makes — milking stools.

"Sell a lot of these now for TV-watching. Folks put the kids down near the set on them. They don't get in the way on a milking stool. Sometimes I sell one for each youngster in a family! Planters I sell mostly in the spring. They go with the season, I guess."

One of the giant-size tubs (they are William Trieb's favorite) went to General Electric, and another was bought by the University of Vermont. The price tag on the ten-foot tub is $64. Not a high price, he feels, since there are six or seven hours' work in a tub that size. He has no idea what they are being used for, but he is pleased that such distinguished organizations wanted them. He originally made them to be water-stock troughs. Rather to his amazement, in recent years, his six-foot-in-diameter tubs have been increasing in popularity. "They're really making quite a comeback. Young people are using them for bathtubs."

In the past from time to time, Mr. Trieb had an apprentice working for him, but he doesn't think much of hired help. "If you work alone, it's less bother. The young lads think they want to learn, but they stay about a week and then you never see them again."

Although he both works and lives alone, in an apartment above the garage, he doesn't, he says peering piercingly through his spectacles, feel lonely. "I have a lot of friends, and we do a lot of reading. We keep changing books around. I like the *Reader's Digest* and *Yankee*. I'm often still reading when other people are getting up, but I get up early too. I never was much of a hand at laying in bed."

Although he has done a little dairy farming ("I had mixed-up brands of cows — just a little place") along with his carpentry and tub making, it is the last two occupations of which he has always been fondest. "I've never really wanted to do anything else," he says, examining and tossing out a stave that displeases him. "It would be a pain in the neck to work for anyone else, and there's always been a great demand for my work anyway. Years ago, I did a lot of repairing of farmers' sleds and wagons, and I made churns and the molds for butter with the print marks on them. When the Depression came, I didn't see any Depression at all."

A scrambling on the shed roof interrupts him. "Cats," he comments laconically. "There are five or six cats I feed here. They climb the tree outside and jump up on the roof and let me know whenever they're hungry."

For cats, he feels an affection; for snowmobilers, anything but, especially when they interrupt him. "They're a damn nuisance. They're out here on this hill and you can't sleep when they start tearing up and down, those damn things."

His own years as a sportsman are long passed, but he used to hunt and fish, though it is with dismay that he remembers the last time he went ice fishing. "I fell in, and I haven't been back. I had on a big mackinaw and mittens and my arms were filled with fishing rods. We were after perch. I walked right into the lake. My brother and another fella fetched me out, or I wouldn't have got out. Oh, it was awful cold! We had a twenty-five-mile ride to get home too."

And he vividly remembers another hairbreadth escape — that one from the Vermont flood of 1927. He and his brother and two friends were doing construction work then on the schoolhouse in neighboring East Bolton. "We camped out there nights because it was easier, though we were boarding with a family in town.

"The night of the flood, somebody came by and told us we'd better not stay there because it was right near the Winooski River, so we came home to Jericho. Don't ask me why we didn't go to the family we were boarding with, but it's lucky we didn't. In the morning, when we went back to work, there was no schoolhouse left, and the flood had swept away everybody in that family we'd been staying with too. That was a terrible time!"

For William Trieb, making tubs is so much a matter of course after six decades that he has difficulty telling anyone else how to make them, but he tries to give pointers to interested visitors to his shop — as long as he is sure they are in earnest. He hasn't much use for fools, he says tartly.

1. Buy 1″ native pine stock — "Never use plywood — it's no good for moisture" at the lumber yard; this will actually be ¾″ thick. Saw the bottom 12¾″ in diameter. If a round of wood 12¾″ in diameter cannot be found, use pieces cleated together on the bottom by affixing an extra stave piece of any reasonable width going across the bottom pieces (Fig. 1).

2. Side staves should be about 2″ wide, and 14″ long, and also of pine. It may be necessary as you come near the end of fitting the staves together to plane down one or two of them so they go together tightly.

3. Approximately twenty staves will be needed for a 12¾″ tub. They should all be beveled at about a 10-degree angle so that they will fit together well. ("Of course, wood swells when it gets wet, but you don't want big cracks between the staves, all the same" [Fig. 2]).

MAKING A PLANTER TUB

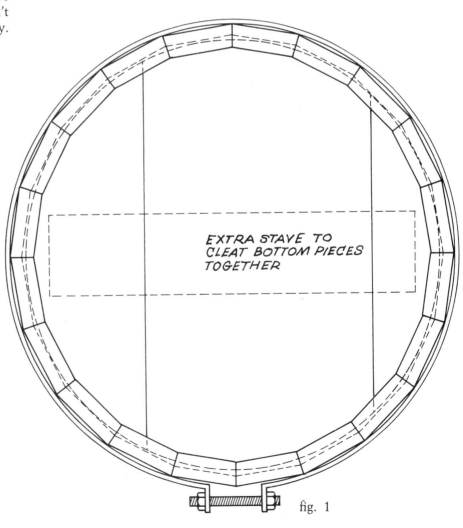

EXTRA STAVE TO CLEAT BOTTOM PIECES TOGETHER

fig. 1

4. Make a ¾″ rabbet in each stave ¾″ from the bottom to provide a groove into which the bottom of the tub will be wedged. ("I cut the grooves out on a table saw I made up. It's just ten of my thin circular saw blades together" is the way Mr. Trieb describes his apparatus, but a dado set or the use of an adjustable dado blade would be better for the amateur tub-maker. A saw and a chisel could also be used, of course [Fig. 2]).

5. When the staves have been beveled and rabbeted, fit them around the tub bottom, planing down if necessary. If the rabbeting has been properly done, the staves should stand erect.

6. With one six-penny box nail for each stave, use a hammer to drive the nails from the outside of the stave into the planter bottom to secure it while you prepare to bind the planter firmly together with steel strapping.

7. Take a piece of steel strapping ¾″ wide and 41½″ long. Clamp one end at the top

fig. 2

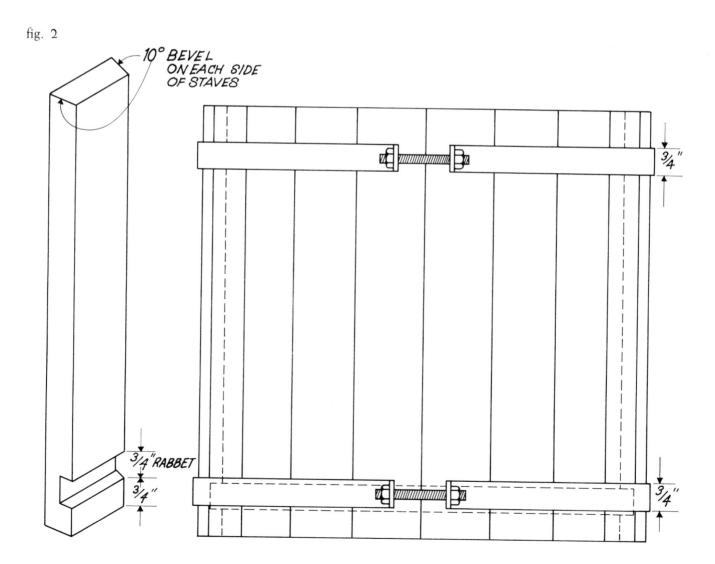

10° BEVEL ON EACH SIDE OF STAVES

¾″ RABBET

¾″

¾″

¾″

of the planter with a C-clamp and fit the strapping tightly around the planter 1″ from the top. It may be necessary to hammer it around the tub. Use a vise to turn up a piece about ⅝″ at both ends of the strapping. Remove the strapping from the tub and drill a ¼″ hole in the end of each turned-up piece. Then return it to its position 1″ from the tub top. Once more hammer it in place, this time joining the two ends with a 3″-long nut and bolt screwed tight. Use a hacksaw to saw off any excessive length from the bolt.

8. Repeat this procedure at the bottom of the tub so the strapping covers the ring of nails (Fig. 2).

9. Chamfer the outside edge of both the top and the bottom of the staves to prevent the tearing off and splintering of wood. Sand or file the flat surface of the staves at the top of the planter so they look smooth.

10. Drill 3 or 4 ½″ holes in the tub bottom to allow draining, and your tub is ready to be planted.

fig. 3 *Measuring the width of a planter*
(Thomas D. Stevens)

When a winter storm is blustering over Southwest Harbor, Maine, or the fog rolls in over green black waters, it is cozy in the workshop above the harbor where Wendell Gilley carves his wooden birds.

There is a touch of spring in his songbirds and signs of a crisp fall, with good hunting, in his wild turkeys, mallards, and black ducks. There is friendly palaver to be shared and a Siamese cat to be stroked.

Wendell Gilley used to be a plumber, always was a hunter, and although something of a taxidermist and a whittler, had never thought about carving birds till he visited the Museum of Natural History on a trip to Boston, where he saw two shelves of birds by Cape Cod's famous carver, the late Elmer Crowell. That was forty years ago, and he came home and carved his first bird and has been carving ever since.

He has been so successful at it that three United States presidents have had Gilley birds, and examples of his work have been shipped to France, Germany, Yugoslavia, Belgium, and Finland. For thirteen years, they were best sellers at the New York sporting goods store Abercrombie & Fitch, and today, Wendell Holmes Gilley ("I suppose I'm a relation of Oliver Wendell Holmes") is the acknowledged dean of New England folk bird carvers.

Wendell Gilley talks animatedly of his forebears — a grandfather who owned the land where Mr. Gilley was born, a great-grandfather who owned a three-masted schooner that sailed all over the world, a great-great-uncle who was drowned in a storm when he was carrying provisions to nearby Northeast Harbor — but he speaks of his own accomplishments shyly.

"I get satisfaction from being just a whittler. That's all there is to it. I don't figure I'm an artist. I can put in a pretty good bathroom though."

While he chats, Mr. Gilley, a white-haired, gentle-voiced man, is likely to be touching up the feathers on a basswood great blue heron or whittling an uppity tail on a basswood wren. He favors basswood for his carvings because it is fine-grained, tough, has neither pitch nor knotholes, and is easy to work with. "And I can get it up here just about fifty miles away. There are no knotholes because it grows straight up with no limbs. Sometimes there are little black spots here and there, but that's all there is in the way of imperfection."

·2·
TWO BIRD CARVERS OF MAINE

Nineteen years ago he gave up plumbing to devote himself full time to carving, and although now, at sixty-nine, he has slackened off a bit and carves just for himself and on order, the Gilley bird workshop is not sparsely populated.

Puffing on his pipe and putting on and taking off his green camouflage hunting hat, he shows off his workshop. But his pride — a quiet kind at best — comes more often from the rare bird that he has stuffed than from his own handicraft. He is a discerning naturalist impressed with unusual finds.

"Up there," he comments, pointing to a shelf of upland game birds, "I have a red-tailed grouse from North Carolina. And there's a cinnamon quail that came from a friend in California. And here's a wood hen that was flying in Florida. Over there" — he motions across the room — "are two blue quail from the King Ranch in Texas. See the differences among all these quail. And up here I've got a boreal owl. They're a very rare visitor from the north. They breed in northern Canada and only occasionally come to this part of the United States. This one dropped out of a friend's apple tree in Ellsworth. Starved to death apparently."

Game birds and birds of prey are Mr. Gilley's specialty, for he knows them well from his years as a hunter. "Oh, I used to go after eiders and black ducks and scoters and golden-eyes. These are good duck-hunting waters here around Southwest Harbor," he said, nodding toward the outside, "and when I went out, I'd always take a newspaper along so if I got a good specimen, I could bring it back and stuff it. You fold the newspaper up like a cone and slip the bird inside to keep it clean. This year, though, I guess I'm getting kind of soft. I only went hunting once. I'd rather see the birds fly."

Gilley birds are often recognized by the naturalness of their poses. "Those just come to you if you're in the woods a lot," he says matter-of-factly. But also, sometimes, there are live birds in his menagerie. "I had a pair of quail one time. This man in North Carolina was going to get me a pair of quail. I thought they would be dead ones, but not at all. He flew them up and the hen laid eggs on the way. I had to send them back though. I couldn't kill them, and I couldn't keep them indoors in winter with the cat."

Although almost all of Mr. Gilley's life has been spent in Southwest Harbor, there have been recent winters that he has spent in Florida, and one of his most memorable excursions among birds was in the Everglades where he went on an Audubon field trip and watched the herons. "That particular day, no one showed up but John Dennis, the guide — he's quite a noted ornithologist — and me, so we just went out alone together. We saw ospreys and spoonbills and also ani, which are called graveyard birds all over the Keys. They're fascinating-looking birds with bills like puffins, coal black in color."

When Wendell Gilley is not watching birds or hunting them, stuffing them or carving them, he is almost certain to be reading about them. One of his most popular carvings is of a mother loon carrying her young on her back, a sight he says he has never actually seen. "But I know about it because I've read about it and seen it on TV. I read all the time about birds," he says, perching on a stool by a shelf filled with bird books. "I've got about every bird book published, I guess. I'm apt to sit down at night and read and read and look at pictures." He urges any potential bird carver to do the same. For information and pictures of waterfowl he recommends *Ducks, Geese and Swans of North America,* published by the Wildlife Management Institute in Washington, D.C., *Birds of Song and Garden* by the National Geographic Society, and Eric Porter's *Birds of North America.* He suggests, too, the National Wildlife Federation in Washington, which has good prints of birds that can be used as models by carvers.

He also proposes that the bird-carver-to-be get plenty of carving practice.

"I whittled all the time when I was a kid. I was never without a jackknife. I made little sleds and ox yokes. My grandfather had horses and I did a funny little old horse and horse sleds and whistles." Today, he finds both X-acto knives and matte knives with adjustable handles particularly useful in whittling.

When you ask Wendell Gilley for advice about bird carving, he is more than ready to give it, to turn on the band saw that he uses for cutting out the shape of most birds that are to be life-size, the belt sander he uses to smooth wings and other flat surfaces, the contour sander that is most effective on rounded surfaces, and ¼" electric drill that he finds handy for drilling holes to insert wires in legs. He emphasizes as he does so, however, that complex, sophisticated machinery is not necessary for the amateur carver; there are a great many birds that can be carved simply with a band saw and a good knife.

He says that he enjoys giving advice, and he has written two books on handcrafted birds, the latest, published in 1972 by Hillcrest Publications, is *The Art of Bird Carving*.

"I like to think that I've helped somebody in my lifetime. A friend said to me one day, 'Wendell, when you die, you will have left something. People will have pleasure for years from the carving you've done,' and I sort of look at it that way too. It's the same way when I'm selling birds. I don't want my prices to be so high people will think I'm trying to roast them. When people write to me about bird carving, I try to answer them at once. It pleases me to help people out."

One of the birds he is most likely to suggest as a starter for a new carver is his famous loon with her young.

CARVING A LOON

1. Use soft basswood or white pine, making sure if you use the latter that it is free of pitch. You can determine this by cutting into it at a 45-degree angle and leaving it in a warm place. If there is pitch in it, it will ooze out. Do not use this piece.

2. You will need a piece of wood about 10" long, about 5" wide, and about 3" from top to bottom for the body and a block about 5" long, at least 3½" from top to bottom, and 1¼" thick for the head.

3. Trace the body pattern (Fig. 1, 2) from the top and side views on the large piece of wood.

4. On the small piece, trace only the horizontal view of the head (Fig. 2). The vertical shape can be easily carved.

5. With a band saw, cut out the vertical shape of the body and fasten the two pieces of wood that are left over when you are finished to the body with Scotch tape. These will be used later to make baby birds.

Duck detail

6. Saw out the side view of the body, and, from the smaller block, saw out the side view of the head.

7. Drill a 1/8" hole in each block where the neck and body will meet and insert an eight-penny finish nail, with both of its ends filed sharp, as a dowel. Next glue the head to the body with Elmer's glue or any good glue in whatever position you wish, facing straight ahead or at an angle. Fit the head and the body together as closely as possible so the seam will not show.

8. When all this is done, it is time to start "chipping" the bird into shape. A rasp, as well as a knife, is useful for this purpose. Sand the bird with medium-grit sandpaper and then cut in the details on the beak, the wings, and tail feathers. It may help if you put the bird in a vise while you are working. To do this, screw a block of wood about 3" long by 1" square to the bottom of the body and put this in the vise jaws so as not to injure your bird.

9. Mark the places for the eyes and drill 1/4" holes for them. Taxidermist's eyes, which come attached on a soft wire, are good. Cut the wire, leaving 1/4" on each eye, and insert the eyes in the drilled holes, or simply paint the eyes on. Use a carpenter's nail set of the appropriate size for the bird to mark the indentation for the eye and twist it to mark the indentation. Paint the whole eye the iris color (red, in a loon). When the iris is dry, paint on the black pupil. Use artist's oils or acrylics.

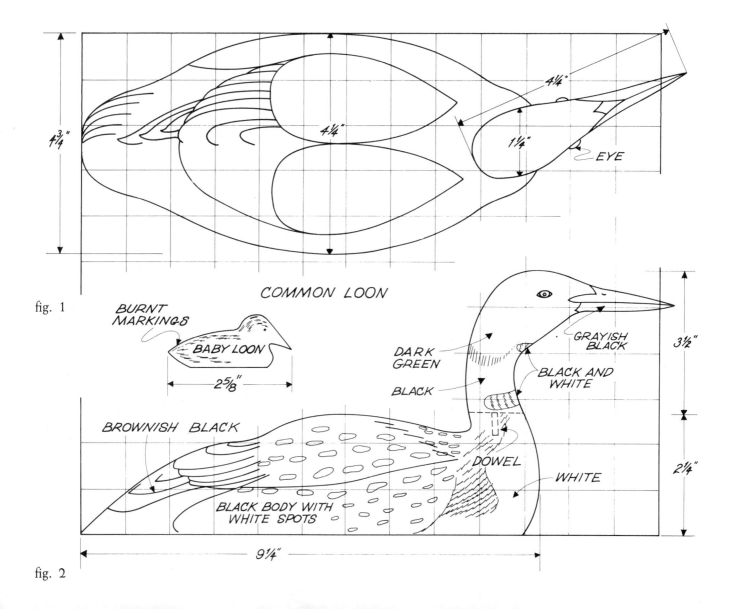

fig. 1

COMMON LOON

fig. 2

10. Prime the bird with gesso. Let it dry and do finish-sanding. Then, following the pattern in Fig. 1 and using the ends of a worn short-bristle brush or a sable brush, paint the breast of the bird white. A worn brush produces a natural effect. For loons, Mr. Gilley prefers acrylics to oils, for they dry faster and white can be painted over black without showing through. Paint the wingtips brownish black, the head dark green stippled with black. Paint the loon's back grayish brown or brownish black. Visit a wildlife sanctuary or consult a color photo for the correct shading. Once the back is dry, paint white spots on it and draw dark breast lines. White spots should also be painted on the throat (Fig. 2) and on the sides of the neck with black lines going through them.

11. Now shape the young birds from the leftover wood. Mr. Gilley does not paint them at all but simply uses an electric burning pen (Fig. 3) and colors the baby birds' bills black with a felt-tip pen. The babies may either be glued to the mother's back or simply set on it.

12. Finally, glue a piece of felt to the bottom of the mother bird to help her sit steadily on a table or mantelpiece.

fig. 3   *Burning bird feathers with an electric burning pen*

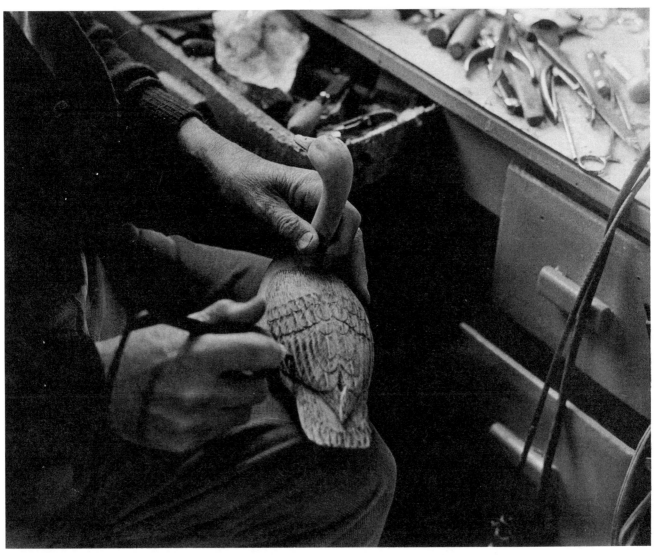

One of Mr. Gilley's staunchest admirers (who is, in turn, admired by Wendell Gilley) is William Godsoe of Bangor, Maine, a jeweler for years until his right eye suffered excessive strain from his use of the jeweler's loop.

About twelve years ago, after his wife gave him a book on carving when he was ill in bed, he began carving birds as a pastime. Now it is his full-time career.

William Godsoe paints a sandpiper

"I learned patience from the jewelry business and was accustomed to working with small things. I'd always liked to whittle and carve," he says. To perfect his technique, Mr. Godsoe got in touch with Mr. Gilley. Soon they were comparing their thoughts on the proper methods of burning feathers, the making of lead feet, the inserting of eyes.

A tall, bespectacled, scholarly looking man who whistles about his work, Mr. Godsoe's shop is a small room off his living room. Although in the past he did some hunting, as a city man he has had less opportunity than Mr. Gilley to be close to nature. And since he is not a taxidermist, it is largely from books that he copies his birds. Like Wendell Gilley, though, he is enthusiastic about sharing his knowledge.

One of the easiest birds to make, he feels, is the sandpiper. "All you need is basswood or native punkin' pine six inches long by two and one-half inches thick by four inches wide and a paper pattern" (Fig. 4).

MAKING A SANDPIPER

fig. 4

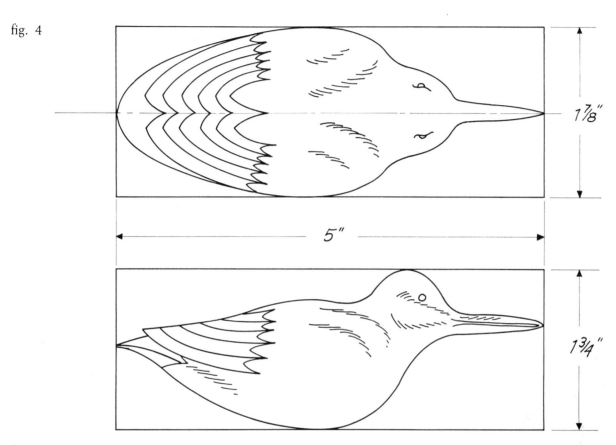

1⅞"

5"

1¾"

fig. 5 *LIGHT BROWN TAIL FEATHERS*

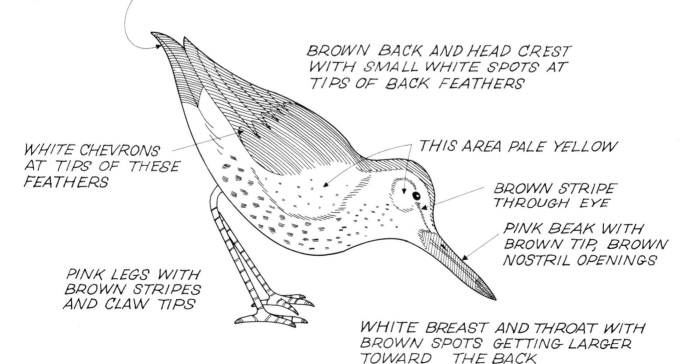

BROWN BACK AND HEAD CREST
WITH SMALL WHITE SPOTS AT
TIPS OF BACK FEATHERS

WHITE CHEVRONS
AT TIPS OF THESE
FEATHERS

THIS AREA PALE YELLOW

BROWN STRIPE
THROUGH EYE

PINK BEAK WITH
BROWN TIP, BROWN
NOSTRIL OPENINGS

PINK LEGS WITH
BROWN STRIPES
AND CLAW TIPS

WHITE BREAST AND THROAT WITH
BROWN SPOTS GETTING LARGER
TOWARD THE BACK

1. Saw the bird body out on a band saw. The head may come from the same piece of wood as the body, but only if, in what remains, there is a piece that will allow the grain to go with the length of the bill. If it runs across the bill, according to Mr. Godsoe, the bill will break.

2. With chisel and knives, perfect the body of the bird. Do rough blocking out at first with a sander if you wish. Similarly, once the bird's head has been cut out with a saw, perfect it with chisels and knives and by sanding finely.

3. Glue the head to the body in a lifelike way with Elmer's glue. To make sure that there is no seam where the two parts are joined together, cut a V shape out of the seam and fill it with plastic wood. When dry it can be filed smooth so that no seam shows. "It used to be," says Mr. Godsoe, "that you made your birds as smooth as you could get them — almost like glass — but then Wendell realized birds aren't like that and began roughing them up. A goose's neck, for example, is quite striated." Paint the bird with an undercoat of gesso white.

fig. 6 *Using two-inch hardwood blocks to make bird feet*

4. Carve the wing feathers and burn in any feathers you wish. (Mr. Godsoe does less burning than Mr. Gilley. On the sandpiper, the only burning he does, with a 5/8″ burning rod as compared to Mr. Gilley's 3/16″ rod, is on the primary and secondary wing feathers. Mr. Godsoe grinds the tip of his burning pen down to a skew edge with a file.

5. To simulate neck feathers, take a box nail filed to a sharp edge and attach it to a flexible shaft. Then, using the nail head like a small grinding wheel, scribe lines on the bird's neck, head and body. When the bird is painted, these lines simulate the fine line of feathers and also break up the sheen of the oil paint. When painting, begin with a flat white paint. When it is dry, paint in the feathers with oils (Fig. 5). Use any good bird book with color illustrations as your model.

6. Attach the legs, being sure to imitate movement.

"Put one foot ahead of the other, or something like that," Mr. Godsoe says. For legs, use No. 12 copper wire. Make sure the pieces you choose are 1/4″ or 1/2″ longer than you wish legs to be, for extra length will be inserted into the base later. For feet, use lead. Attach the legs to the bird by drilling a 1/8″ hole into the torso. Fasten them in place with Elmer's glue.

7. To make the feet, take 2″ hardwood blocks (Fig. 6) and, with a gouge, dig out a footprint in one of the blocks. Then make a small channel in the interior surface of the sides of both blocks of wood so liquid lead can be poured in. Melted lead pipe is fine for this purpose, melted in an old, stainless steel spoon with a propane torch. The molten lead will cool immediately and can be removed. Drill a hole in the lead foot after you have removed it from the mold. Put the leg wire through the hole and solder it to the foot, being sure to leave 1/4″ to 1/2″ of wire below the foot to go into the base. Paint the legs and feet with oil paint.

8. Select your base. (Mr. Godsoe likes to go searching for driftwood that goes well with his birds.) Finish the base or leave it unfinished, as you choose. Mark the spots on it where the feet will go, and drill holes to correspond with them that are one size larger than copper leg wire. Then, to attach feet, cover the extension of each leg wire with Elmer's glue and insert them into the holes in the base. Push down on the bird so that its feet are resting directly on the base and the leg wire has disappeared.

"If you really want to make a bird, work at it and work at it and your efforts will pay off" is Mr. Godsoe's advice.

Andrew Marks was sitting in the sun in Carmel Valley, California, with a guitar-maker friend when he decided to become a pipe maker.

"My friend had a nice house. He was able to support himself. He was doing something he liked to do. I'd been through college. I'd spent two and a half years in Vista in Appalachia and Philadelphia. I'd decided it was time to take off and had trundled everything up and gone out to California. But I still hadn't found what I wanted to do.

"There I was sitting looking at my old friend pipe. All of a sudden I began thinking about pipes. There are only a couple of dozen pipe makers in the country. I was familiar and friendly with pipes. I've been smoking a pipe for ten or twelve years, I guess. I knew I had to make a living at something. I'd grown up around good design. My father is in the architectural metals business and my mother is a writer. So I went to see a pipe maker who was going out of business and was willing to teach me the fundamentals."

Mr. Marks, a 1966 graduate of Middlebury College, of course puffs on a pipe as he talks in the Frog Hollow Crafts Center in Middlebury, Vermont, where he has now established his own pipe-making shop. He is a tousled, earnest young man with dark, curly hair and a dark, curly beard, and his smooth red brown pipe pokes cheerily out above the beard.

"This life has proved very pleasant for me," he says. "I make about a pipe a day and they sell for twenty-five dollars to five hundred dollars. I use the best briar in the world, and it's nice to be working with fine things."

Andrew Marks chose Vermont to return to because he had loved its peace and beauty when he was a student. When he first decided to establish himself in the country, he bought a 16' x 22' motel unit in neighboring New York state, had it floated across Lake Champlain, and built a workshop in the woods in Pittsford, Vermont. But that proved a little more isolated than he wanted, so he moved to Middlebury.

"I'm a little worried about the future for Vermont though," he says sadly. "The face of the state is changing. It's threatening to become ex-urban. Back in the sixties, I had the feeling I was a unique breed here, but no longer. Land prices used to be one hundred dollars an acre and now they're one thousand dollars. That gives you

• 3 •

"MY OLD FRIEND PIPE"

some idea what's happening. But I still like it here," he adds quickly before launching into a long and loving discussion of pipes and how to make them.

"I remember my first pipe," he reminisces. "I was fourteen or fifteen and I was at home for a day or two. My father smoked a pipe and I thought that was nice, so I went down to Eighty-sixth Street and Broadway — I grew up in New York City — and I bought a two-dollar-and-fifty-cent thing and a pack of Bond Street tobacco and I went home feeling like the cat's pajamas — doing a sneaky thing behind everyone's back. From then on, I liked having my pipe and tobacco."

Briar, Andrew Marks says, is the king of pipes; meerschaum the queen. "Corncob is a damn nice material that may get bitter fairly quickly but gives a good smoke for the time that it lasts." And apple and cherry make decent pipes easily produced by the amateur.

Mr. Marks tugs at his beard and his hazel eyes grow thoughtful as he explains that he is trying his best to do very good work in his pipe making and is delighted to pass on any tips that he knows to others.

"But it just isn't feasible for the ordinary person to make a briar pipe. It's terribly expensive to buy briar, and it's hard to work with. I pay ten dollars a block for my briar and I only get one pipe out of a block. Briar comes from the burl that grows right above the root system of the heath tree, they call it, that grows in Algeria and Greece and Spain and Corsica and Italy. Algerian briar is the most famous, but it's almost nonexistent now.

"Anyway, the heath tree takes 100 years to grow a usable burl. And after it's grown and before the pipe maker buys it, there's a long curing process. After it's cut, it's put in the soil, covered with burlap and leaves and more soil and left there for half a year. Then it's taken out and boiled for twenty-four hours and buried again for six months." Mr. Marks pulls an ugly chunk of it out of a basket to illustrate what it looks like in its rough state. Beside it he lays a graceful, polished, finished pipe and smiles.

"What makes a good pipe? For me, you need briar of very good quality. Then it must be cut correctly and drilled correctly with walls of the proper thickness to allow the pipe to smoke coolly without being overly heavy. If you get the walls too thin, they'll burn through. If they're too thick, the pipe will be unwieldy. You want a graceful, well-balanced bowl.

"Then, of course, you have to know how to pack a pipe properly for a good smoke. 'Pack the bottom like a baby; the middle like a woman; the top firmly like a man' is what they say. There should be a springiness in the tobacco when the pipe is packed but not airiness."

To make a cherry or an apple pipe, a minimum of equipment is needed — an electric drill, drill bits, two wood rasps (rough and fine half-round), lots of sandpaper, and vegetable oil. "Then you cut a limb off a tree — a chunk big enough to make a pipe — six inches by three inches, I'd say. Apple tastes pretty good. Cherry has a nice grain to it. Make your own choice."

One of the things that makes pipe making such a satisfying experience for Andrew Marks is experimenting with design. Often the shape or grain of the briar determines what the pipe should be.

SELECT YOUR PIPE OF APPLE OR CHERRY LIMB OR ROOT.

fig. 1

"Each briar is sculpture. Before I came to pipe making, I'd been looking and looking around for something I could like doing and be my own overseer. I don't think I could have found anything I'd enjoy better."

Mr. Marks believes firmly that "a pipe should fit its smoker." He refuses, for example, to sell a pipe without some idea of the person it is for. "How tall is he? How much does he weigh? Does he wear glasses? Does he hold a pipe in his teeth or his hand?" are a few of the questions he asks as he lays out a selection of big and small pipes for a potential buyer. He displays them, rough-topped and smooth-topped, on velvet on top of the worn braided rug on the floor of his sunny pipe studio.

If his advice on pipe cleaning is asked, he will readily give it, but he never foists it if it isn't sought.

"You should ream the pipe out so the carbon on the inside doesn't exceed the thickness of a dime," he says. "Never take the stem out when the pipe is hot because the wood expands and there's a danger of its cracking. What's the difference between a good pipe and an ordinary one? The difference between tequila and fine wine."

Apparently, Andrew Marks makes the fine pipe grade, for he is known among pipe connoisseurs as the "Bach of Briar."

Here are his directions for making a cherry or apple pipe.

1. Select your pipe material from an apple or cherry limb or root (Fig. 1).

2. Saw your wood to a workable size. Cut off 1, 2, and 3 (Fig. 2).

3. Look at your wood and draw the design for your pipe on the side (Fig. 3).

MAKING A SMOKING PIPE

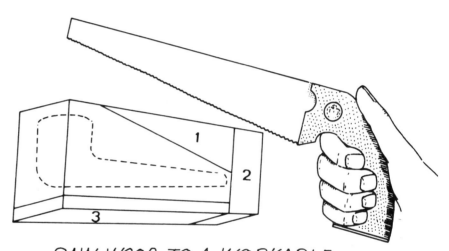

SAW WOOD TO A WORKABLE SIZE. CUT OFF 1, 2 AND 3.

fig. 2

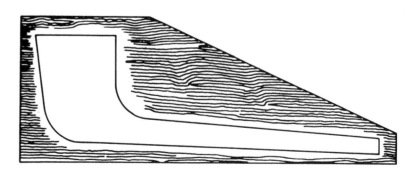

LOOK AT YOUR WOOD AND DESIGN YOUR PIPE ON THE SIDE.

fig. 3

4. Drill your pipe with an electric hand drill, 5/32″ bit for stem, large bit for bowl. Try to get the holes to meet at the bottom of the bowl for good draw (Fig. 4). Put a stop mark on your drill bits so you don't drill too far. If you do, it's off to the woods again.

5. Take your rough rasp and start rasping until you get your rough shape. It's a good idea to put your pipe in a vise while you're doing this. "It took me fifteen hours to make my first pipe," Mr. Marks says, "so don't get discouraged. If you really want to save time, you can use a coping saw here" (Fig. 5). Then you fine rasp for smoothing and firming your shape. Use the half-round rasp to get into the curves and do the major shaping. While you're rasping, leave about a 5/16″ neck around the bowl so it won't burn too hot.

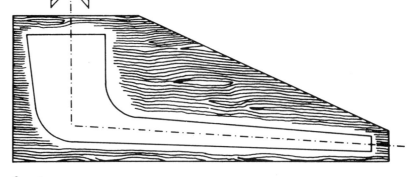

DRILL YOUR PIPE WITH AN ELECTRIC HAND DRILL. 5/32″ BIT FOR STEM. LARGE BIT FOR BOWL. TRY TO GET HOLES TO MEET AT BOTTOM OF BOWL FOR A GOOD DRAW. PUT A STOP MARK ON YOUR DRILL BITS SO YOU DON'T DRILL TOO FAR. IF YOU GOOF, IT'S OFF TO THE WOODS AGAIN.

fig. 4

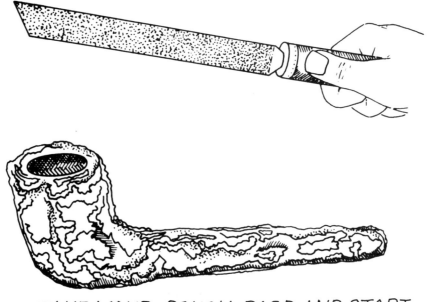

TAKE YOUR ROUGH RASP AND START A'RASPIN. 'TIL YOU GET YOUR ROUGH SHAPE. THEN YOUR FINE RASP FOR SMOOTHING AND FIRMING YOUR SHAPE.

fig. 5

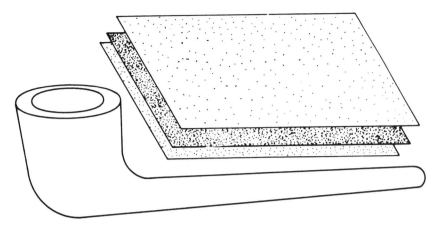

SAND, SAND, SAND AND THEN OIL.

EQUIPMENT NEEDED:
1. ELECTRIC DRILL – 2. DRILL BITS
3. TWO WOOD RASPS (ROUGH AND
FINE, HALF ROUND) – 4. SANDPAPER,
AND LOTS OF IT – 5. VEGETABLE OIL.

fig. 6

6. Start rough sandpapering (Fig. 6). Take your time. "This is *your* pipe!" Mr. Marks emphasizes. Then gradually use finer and finer sandpaper. The higher the grit, the finer the sandpaper. If you begin with 50-grit, you will gradually use a larger grit to remove rough sanding marks. Each grit should remove the marks of the grit before it. Finish with No. 600-grit sandpaper (if you have the patience)!

7. Use a little nose grease to bring out the grain of the wood. "Just rub your pipe lovingly against the side of your nose. If you're fastidious, use Mazola or peanut oil instead. Then fill up your pipe and enjoy it!"

A burl and the pipes it makes

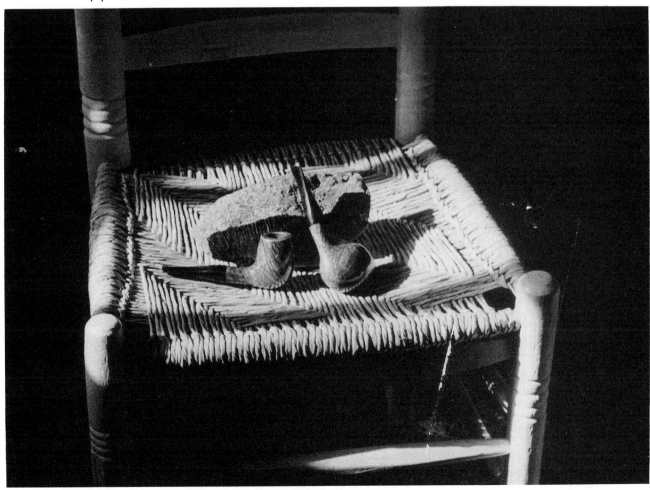

We found a good, deep hole and put *The Cricket* in it," Dick Gardner says. "I loaded her full of rocks. I sailed her there off the spar buoy to where it was two hundred and eighty feet deep. It was a breezy, sunny day. I took a big auger bit and drilled her full of holes and climbed into the skiff with Carol. *The Cricket* went down as straight as an arrow. I was crying. We both were crying. I wouldn't sell that boat. She was as old as I am. She was one of the original Beetle catboats — thirteen feet overall with a six-and-a-half-foot beam. It was time to get rid of her, but I couldn't stand letting anyone else have her and maybe let her rot on a lonely beach somewhere. So we had a Viking funeral, and there she is half a mile out there."

Dick Gardner, toy boat maker and marine hardware producer, nods toward Maine's West Penobscot Bay. Friendship sloops tacked in the distance, and a 50,000-ton cargo vessel puffed its way in the shipping channel that leads to Bucksport, Searsport, and Bangor.

Richard Gardner is a stocky, rugged mechanical engineer, but his voice grew tender as he talked of *The Cricket*.

Ever since he was a youngster leaving the busy streets of West Roxbury, Massachusetts, to spend his summers in Stockton Springs, Maine, he has had a soft spot in his heart for boats.

"I remember how we used to sail on the Eastern Steamship Line. We'd board at night in Boston and be on Penobscot Bay by morning. And as soon as we got here, we'd go to see 'Uncle' George Hopkins. He was Stockton postmaster in those days and one of those honorary uncles kids have. He'd always have toy sailboats for us that he'd made in the winter. And those little boats really sailed! They turned us into shore rats, that's what they did. We'd put on our bathing suits and go out with them and just stay for hours and hours. I guess I learned a lot about sailing from those little boats. When I was ten or twelve and my dad bought a couple of skiffs with centerboards, I knew how to rig them up with burlap bags and steering oars, and we'd go offshore and come tearing in!"

One boat led to another, and for a good part of his life, Dick Gardner has made his living from them — sometimes from sailing, sometimes from boat building, today from the hardware he makes in his machine shop and from his ver-

• 4 •

A LOVE AFFAIR WITH SAILBOATS

sion of "Uncle" George Hopkins' toy sailboat — a twenty-four-inch-long model with a jib, mainsail, and deckhouse that was a best seller in the years he was making them in large quantity for the children's toy store, F.A.O. Schwarz.

Mr. Gardner began making the toy sailboats of his childhood in the 1950s when he and his wife, Carol, quit the city. He had finished army service in the Signal Corps and had been studying engineering at Northeastern University; his wife was a student at the Boston Museum of Fine Arts School. On a schooner cruise Down East they read about subsistence farming.

"And we were impressed by the idea of it," Dick Gardner recalls, "so we bought a couple of goats and a couple of hens. We came up to Stockton Springs because we'd both known it as kids. We had about an acre of land and we grew beets and turnips and potatoes and tomatoes and beans and carrots and cabbages. I'll admit it was just subsistence farming in a small way, and I had to take a job, too, in a mill supply house in Bangor, but we were able to enjoy the good life, and that's what we wanted."

The Gardners also discovered that "you can reach back so easily in Maine," as they put it. "We look out on the same landmarks here that people did in the seventeen hundreds," Carol Gardner says. "In Maine, especially in this area, you can go to a particular place and say 'so and so was here a generation ago' and it's just as if he still was."

In the settlement of Lincolnville Beach, where they live, there are only two dozen year-round families, a general store, and a post office. Even in summer, the population only increases to about 100. The Gardners' cottage is a former fisherman's shack where Carol Gardner has planted both indoor and outdoor gardens that glow with gay blossoms, has painted the walls buttermilk blue, arranged Sandwich glass on the mantelpiece, covered the beds with pink patchwork coverlets, and hung antique maps of the county and oil paintings of family-owned schooners on the walls.

"I guess there's no doubt about our having been drawn back by the ancestral ties," she admits.

In nearby Sandy Point, where green-shuttered white houses face the bay, her great-great-grandfather — a blacksmith, boat builder, and merchant mariner — built a homestead in 1820. It passed out of family hands, but the Gardners have now bought it back and are restoring it.

Dick Gardner chuckles over his wife's enthusiasm for history and is inclined to polish his glasses self-consciously when she begins to relate how his great-great-grandfather built America's first commercial railroad in 1826 to carry the granite needed for the Bunker Hill Monument from the quarries in Quincy to the hilltop.

"The railroad was four miles long and could lift five tons," she quotes brochures of the day as saying. "Gridley Bryant was the name of Dicky's great-great-grandfather."

At such times, Dick Gardner is likely to try to tell adventure yarns instead about the two years after high school when he took jobs on yachts.

"The first boat I sailed on was a 120-foot twin-screw motor vessel out of New Bedford called *The Galaxy*. With the second one, a ninety-six-foot Dutch pilot schooner made of iron for North Sea Service, we had quite a time. We almost lost her in that boisterous stretch of water off Diamond Shoals along the Carolina coast. It's always bad there in wintertime and this wasn't any exception. We were going from City Island, New York, to Nassau in the West Indies. I remember I was below eating and all of a sudden the boat took a list to port and everything got dark. Water came pouring in through the vents.

"But we were lucky. We had a Gloucesterman named Johnny Veeder at the wheel, and he'd had foresight enough to put his arms through the wheel and hang on for dear life. You know, at sea, they say every seventh wave is larger than usual, and this one that hit us was a seventh one and she just pooped over us. When the wave was gone, Johnny no longer had a binnacle in front of him, but at least he had the wheel.

"After that, there was one more schooner I sailed on, and then it was wartime and everyone was selling his yacht to be an antisubmarine boat."

In postwar years, after he moved to Maine, Dick Gardner tried his hand at boat building as well as sailing. He worked in several yards. He also built himself a salmon wherry and his daughter a turnabout. But five years ago, he decided to become a full-time craftsman, cleared off some woodland behind his cottage, had the lumber sawed, and built himself a shop with the wood.

For $600 at an estate clearing, he purchased all of a machine shop of the 1920s. "It was put together as a hobby shop by a retired engineer, but he almost never used it," Dick Gardner explains as he ducks out the kitchen door, crosses a few feet of grass, and is in with the whirring machinery of the past.

"I have five machines all powered with one electric motor that drives a line shaft through a six-inch-wide leather belt that puts everything in motion," he shouts above the commotion. "It's a method of operation that was discarded in the early nineteen forties, but, at the price I paid, it suits me fine. It allows me to have that personal satisfaction that comes with craftsmanship — with evolving the idea of what you're going to make, then making the finished product, and — hopefully — selling it."

On his machines, Dick Gardner makes his marine hardware. On the workbenches that edge the shop, he fashions his toy sailboats. Here are his directions for the boat.

Materials Needed

Hull: clear pine or cedar piece 3″ x 5″ x 24″ long can be glued up from stock width boards

Deck: clear pine or cedar planed to ¼″ thick x 5″ wide x 24″ long

Deck house: scrap mahogany or stained pine

Mast and boom: one ⅜″ round birch dowel 36″ long, one ¼″ round birch dowel 36″ long

Keel and rudder: scrap galvanized metal approximately 1/32″ thick, sheet lead strip ⅝″ wide x 24″ long

Rudder stock, mast spreader, and sheet horse: brazing rod 1/16″ and 3/32″ diameter

Paints and varnish: any outside enamels of suitable color

Glue: Weldwood plastic water resistant powdered glue

Sail material: lightest sheeting, silk or rayon

Rigging: braided nylon fishline about 25 or 30 lbs. test

Construction Steps

1. Make up a template of the hull profile, and deck outline, from cardboard or heavy paper and trace the outline on a 3″ x 5″ x 24″ hull piece (Fig. 1). Shape the block to your pencil outline with hand saw and plane. To facilitate hold-

MAKING A TOY SAILBOAT

fig. 1   *Tracing the hull's profile from a template*

ing the hull piece clamp a short block of wood 2″ x 4″ x 5″ long in the vise so that you can work on the hull sections. To obtain the correct curved cross sections of the hull at the three points, A-A, B-B, and C-C, make three cardboard templates from the plan (Figs. 2, 3b) and cut the excess wood away with a spoke shave, draw knife, or small block plane. Do not bring the hull to a completely smooth condition at this point as you should hollow it before final finishing and deck assembly.

2. With a sharp gouge chisel, hollow out the hull piece (Fig. 3). The shell thickness should be about ⅝″ thick at the bottom where the keel attaches, tapering to about ⅜″ thick at the point where the deck attaches.

3. Lay out on the ¼″ x 5″ x 24″ deck piece the deck outline traced from the deck template made from the plan.

Roughly cut the piece to this shape, allowing about ⅛″ to finish.

4. Glue the deck piece to the hull, using the Weldwood plastic glue. Allow the glue to cure for twenty-four hours and shape the deck outline to conform with the hull piece.

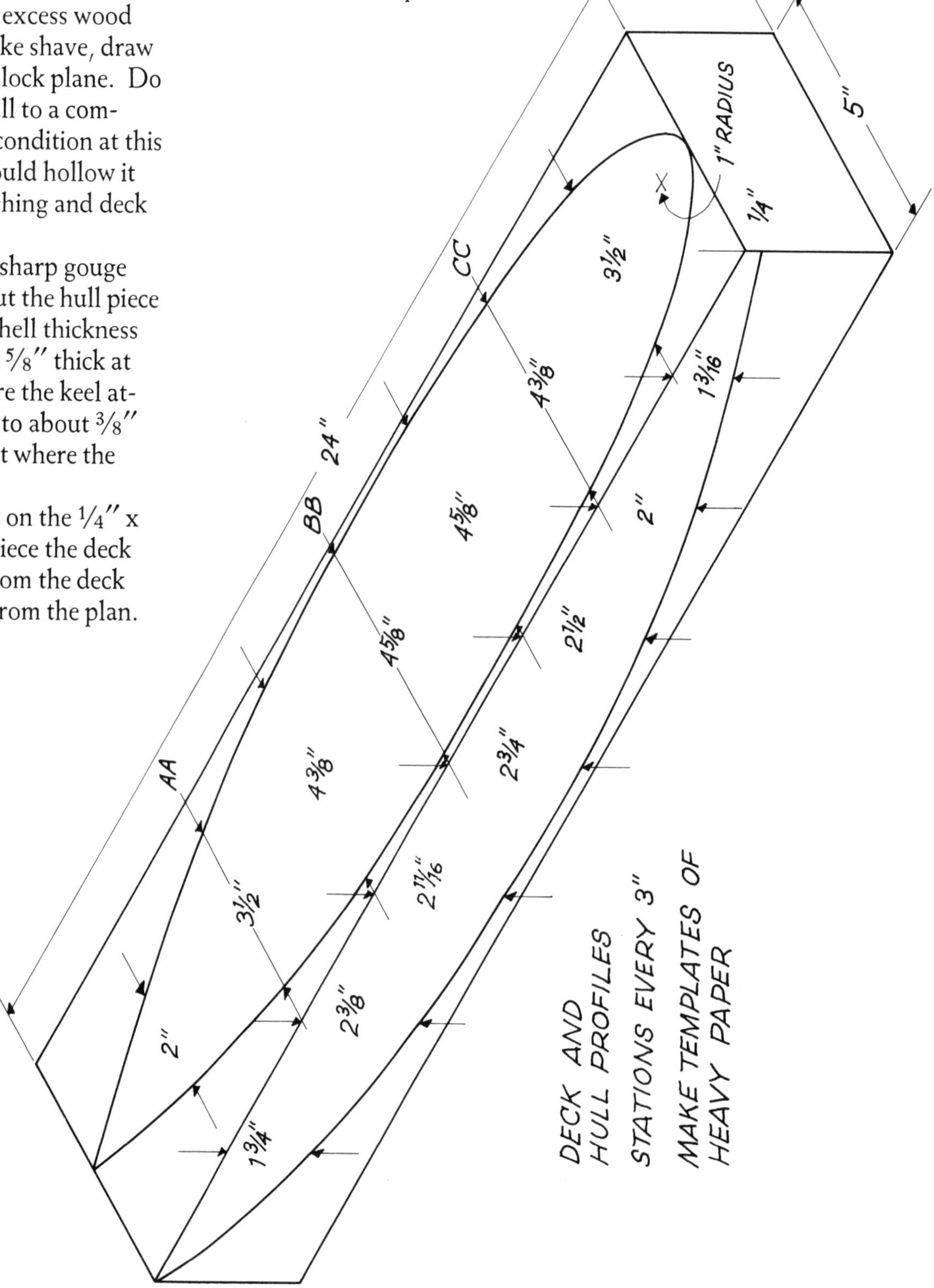

fig. 2

DECK AND HULL PROFILES
STATIONS EVERY 3″
MAKE TEMPLATES OF HEAVY PAPER

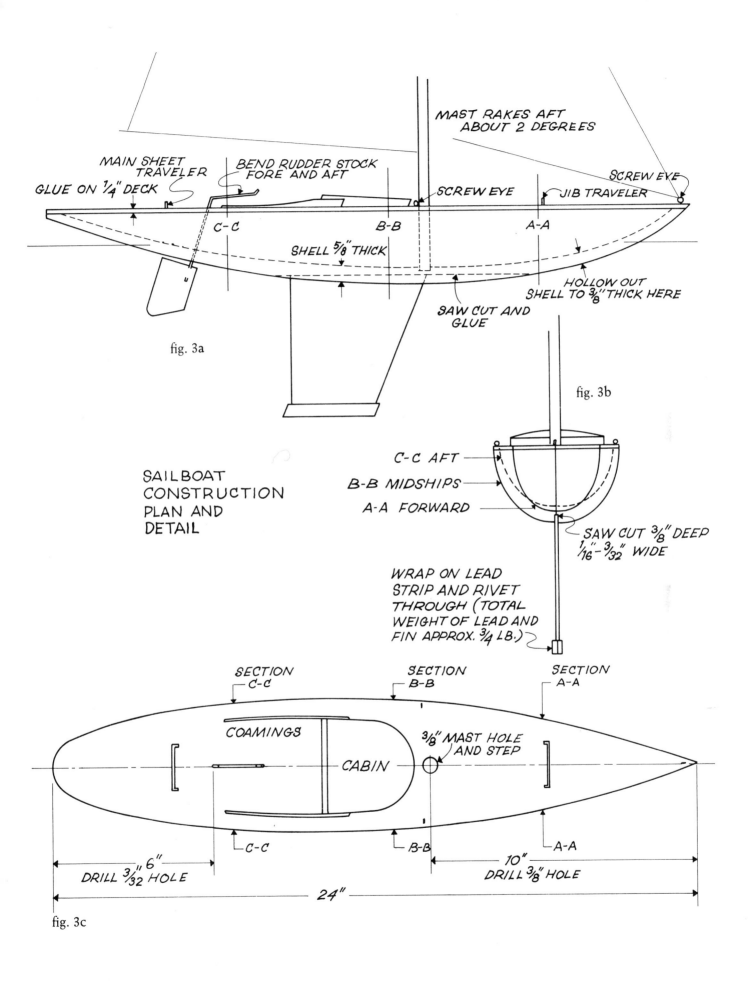

MAST RAKES AFT
ABOUT 2 DEGREES

MAIN SHEET
TRAVELER
BEND RUDDER STOCK
FORE AND AFT

GLUE ON ¼" DECK

SCREW EYE

SCREW EYE

JIB TRAVELER

C-C

B-B

A-A

SHELL ⅝" THICK

HOLLOW OUT
SHELL TO ⅜" THICK HERE

SAW CUT AND
GLUE

fig. 3a

SAILBOAT
CONSTRUCTION
PLAN AND
DETAIL

fig. 3b

C-C AFT

B-B MIDSHIPS

A-A FORWARD

SAW CUT ⅜" DEEP
1/16" - 3/32" WIDE

WRAP ON LEAD
STRIP AND RIVET
THROUGH (TOTAL
WEIGHT OF LEAD AND
FIN APPROX. ¾ LB.)

SECTION
C-C

SECTION
B-B

SECTION
A-A

COAMINGS

⅜" MAST HOLE
AND STEP

CABIN

C-C

B-B

A-A

6"
DRILL 3/32" HOLE

10"
DRILL ⅜" HOLE

24"

fig. 3c

FIN KEEL

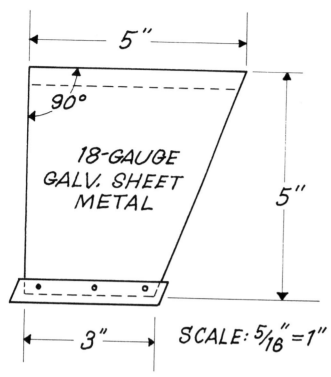

5"

90°

18-GAUGE
GALV. SHEET
METAL

5"

3"

SCALE: 5/16" = 1"

fig. 4a

RUDDER

fig. 4b

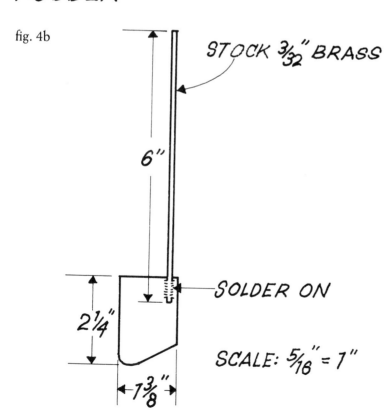

STOCK 3/32" BRASS

6"

SOLDER ON

2 1/4"

1 3/8"

SCALE: 5/16" = 1"

5. To make the fin keel and rudder (Fig. 4a), obtain from the plumber or a sheet-metal shop some 18-gauge scrap galvanized metal about 1/32" thick. Cut the material to the shape shown on the plan.

6. For the keel weight, take a strip of sheet lead 5/8" wide by about 24" or 30" long and wrap this lead ribbon around the lower edge of the keel, tapping it into shape with light hammer blows. Once in place, drill two or three 3/32" holes through the lead and the lower edge of the keel. Rivet lightly into place, using some of the 3/32" brazing rod material for rivet stock. Push the keel piece down into a saw cut made in the hull to a depth of about 3/8" and bedded with Epoxy cement or plastic resin glue. Make the rudder from the same galvanized metal as the fin keel and cut to shape as shown in Fig. 4b. Leave the rudder stock straight with the end chamfered to allow it to be pushed through a 3/32" hole drilled through the hull and deck. Once it is in place, bend it over at right angles to the deck.

7. For the mast drill a ⅜″ hole 10″ back from the bow and on the center line of the hull (Fig. 3c). The mast hole should be drilled raking aft a couple of degrees to improve the appearance of the model. Drill this hole carefully, allowing the auger bit to continue down through the deck and into the wood at the bottom of the hull about ¼″ to form the mast step.

8. The cabin and coaming rails can be made to the builder's taste or ideas (Fig. 3c). A cabin and coaming made of scrap mahogany, when varnished, will contrast nicely with the natural finish of a varnished deck.

9. The sheet travelers for the main and jib are made from the 1/16″ diameter brazing rod about 2½″ long. Bend the rod to shape with pliers and press it into 3/64″ holes drilled in the deck at locations shown in Fig. 3a.

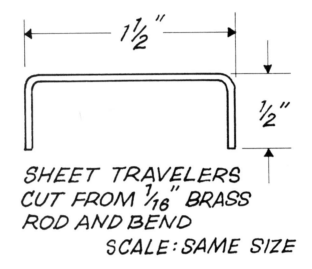

SHEET TRAVELERS
CUT FROM 1/16″ BRASS
ROD AND BEND
SCALE: SAME SIZE

OPEN SCREW EYE — JIB BOOM ¼″ DOWEL 9″ LONG — 3/32″ DRILL

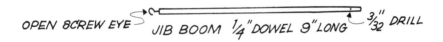

OPEN SCREW EYE — MAIN BOOM ¼″ DOWEL, 11″ LONG — 3/32″ DRILL

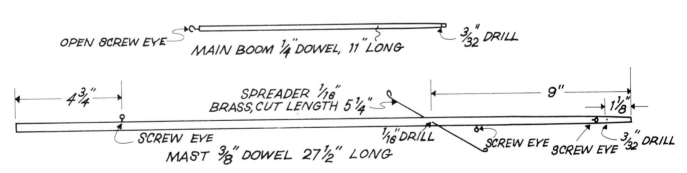

4¾″   SPREADER 1/16″ BRASS, CUT LENGTH 5¼″   9″   1⅛″

SCREW EYE   1/16″ DRILL   SCREW EYE SCREW EYE 3/32″ DRILL

MAST ⅜″ DOWEL 27½″ LONG

fig. 4c

SAILBOAT ASSEMBLY PLAN

1. HOLLOW HULL PIECE
2. FIN KEEL
3. LEAD STRIP (WOUND ON AND FASTENED)
4. RUDDER
5. 3/32" BRASS ROD RUDDER STOCK
6. MAST STEP 3/8" DRILL THROUGH DECK
7. JIB BOOM AND SAIL LACING
8. JIB SHEET TRAVELER 1/16" BRASS ROD
9. MAIN SHEET TRAVELER 1/16" BRASS ROD
10. RUDDER STOCK, BENT AFTER ASSEMBLY TO FORM TILLER
11. BRASS SCREW EYE FOR FORE-STAY AND JIB BOOM END
12. BRASS SCREW EYE FOR SHROUD ENDS, BOTH SIDES
13. FORESTAY, NYLON FISHLINE
14. 1/4" DOWEL, MAIN BOOM
15. HEAVY THREAD, TOPPING LIFT
16. SAME FOR JIB LIFT
17. CABIN AND COAMING
18. 1/16" HOLE THROUGH MAST FOR SPREADER
19. SCREW FOR UPPER ATTACH. FORESTAY
20. BRASS SCREW EYE FOR HEAD OF SAIL
21. 3/32" HOLE FOR SHROUDS
22. MAIN SHEET, ATTACH TO TRAVELER 9.
23. 3/32 SAW CUT RUN OUT AND FILLED WITH PLASTIC WOOD AND GLUE
24. SEW ON JIB AT 1" INTERVALS WITH LIGHT THREAD
25. SIDE SHROUDS, NYLON FISHLINE

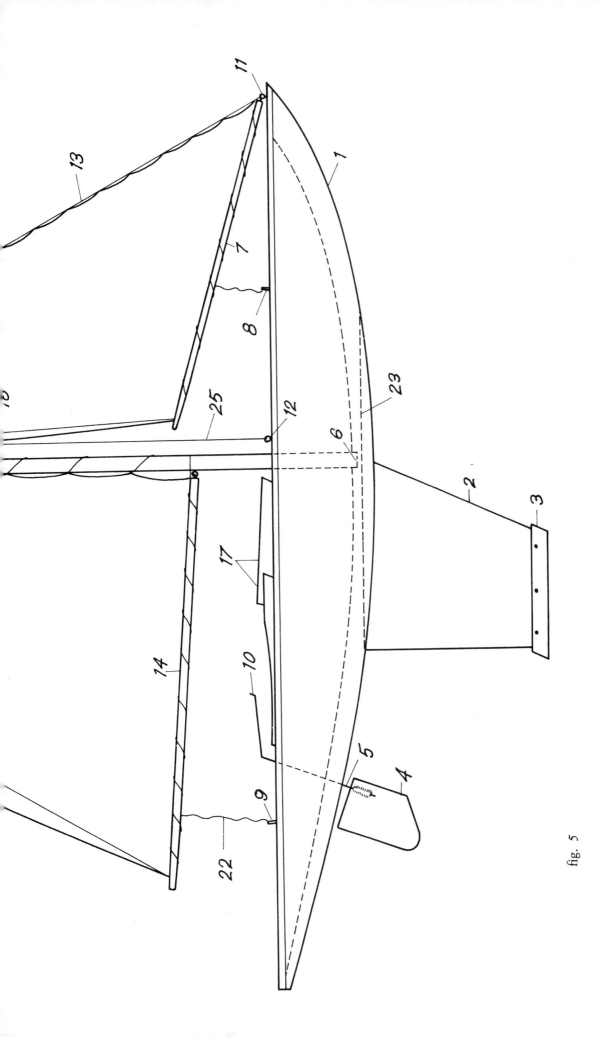

fig. 5

10. Sand the hull smooth and apply a coat of white primer to the hull and fin keel. The deck and cabin should also be varnished at this point.

11. Cut the main mast to length as shown on the spar plan, tapering the top portion of the mast slightly (Fig. 4c). Drill holes through the mast at the points shown for the spreader and shrouds (Fig. 5). Cut the boom to length from the ¼″ dowel and taper it. Use small screw eyes to attach the main boom and jib boom to the mast and stem. Make the spreader from 1/16″ brazing rod and bend the ends to form eyes for the stays to pass through. Mount the screw eyes at the head of the mast and just under the spreader on the forward side of the spar for the forestay attachment.

12. Rig the model (Fig. 5) using braided nylon fishing line for the shrouds and forestay. If you can obtain a small length of brass chain of about 3/16″ pitch, the chain links can be opened up to form suitable brass hooks for attaching the sheets and stays. After the nylon line is in place, a small dab of varnish on the knot itself will cement the connection so the knot is not likely to untie.

13. The sail material should be the lightest obtainable. Percale sheeting is all right but is heavier than necessary. Cut the sails as shown in Fig. 6 and tape the edges with iron-on-tape as neatly as possible. Sew the jib to the forestay at intervals and lace it to the jib boom with heavier thread. Make the jib sheet from nylon fishline; this sheet leads to the sheet traveler forward of the main mast.

14. Lace the mainsail to both mast and boom. If you can find some small brass curtain rings, use them as sail hoops to secure the mainsail to the mast in a conventional manner. Make the main sheet from the same nylon fishing line; this sheet leads to the sheet traveler just aft of the rudder post. Leave several inches of extra sheet length so you can adjust the trim of the sails.

Sailing Directions

15. Since this model does not have the automatically correcting wind-vane type of steering found on more elaborate sailing models, some experimentation with the rudder settings is in order. For sailing across the wind, the jib should be fairly flat or close-hauled and the mainsail somewhat slacked away. The rudder setting should be such that the boat is prevented from sweeping up into the wind as the breeze increases in puffs. Models of this type generally have a strong "weather helm"; they come up sharply into the wind on heavier puffs and even may tack over and then immediately go back on the original tack because of the rudder setting.

For sailing downwind, let out both jib and mainsail nearly at right angles to the center line of the hull. With the rudder set amidships the model will maintain a fairly straight course downwind. Very light or moderate breezes will give the best results. Heavy winds will generally overpower a small model such as this, and not much can be accomplished under such conditions. For a child who wants to become or is a novice sailing student, the model is a useful demonstration tool.

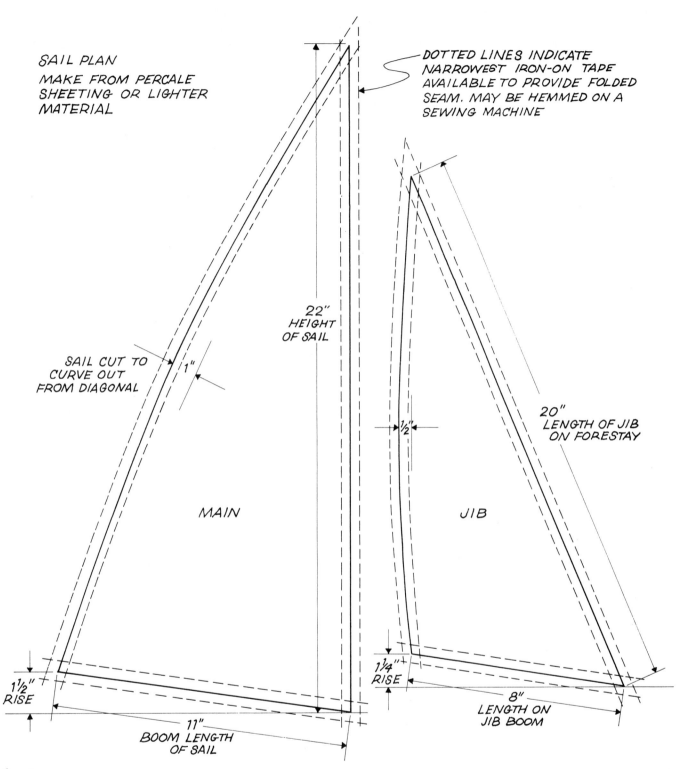

SAIL PLAN
MAKE FROM PERCALE
SHEETING OR LIGHTER
MATERIAL

DOTTED LINES INDICATE
NARROWEST IRON-ON TAPE
AVAILABLE TO PROVIDE FOLDED
SEAM. MAY BE HEMMED ON A
SEWING MACHINE

22"
HEIGHT
OF SAIL

SAIL CUT TO
CURVE OUT
FROM DIAGONAL

1"

MAIN

1½"
RISE

11"
BOOM LENGTH
OF SAIL

20"
LENGTH OF JIB
ON FORESTAY

½"

JIB

1¼"
RISE

8"
LENGTH ON
JIB BOOM

fig. 6

I get my birdhouse ideas mostly from the ladies," Jeremiah Thibault says. "They tell me how many compartments purple martins like in their houses and how bluebirds will not accept a birdhouse that has a perch protruding. The perch must go inside. One little lady was going on vacation and was so afraid that her birds would get hungry that I designed a ten-pound bird feeder for her and it's gotten to be quite a thing. When neighbors were having trouble with rodents and cats I came up with a bird station with two barrels in it to stop them. That's just the way it goes. Me — I just don't have that much time to watch birds and find out all their habits."

Jeremiah Thibault of Winchester, New Hampshire, is a jolly retired U.S. Army bass tuba player who moved to New Hampshire in 1967 and has been designing birdhouses almost ever since. He makes about 2000 houses and feeders a year in the barn behind his 200-year-old farmhouse. The Massachusetts Audubon Society buys his windowsill and gable feeders and his jumbo 9" x 11" x 18" feeder.

"There's a little chickadee house they've asked me to put together too," he says in his melodiously lilting voice one afternoon in his workshop, as he pounds together a blue birdhouse and explains that birds, his customers tell him, "like their houses unstained on the inside but stained on the outside, so making houses that way has become my trademark." And then he sighs with mock sadness and remarks that, despite all the work he does for the birds, "They just don't sing my songs and I wish they would. I guess they just don't realize I'm a musical man. Beethoven — he's definitely number one with me."

When he was eleven years old, and growing up in Fall River, Massachusetts, where his father was a carpenter ("I was there with him when he made his superduper outhouse"), Jeremiah Thibault learned to play the fiddle. Then he learned the baritone, the trombone, the bass viol, and finally the tuba. "And that seemed to be my instrument. I played under Koussevitsky of the Boston Symphony and Meredith Wilson at NBC Studios and Toscanini, and Pierre Monteux in San Francisco, and Stokowski for a film on Long Island, New York. Since symphony orchestras only have one tuba player, if he gets sick they're likely to call on someone they know and that's how I got in," he explains as he hammers another

• 5 •
HOUSING FOR BLUEBIRDS

nail into the birdhouse roof and pops a chocolate-covered cherry into his mouth. Mr. Thibault is a widower, inclined to favor chocolate-covered cherries to fill in the meal gaps in his day. He attributes his woodworking ability to his French-Canadian ancestry.

"When I was a young man," Mr. Thibault continues to reminisce, "being full-time in the Boston Symphony — that was my aim. But those were Depression days, so I enlisted in the army because I had to make a living. But I did play with the symphony for six months in nineteen forty-one, before I went to war.

"After the war, I went to Symphony Hall one day because the old man — that's what we always called Koussevitsky — had promised me a job if and when I got back. There was a rehearsal going on and I listened. They had a young tuba player there and he was tremendous so I thought I'd better go home and practice before I asked for an audition. But I never got around to it because it wasn't long after that that they changed the army retirement plan so you could retire after twenty, not

thirty, years. I already had twelve years of service so I figured I'd re-enlist. It hurts me now that I never did more with my music, but to do it further I would have had to establish myself in a city, and I abhor cities," Mr. Thibault says, and looks out across a broad expanse of pine-bordered field. "And anyway" — and his blue eyes sparkle merrily from behind his horn-rimmed glasses — "I like to do a lot of things, and I guess I have brought some comfort to the birds."

Mr. Thibault calls his present home his "cosy little nook" and expresses his pleasure at having found it after travel in the service in eighteen foreign countries and every state but six.

"I started out in the service assigned to an antiaircraft gun in the Hawaiian Islands and, boy, I loved that little gun, but somebody found out I had some musical experience and so I was called in to find out if I should be in the band.

"'What do you play?' they asked me.

"'All I play is the violin,' I said, because I wanted to get back to my gun.

"'We have no use for a violin, but we'll let you play the trumpet,' they said. 'How about that?'

"'Maybe,' I said, but I wasn't very pleased about it.

"'Well, then, how about the baritone?'

"'Maybe.' But then I saw the tuba and I said to the boss, 'I can play that a little bit.' And that was my mistake because, although I love it, I ended up carrying it for the rest of my army life!"

After a day in his workshop, Mr. Thibault likes to have a tumbler of whiskey, fry himself a steak, and boil a pot of potatoes and a kettle of water for tea. After dinner, he settles down in his Morris chair by the TV and thinks back again to his army days, as he rolls a cigarette and sips his whiskey.

One of his fondest recollections is of a celebration of the liberation of Charleroi, Belgium, freed by the First Division of which he was later a member.

"It was about nineteen forty-seven that we went there for the celebration. When the band arrived, we had a parade into town, and that afternoon we gave a concert on the town common. We were so popular we were almost like returning prisoners. They had to have the militia around us to keep the people away. After the concert, we started to parade again — up the cobblestone roads and down the valleys. I was the first sergeant of the outfit. I was up ahead and all of a sudden I realized the band sounded pretty tinny. I looked behind and there were only three lines of us left where there should have been a platoon of troops and color banners and a fifty-piece band. The villagers were picking everyone up and taking them home to dinner. Finally, I was left all alone playing and some people came up and said, 'Look at this, this poor, forlorn soldier!' I turned around and answered them in French, and they took me off to a restaurant with great gusto and then to their home. It turned out my host and hostess were the mayor of the town and his wife!"

Mr. Thibault will also, at the end of a day, with the radio or television news on faintly in the background, tell what he knows about birds. "But it isn't much," he continues to insist. "I know more about fish. I generally go to Nova Scotia after fish in the summertime, and — would you believe — I picked up a seven-hundred and thirty-pound blue fin tuna last time!"

It was one of the "neighborhood ladies" who got him started making birdhouses. "After we moved here and fixed up the house and I set up my little shop, somebody saw that I was woodworking and said she wanted a birdhouse. I made that one and then somebody wanted a feeder. Then my wife wanted some feeders, so I worked up about a dozen items. The best seller is my jumbo feeder, but people also like the squirrel discourager. I, myself, am fond of the bluebird house — tree swallows will nest in it too. Last year I counted six bluebird families in my houses. What bluebirds need is a large area — about a six-by-six-inch cube. They're not very smart, though, and they're easily discouraged, so you have to be very careful when you're making them a house to have it just what they want. The entrance hole, for example, must be one and a half inches in diameter or they'll reject it, and there's that matter of their not accepting a perch on the outside of the box — just inside. For any bird, of course, you have to have ventilation."

Here are Mr. Thibault's plans for his bluebird house and a few general directions on birdhouse building. Complete, step by step, instructions, he feels, take the fun away from building. "Use your imagination, but make the measurements meticulous," he says.

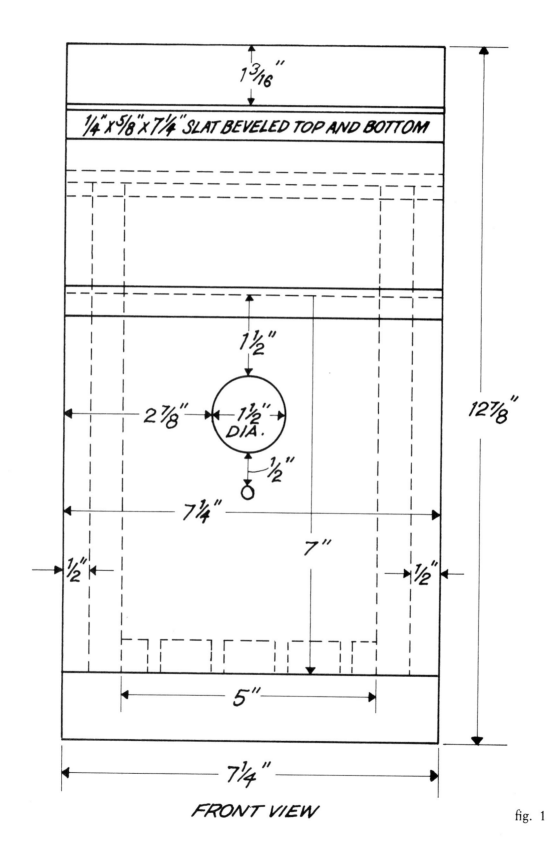

$1\frac{3}{16}''$

$\frac{1}{4}'' \times \frac{5}{8}'' \times 7\frac{1}{4}''$ SLAT BEVELED TOP AND BOTTOM

$1\frac{1}{2}''$

$2\frac{7}{8}''$

$1\frac{1}{2}''$
DIA.

$\frac{1}{2}''$

$12\frac{7}{8}''$

$7\frac{1}{4}''$

$7''$

$\frac{1}{2}''$

$\frac{1}{2}''$

$5''$

$7\frac{1}{4}''$

FRONT VIEW

fig. 1

1. Buy a 1″ x 8″ white pine board, 5′ long.

2. If you feel you need to, make templates of the right sizes from the accompanying plans and trace them on the wood (Fig. 1).

3. Cut out the parts. (Mr. Thibault uses a table and a radial saw, but other saws will do.)

4. Use an electric drill with a bit that has a 1½″ cutting end to drill an entry hole in the front piece. Also drill a hole to insert a ¼″ dowel ½″ below it.

MAKING A BLUEBIRD HOUSE

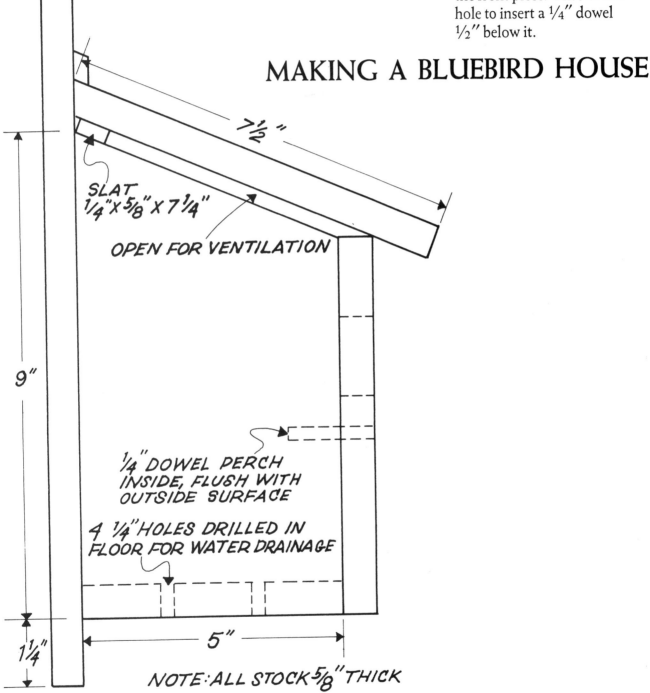

7½″

SLAT
¼″ X ⅝″ X 7¼″

OPEN FOR VENTILATION

9″

¼″ DOWEL PERCH INSIDE, FLUSH WITH OUTSIDE SURFACE

4 ¼″ HOLES DRILLED IN FLOOR FOR WATER DRAINAGE

1¼″

5″

NOTE: ALL STOCK ⅝″ THICK

SIDE VIEW

fig. 2

fig. 3   *The first step in assembling a birdhouse*

5. Either drill four ¼″ drainage holes in the bottom of the house (as shown in plans) or cut off the corners of the bottom piece at a 45-degree angle. The space so created will also make drainage areas.

6. Start assembling the house by nailing the two side pieces to the bottom piece with 1¼″ corrugated brass nails or 1½″ finish nails (Fig. 2). Altogether, you will need twelve nails. Mr. Thibault prefers the corrugated brass nails because they hold the house together sturdily. "For ten years," he

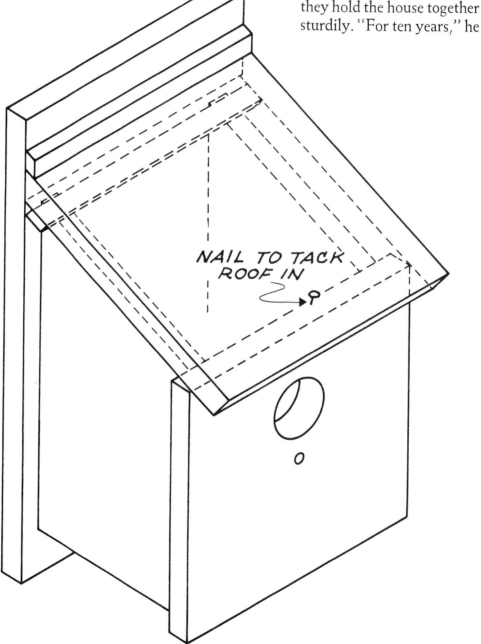

NAIL TO TACK ROOF IN

fig. 4

says. Once the sides are attached to the bottom, nail the bottom to the back. Be sure, when the house is put together, that the grain of the wood all runs in the same direction.

7. Attach a slat to hold the top down and attach a slat underneath the top for ventilation (Fig. 1). Use three ¾″ brads to attach each of these pieces. Attach the roof with corrugated nails (Figs. 5–6).

8. Insert a ¼″ dowel under the entrance, making sure that it fits snugly and that none of it protrudes outside the house. The dowel should be 1¼″ to 1⅓″ long (Fig. 2).

9. When assembled, coat your house with wood preservative. One heavy coat will do. When it is dry, stain it with redwood stain or whatever stain you like.

fig. 5   *Preparing the birdhouse roof*

fig. 6   *The birdhouse roof in place*

When it rains in the state of Maine and fog settles into the harbors, summer visitors are wont to complain about their bad fortune. One day in 1970, some of them expressed their complaints to a dark-haired young manufacturer who was making and selling portable lecterns out of a red cement block building in South Windham.

It was the sort of building where idle travelers were likely to stop when skies were lowering. It said Glencraft on it and that sounded enticing to city folks looking for country crafts. But their disappointment became apparent when they opened the door to a roomful of binder-board lecterns and cardboard book covers.

The owner of the concern always greeted visitors warmly, though, and offered coffee, and chatted about his fondness for Maine, and told how he had moved to the Pine Tree State from the Boston suburb of Newton because Maine had "what the people in the cities go to the museums to see — the seascapes and the landscapes and the handcrafts."

The visitors pointed out to the tall, pipe-smoking manufacturer of Glencraft Products, Jeremy Guiles, that that was all very well, but that if you took one week's vacation in Maine and a northeaster brought only high seas and cold winds and downpours, you didn't feel like enjoying the scenery, and there wasn't very much else to do in small Maine towns.

"So I tried to think of what I could make that might improve wet vacations and help pay the rent too. After all, people were bringing their money in the door with them. What could I make that they'd get enthusiastic about?" Mr. Guiles recalls one afternoon in the red block building, as he saws away at his solution — jigsaw puzzles.

"We'd always had wood puzzles in my family. I was sitting home doing a jigsaw puzzle one night, and I thought 'why not?' I found out only one dealer in the state of Maine was selling wooden puzzles and his computer had told him to get out of business, so I bought one thousand dollars' worth of his stock of puzzles and put them in the window."

But the puzzles Mr. Guiles had bought were not handcrafted Maine products, and many tourists continued to ask, "Why don't you make your own here?"

"I tried every excuse I could think of," Mr. Guiles remembers, "and finally I went out and bought a jigsaw." He also purchased a

• 6 •

HEIRLOOM JIGSAW PUZZLES

puzzle by one of the leading puzzle-makers of the past, studied it, and tried his hand at making his own. Ever since then, he has been able to offer passers-by hand-crafted Maine puzzles. He offers seascapes and farm scenes mounted on bass plywood that, he says, should be 3/16″ or more thick to feel and fit right.

He calls wooden jigsaw puzzles the "heirloom type" and notes that, for serious puzzle-doers or collectors, they are the only kind worth having.

Cardboard puzzles are "clicked" out or cut with a die. If the die is dull, as it is bound to be after a while, the perforations won't be complete and the puzzle rips. And then cardboard puzzle pieces blow off tables, and cardboard gets wet and useless after a while. In contrast, good wooden puzzles become collector's items.

"One woman wrote to me and told me about the sixty-three puzzles she had. Some of them were made by Par Company Ltd. that has existed in New York since the thirties. They were known in those days as the "Puzzle Cutters for Kings." Some of their puzzles today are worth thousands of dollars. They specialized in custom art and photo work. Some member of the royalty of Europe, for example, might have a photograph taken of a state visit, and he'd send the photograph to Par, and it would be turned into an exquisite jigsaw puzzle mounted on mahogany and the king or prince would give it as a memento to the dignitary who had been his guest. Their puzzles were cut into lovely and very special shapes too — mythological charac-

ters and ballet dancers and milk-maids in bonnets. And there were two seashore shapes in their puzzles — that was their trademark.

"And that woman also had some U-Nit puzzles. That was a brand started in New Jersey in nineteen thirty-four. It was famous for its mahogany backing and its unique shapes too. I was tempted to write back to that lady and tell her she'd better up her house insurance with treasure puzzles like those on hand!"

The heyday of American jigsaw puzzles, according to Jeremy Guiles, was in the 1930s when milkmen and other routemen would take puzzles with them when they made their rounds and rent them for $1 a week or so. In those Depression days, puzzles gave the unemployed something to do with their time and were an activity the entire family could enjoy together.

"Lending libraries also had them," he recounts, "and when they lent them out they would ask the borrower — if he lost a piece or found one missing — out of courtesy to indicate the section around the missing piece to show where it belonged. Then the library could get someone to make the replacement piece."

Many early puzzles, Mr. Guiles has learned, were cut along color lines. All red segments would belong in one area; all blue sky or water in another, etc. Many of them also had parts cut in recognizable shapes — like Par's ballerinas and gods and goddesses. One man was known for his kewpie dolls. Dogs, bears, arrows, and squirrels were especially popular shapes. Mr. Guiles is beginning to introduce his own special shapes into his puzzles — "state of Maine pine trees and sailing ships and seagulls" among them, he says.

Jeremy Guiles describes himself as a dreamer. He majored in philosophy at Colby College in Maine and had planned to enter the ministry. He likes puzzle-making for the same sort of reason that he almost became a clergyman — "because it can bring people joy." He also finds that he gets the same "sense of creation that a builder would get" from cutting puzzles. "It's a little bit like an architect designing a building. I know what I do is going to last."

Puzzle "nuts," he says, are people who would rate high on a spatial relations test. To that sort of person, working a puzzle becomes as addictive as eating peanuts. The extent of Mr. Guiles's correspondence and the number of telephone calls he receives from potential customers are both phenomenal.

"One woman called me frantically from Washington, D.C., one night. She said her nerves were bad and would I please send her any new puzzles I had. 'They do a much better job of calming me down than pills,' she said. And in the height of the gas crisis, I got a letter from a woman in Florida who said to please send her twenty-five dollars' worth of puzzles or of gasoline — it didn't matter which."

The size of a puzzle, as well as the picture on it, is what most puzzle-doers look for, according to Mr. Guiles.

Aside from the wood on which the picture for a puzzle is mounted, the materials necessary for making puzzles are minimal. "But if you plan to make your own puzzles, remember that it can be like painting yourself into a corner," Mr. Guiles warns. "You've got to think ahead and you have to think fast. The puzzle is cut on the principle of locks — you should have four of them in each piece. You can't, all of a sudden, as you're running your saw down the puzzle, say to yourself, 'My, my, there's no room for a nub.' You have to have your mind on your work and your eye on the puzzle all the time. It's like whittling or sculpture. You can't cut too much or too far."

Mr. Guiles also warns that the puzzle-cutter should never work when he is tired or until he is tired because of the dangers of using a jigsaw. "And puzzle-cutting is tiring because you're working in such a tight space; you must have first-rate muscle control and very good light because you use your eyes so much."

CUTTING A JIGSAW PUZZLE

1. Begin with small puzzles. Use 4″ x 5″ squares of bass plywood 3/16″ or more thick. "If the wood is thinner than that, you can't control the blade." This wood, according to Mr. Guiles, can usually be obtained from Constantine and Son at 2050 Eastchester Road, the Bronx, New York, in 2′ x 2′ or 2′ x 4′ square boards.

2. Buy prints on lightweight paper from an art store, or use lightweight calendar pictures. "Don't use magazine pictures because there's too much clay in them — that's what makes them shiny — and they're hard to work with. The edge of a picture with clay in it cracks or shreds when it's cut."

3. Mr. Guiles uses Peter Cooper's Flexible Hot Melt Animal Glue to attach his pictures to the wood, but it is an industrial product hard to obtain except in bulk, and must be heated when it is prepared. An easier way of gluing is to use thinned wallpaper paste applied with a long-bristle brush. Be sure, however, that it is free from lumps. Elmer's glue is not advisable, for it is usually too thick for this purpose.

4. Spread glue or paste evenly over the back of the picture. (Mr. Guiles has a sheet-gluing machine that he uses for this, but it is not necessary.) Let the glue stand until it is tacky (sticky, but not wet). This should take thirty seconds to two minutes. Carefully lay your picture on the wood. Press it down with a rolling pin, rollers from an old washing machine, or rollers from an old printing press to make sure no air bubbles are left. Let the picture dry. Then trim the board down, sand the edges and start cutting.

5. The blade to be used in your jigsaw will depend on the thickness of the plywood, but for "strip" cutting — the kind the beginner should experiment with — a fine-tooth scroll blade is best.

6. Start by dividing your puzzle into even segments across the top, usually 1" to 1½" wide. Divide by making small marks with a pencil. Then make your first cut about halfway across the puzzle. Start moving your board through the saw from the top to the bottom of the wood in reverse French curves end to end (see Fig. 1). Cut with the picture face up. Remember that when the puzzle is completely cut, you will need a lock (either a nub or a void) on each of the four sides of the puzzle pieces (except on outside edge pieces).

7. When you have cut even strips from top to bottom of the puzzle (Fig. 2), turn it sideways and start cutting across between the nubs you have fashioned as you cut down. You may wish, once

REVERSE CURVES

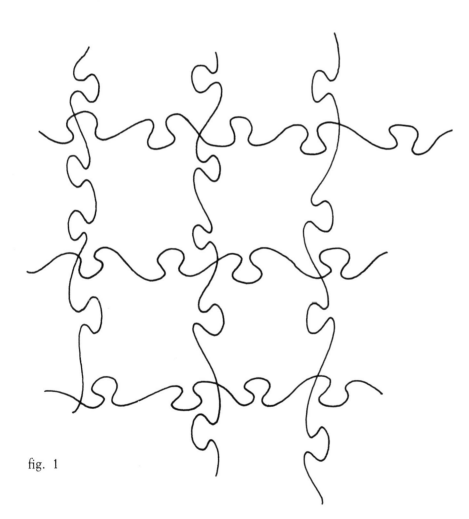

fig. 1

you are making larger puzzles, to cut only half of the puzzle at a time, but cut that half completely. If the puzzle is large, it is easier to manage cutting it in halves or quarters. Mr. Guiles warns that the tendency of the first-time puzzle-cutter is to cut pieces that are too large. When he cuts a 12″ x 18″ puzzle, he has from 325 to 350 pieces. For a 4″ x 5″ puzzle, you will want 20 to 28 pieces. If you mistakenly cut off a nub, it can be glued back into the void with Elmer's glue.

8. When the puzzle is completely cut, sand the back before disassembling and put the pieces in a box.

9. It is also possible to cut puzzles by the "random" method — with no predetermined process, simply starting your cuts at one corner of the puzzle and going on, but this is difficult and takes time. Even Mr. Guiles only does it occasionally.

fig. 2   *Cutting a mounted picture from top to bottom for a jigsaw puzzle*

As early as I could tie a shoestring, my father taught me how to knit lobster pot funnels," Vincent Clark recollects. "He taught me everything he knew about lobstering, and I enjoyed it. He was well known among Connecticut lobstermen, my father, Willy Clark, was. He told me about the nature of the lobster and how climate and season affect them. Like us when we get old, they like a comfortable climate. They like a water temperature of forty-five to fifty-five degrees approximately, he used to say.

"Lobsters, you know, were the first creatures with TV antennae. They do most of their seeing with them. They sense air waves and sound. They even seem to have a sense of smell because they seem to know when their chums are there. Here's another thing about lobsters. Whenever there's a thunderstorm, you don't catch lobsters the next day. And when there's a full moon, you catch them on the shady side of the rocks, not the bright side."

Vincent Clark pounds nails into lobster pot laths as he talks. Outside his red clapboard workshop in Guilford, Connecticut, Connecticut Turnpike traffic zooms by.

"My hands tell the story of my work," Mr. Clark says, and looks down at his sturdy fingers and broad palms. "We used to go out in a fourteen-foot rowboat and pull two hundred and fifty pots by hand all day, Pop and I. We'd start at daybreak and work till two or three in the afternoon. There are more lobsters around here now, though, than there were then. This is back in the Depression days I'm thinking about. Up north around Maine it seems to be getting too cold for the lobster, so he's pushing south. I, myself, think there's another Ice Age coming on. Now they're as far down as South Carolina where they never were before. And we have a lobster pot customer in Maryland demanding pots wholesale! That would have been unheard of forty years ago."

Vincent Clark is six feet tall and broad-chested from his years of heaving lobster pots.

"I left the water to make lobster pots," he recounts, "because friends said they were sick and tired of getting bundles of laths with knots in them for pots. A knot just won't do in a lobster pot. It makes the wood weak. Pot wood has to be perfect. The way most lobstermen make pots, of course, is to get materials all cut up by someone like me and put them

·7·
HOW TO CATCH A LOBSTER

together themselves. And I'm fussy. I'm particular with what I make, whether it's just materials or a whole pot. I burned out a lot of saw blades and motors and did a lot of experimenting on how to get pots made the way I wanted them done. I found out, for example, that galvanized staples which can be pressurized to countersink, are tighter than pot nails. And on the edge of the pot where the strain is, if you're using pot nails instead of staples, you should have double nails.

"Then I use four wooden funnel strips around the entrance to my pots [Fig. 1]. I like them because that way you don't have to nail each mesh of the net and risk the possibility of the nail tearing the twine. Wood strips are a lot tenderer on the twine. The other thing I do, I've designed my funnel to be more efficient than any other. It has more twine and more knots than others. As I said, I'm fussy."

Clark's Pots — a black and gold handcarved sign on his red shed reads just that way — is only a three-man operation, though as many as 5000 pots are produced in the little shed outside Mr. Clark's white house each year. Production is virtually around the clock, however, with Sundays working days for Vincent Clark, too, unless something like an especially fine day for boating lures him to his birthplace, neighboring Short Beach.

"I don't get much time for it these days," he says. "Sometimes I work from eleven A.M. till two or three in the morning, but I always anticipate going out on the water. That's all right, though, I love people and I love my work, so I don't mind working hard."

Before he went into lobster-pot-making full-time — in the days when he was lobstering himself — Vincent Clark was also working nights in a factory. And before that he had worked as a salesman, and before that for the WPA.

Mr. Clark leans on a pot and begins threading the net funnel that befuddles the lobster. "When I figured I'd do this all the time, I advertised in the *National Fisherman* and I got responses from all over the world. There are even letters from the South Seas requesting information about catching not just lobsters, but crabs."

Mr. Clark, an amiable, talkative man, continues, between drilling and stapling operations, to offer lobster lore and information.

"Trap is the proper name for these things I'm making," he says. "Pot's just a nickname. And here's another nickname. The old-timers call lobsters 'bugs' — that's right, just like the beetles that go on roses. They'll always say to each other, 'Bill, you got any bugs today?'"

Clark's Pots makes pots in all sizes and shapes depending on the needs of the customer. "It's the nature of the northerner to make and want round pots. Down here we've gotten used to rectangular pots — I don't know quite why. Maybe it's because they pack easier. The average pot we make is thirty-six to forty-two inches long and twelve to fourteen inches wide, but there have been some as much as five-foot long. These are for deep sea fishing. In one case like that, with a double entrance and double parlors, you can catch as many as eighty or one hundred lobsters."

Mr. Clark stops in his work to chat with a gold cat that ambles in — one of three cats that keep him company during his long working hours. "They're always climbing in and out of the pots," he says, and chuckles. "You know, if you get unsettled, all you have to do is to look at a cat. It makes you peaceful to see how settled they are."

"I used to write poetry," he says. "That's a good way to get peaceful too. I'd lie out there under the wild cherries" — and he nods toward the white blossoms in his yard — "and write a little. I still do it when I have time — things like 'I think God loved pale blue the best; He made it lovelier than the rest. It isn't gay and proud like red. It's just a little sad instead. I like it in the summer skies. But best of all in thoughtful eyes.' It was always rhyming poetry that I wrote."

He picks up a pot and carries it out under the trees, where stacks of other pots already rise.

"Oak," he says, "is what you've got to make a pot of. It's the best material underwater. And I use nylon net. In the old days, they used cotton, but you had to tar it and change it twice a year.

"The era after that was five-pound balls of hemp-treated green, and after that they came up with nylon. I use No. 21 and No. 30 Brownell-treated nylon — the top grade, three-ply long.

"There sure are a lot of people lobstering today," he says. "Down around Norwalk, you can't hardly get in and around the pots and buoys. And everybody says down in New York that they catch a lot of lobsters around the Statue of Liberty where there's a garbage dump. I'm guessing and wondering if our polluted waters and the change in the weather aren't the reasons why the lobsters are coming in heavier around here. After all, lobsters are scavengers, though they like fresh bait too — sand flats, sea robins, menhaden. You feed them the whole fish, that's the way you do it. Most fishermen try to use a minimum of bait, but I was taught by my father to put four or five fresh fish to a pot — enough to attract the lobster's attention, but not enough to block off the back funnel. The kitchen is the first compartment of the pot where the lobster comes waltzing in to eat his fill. Then he goes into the second compartment — the parlor — to digest it. You know," he continues, "I know a lot about lobsters not just because my father lobstered, but so did my grandfather and my great-grandfather. My great-grandfather owned the four-masted cargo ship, the *Robert M. Clark*, and my grandfather owned the S.S. *Scranton*, a two-masted vessel that used to travel back and forth from Point Jude in Rhode Island to the West Indies carrying limestone and cargo. And then when my grandfather and my great-grandfather retired, they went lobstering. I'm a Yankee from way back."

Mr. Clark takes off his horn-rimmed glasses and polishes the sawdust off them on his yellow sweatshirt.

"Lobsters are about the toughest creature to catch there is," he continues. "You never catch all the ones out there. A lobster will walk around a pot for two or three days and never go into it, and then sometimes they'll get out of a pot. No amount of lobstering is going to make them extinct. Only natural climatory conditions will do that.

"I do think they're changing some of their habits though. I've always said in the spring when lobsters come out of the mud from hibernating, or are coming into Long Island Sound from offshore, that they're looking for food on the rocks, so that's where I always tried to trap them. But this was previous. Now they tell me you get them most anywhere. In a pot like ours if there are any around, you'll get some."

A car door slams, and he waves a hand in greeting to a young couple approaching.

"I think I remember they bought pots last year," he says. "How'd you like my pots?" he hails them.

"Well enough to come back for six more," the prospective buyer replies with satisfaction. "We got thirty-three lobsters in one week. This guy is a perfectionist in his pots!"

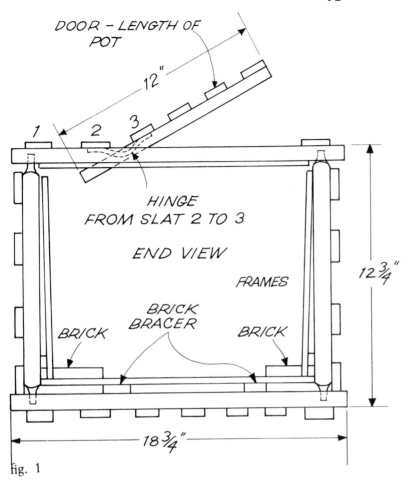

DOOR – LENGTH OF POT

12"

1   2   3

HINGE
FROM SLAT 2 TO 3

END VIEW

FRAMES

BRICK
BRACER

BRICK   BRICK

12¾"

18¾"

fig. 1

1. From a lumberman, buy green oak, which is easy to work, or cottonwood. Get 1½" wide, ⅜" thick laths. (If you are in a seaside area, ask specifically for lobster pot laths.) They should be 36" long for an average pot. You will need enough of this material to make four laths for each side of the pot; seven laths of that size for the bottom; three for the top and four for the door. You will also need three laths 17" long for one end of the pot. At the other end is the net. Materials for three 18" x 12" frames (Fig. 1) of 1" x 1¼" wood are needed, for it is to these that the laths are attached. Two or three 1" square pieces of wood 12" long will be required, too, to strengthen the door laths.

2. Erect frames. Six of the pieces for the frames should be 18" long with holes to receive the dowels (Fig. 1).

MAKING A LOBSTER POT

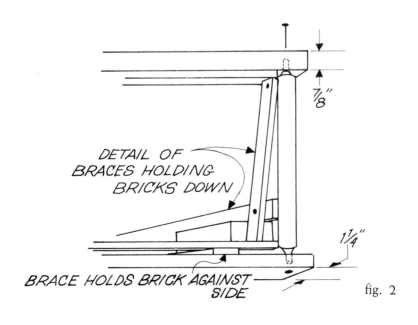

DETAIL OF
BRACES HOLDING
BRICKS DOWN

⅞"

1¼"

BRACE HOLDS BRICK AGAINST
SIDE

fig. 2

3. Fit two of the frame pieces together with two corresponding shorter doweled pieces. Pin frames. (Drive galvanized lobster pot nails from the undoweled part of the frames into the doweled part. So that the oak does not split, drill the pilot holes first.)

4. Set three frames on their sides, spread equally apart, and then nail four laths to frames, spacing evenly. Turn them over and repeat the process on the other side.

5. Nail on seven bottom laths (drilling pilot holes first). The two outside laths of the bottom are the runners used to pull the pot in on, and they should be thicker and wider than the other laths : 3/4″ thick and 1½″ to 1¾″ inches wide.

6. Put the pot on its end and nail three laths on one end, spacing evenly and predrilling.

7. In all instances, be sure that there is double nailing at corners for strength.

8. When the rest of the pot is complete (except for the top and the door) prepare to put in ballast. At a right angle to the bottom laths, 7″ from the lath end of the pot, nail two short pieces of 1″ square x 6″ long wood across the tops of the three bottom laths (Fig. 3) on both sides of the pot. To these pieces, and parallel to the bottom laths, across the middle frame and the frame that will be at the funnel end, nail a 27″ long lath on each side (Fig. 3).

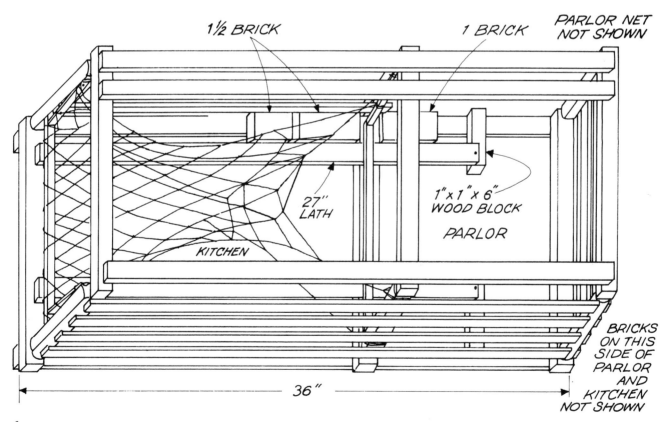

fig. 3

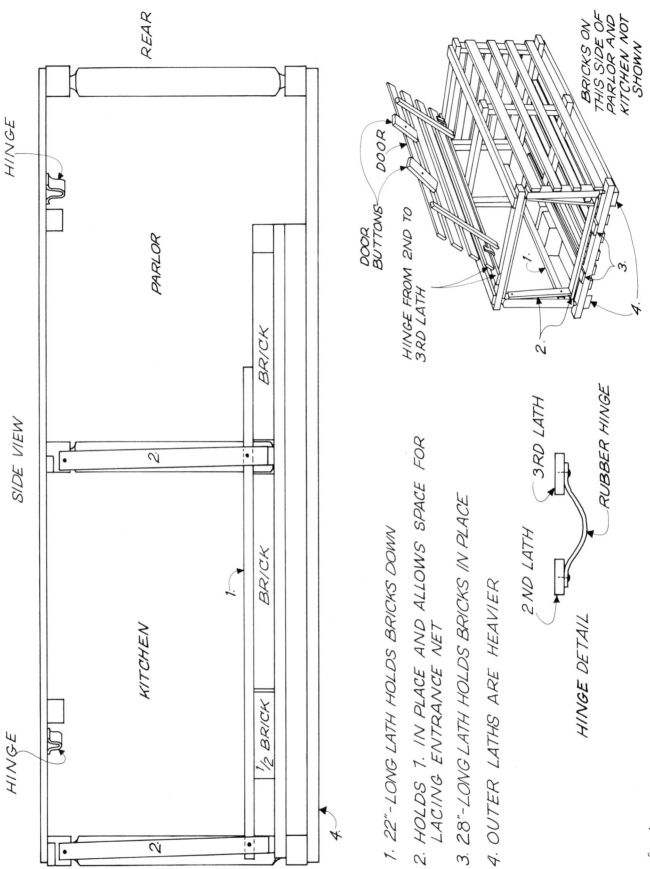

SIDE VIEW

REAR

HINGE

PARLOR

BRICK

HINGE

FRONT

KITCHEN

BRICK

½ BRICK

1.

2.

2.

4.

BRICKS ON THIS SIDE OF PARLOR AND KITCHEN NOT SHOWN

DOOR

DOOR BUTTONS

HINGE FROM 2ND TO 3RD LATH

1.

2.

3.

4.

3RD LATH

RUBBER HINGE

2ND LATH

HINGE DETAIL

1. 22"- LONG LATH HOLDS BRICKS DOWN

2. HOLDS 1. IN PLACE AND ALLOWS SPACE FOR LACING ENTRANCE NET

3. 28"-LONG LATH HOLDS BRICKS IN PLACE

4. OUTER LATHS ARE HEAVIER

fig. 4

Insert two and a half bricks in the enclosure you have made, lay them flat side down, one on each side in the parlor, one and one-half on each side in the kitchen. To hold the bricks in place, nail a 22″-long lath set on its edge to the side of the funnel frame and the side of the middle frame on both sides (Fig. 4).

9. Nail two laths on the outer edges of the top of the pot, one on the side where the door hinge will be, one on the side where the door will open. They should be ¼″ from the frame corners.

10. Make the door out of five laths, 36″ long. To keep it from warping, nail two or three 12″-long, 1″-square pieces of wood across the bottom of the laths, 7″ in from both ends.

11. Get some scrap rubber pieces 4″ to 5″ long and nail them to two of the door laths on the underside, beside each of two of the 1″ x 1″ x 12″ squares (Fig. 1). To the bottom of one of the permanently installed top laths, nail the other ends of the rubber strips. These will act as a hinge for the door.

12. For the funnels, buy a net of No. 21 Brownell-treated twine (Mr. Clark sells it). Funnels also may be made of some other nonrotting, waterproof material. Take two 15″ x ¾″ laths and weave them through the bottom of the funnel to become funnel strips Fig. 5). Take two 8½″ x

¾″ laths and weave them through the sides of the funnel to become funnel strips. Repeat the process for the second funnel. Nail the strips (with the attached funnel) to the bottom, top, and sides of the middle frame. Nail the funnel to the outer corners of the end frame with four additional pieces of treated twine. Nail the kitchen funnel frame into place. The kitchen funnel

fig. 5 *Weaving strips into a lobster pot funnel*

should have four twine lines connecting it to the upper corners of the middle frame and two connecting it to the lower corners of the middle frame. (Using four twine lines will open the funnel wider and make it more welcoming to the lobster.) Pull taut.

13. Attach two 6″-long laths to the lath where the door opens. Use a pot nail cleated over for this purpose. These laths can then be twisted backward and forward and will serve as buttons to keep the door closed (Fig. 4).

14. Buy ¼″ nylon line and a buoy for the pot. Attach one end of the line to either the right or left side frame at the funnel end of the pot. (Some people recommend a small additional buoy adjusted to show at the low tide level to lessen the chance of the main buoy's being pulled under or of losing the pot should the top buoy be clipped off by passing boats.) In buying line, bear in mind that you will need one-third more line than the depth of the water at high tide into which you plan to sink your pots.

The completed pot is shown from two views in Figs. 6 and 7.

fig. 6   *The interior of a finished lobster pot*
(Shirley Mayhew)

fig. 7   *A finished lobster pot from the side*
(Tom Cocroft)

Build it like it was, then it's real." That's the way Captain R. D. (Pete) Culler of Hyannis, Massachusetts, makes boats.

"I like and design boats in the classic style, and I build them that way, and there are not many nowadays who do," he asserts firmly as he pauses in his construction of an eighteen-foot outboard, lights up his pipe, and sits down for a spell on the end of a sawhorse in the boat shed behind his house.

"That boat there has good oak and cedar and pine in her. There's oak for the framing because it holds fastenings well — that's been known since Norse times. And cedar is used for the planking, and pine for the finishing out. I like Eastern white pine the best. It's been the standard wood of New England for ships and houses for generations. That's partly what the Revolution was about, of course. King George wanted the pine for ship's masts and the colonists said, 'To heck with him!'"

Pete Culler is not, himself, New England–born. His birthplace was Oswego, New York, and he has lived in California and in the Chesapeake Bay area. "When you sail," he puts it, "you end up lots of places." He is a retired yacht skipper, but for the past twenty-six years, Hyannis has been his home, and he says he doesn't care to go to sea anymore. "The constant motion and the narrow bunks and having the vessel on your mind all the time, I've had enough of that!"

But the boats he builds and designs today are never off his mind either — not even years after they have left his loft or the Concordia Company Boatyard in Dartmouth for which he designs.

"You know, it's funny. I wake up sometimes at night and I wonder how so-and-so's bowsprit is," he says, and takes off his plaid wool cap and scratches the top of his head thoughtfully.

It was not until he was past fifty — he is now sixty-five — that Pete Culler began designing boats. "It wasn't till then I thought I knew enough about them," he says. "Designing is something you don't get altogether out of books. You have to put in time with boats, both sailing them and building them. Before you lay pencil to paper you've got to know what that boat's going to be about. It's like the old fellow who'd commanded the last of the deepwater vessels, who, when World War Two came along, went to the shipyard looking for a job. There was a sign posted

· 8 ·

A BUILDER OF
CLASSIC BOATS

that said they needed a rigger. The personnel man interviewed the old captain. 'How old are you?' he asked. 'Sixty-five,' said the captain. 'I'm sorry,' the personnel man told him, 'you're too old.' 'Hell, man, don't you know it takes sixty-five years to make a rigger?' the captain replied. And he got the job."

But building a boat, even Pete Culler will admit, is something that one can try one's hand at doing at a younger age than that.

"I started the first skiff I built when I was ten with a crosscut saw and a hammer, a ripsaw, a screwdriver, a brace, fittings, a plane, and a few bits — I might even have borrowed the bits from neighbors, I can't remember. You really don't need much in the way of tools, though, for boat building. After

all, aborigines built their canoes with stone axes and hot water to soften the wood, didn't they?"

You do, though, need training in the ritual of boat building, Captain Culler maintains. "Boat building is as stylized and as ritualistic as a High Mass," he says, "and if you break the continuity of it, something goes wrong. How do you learn all that? With a boat builder."

The continuity for Pete Culler, who has designed more than eighty boats and built more than forty, starts with the carving of a half model of the craft he plans to build once he has the plans for it

in front of him. First, he takes the lines — measures the sheer of the boat (how much the gunwale rises at both ends), the run (the amount the bottom curves up at the stern), and the rake (the amount the bottom curves up at the bow) from his half model to make drawings for the boat. Then he "lofts" the boat — draws a full-size pattern of it either directly on the floor if he is building indoors and the floor is unmarred enough so marks can be seen on it, or on a piece of plywood that he will put down if he is building outdoors, or on plywood on sawhorses.

This method, he explains, takes out any errors that might be caused by as simple a thing as the

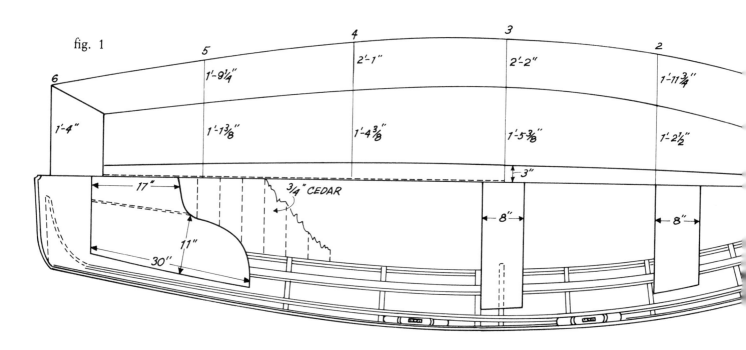

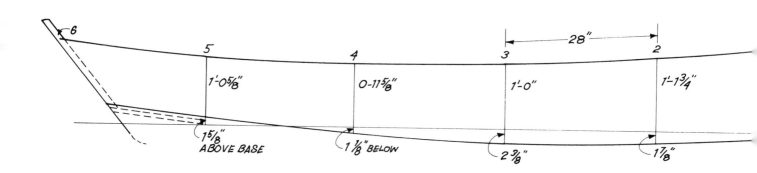

width of a pencil line in his plan. On this floor plan, he puts all the measurements that are on his paper plan, after figuring from the paper plan's scale what their actual size on the boat will be.

Here are Captain Culler's plans for a 14'6" rowboat, but he emphasizes that anyone planning to build it should have some basic knowledge of boat building. He estimates that the materials required could, with careful looking, probably be bought for about $100. "But of course if you go right out and buy things the way most people do nowadays you're going to pay top dollar. If you do that, materials could come to as much as two hundred and fifty dollars." Bought from a boatyard, however, a skiff like this would cost $800 to $1000.

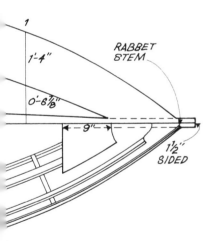

BUILDING A PETE CULLER SKIFF

1. Draw a base line on the floor to represent the planned water line of the boat, or, for convenience sake, so you need not bend down for the building, lay two sheets of 4' x 8' plywood end to end and nail them on top of three sawhorses. Use this as your building "floor."

2. Mark "stations" — vertical lines at which you can gauge the varying shape of the boat (a boat is not, after all, the same width from stem to stern) on the floor or plywood and erect molds at these stations. Molds should be only as wide as the width of the boat from inside planking to inside planking. These will be removed when the boat is done, but they are essential as a base for the boat's construction (Fig. 1). They are made, Pete Culler says, "of any wood you can get," but he is inclined, himself, to use 1"-thick rough spruce, 6" wide. The sides of the boat will be built around the uprights of the mold and the bottom over the shorter of the mold's two horizontal

pieces (Fig. 2, 3). When positioning the molds at the stations, it is helpful to keep them in place by tacking 1" to 1½" strips of pine on the floor or plywood on both sides of them. "Don't build a boat on a cement floor," Pete Culler warns at this juncture. "You can't nail to it. It wears out your shoes, and if you drop a drill on it it's finished." Captain Culler's flat or V-bottomed boats are always built upside-down. "They take kindly to this construction," he says, and adds that it is easier to build them this way if you are building alone, since, if the building is done right-side-up, you must crawl under the boat to put the bottom planking in place.

3. When the six molds you will need (Fig. 2) are made (including the transom) and positioned, the stem and transom should be cut out (Fig. 3). For the stem of his 14'6" skiff, Captain Culler uses 1½" thick x 8" wide oak, which he cuts with a band saw. As in all building with wood, when you are cutting it, the

fig. 2

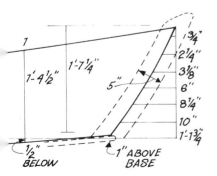

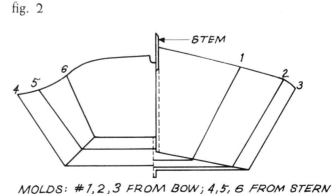

MOLDS: #1,2,3 FROM BOW; 4,5,6 FROM STERN

STEM

CHINE

1

2

3

28"
ON CENTER

4

5
CENTER LINE

PLANKING

6

TRANSOM

fig. 3

14'-6"

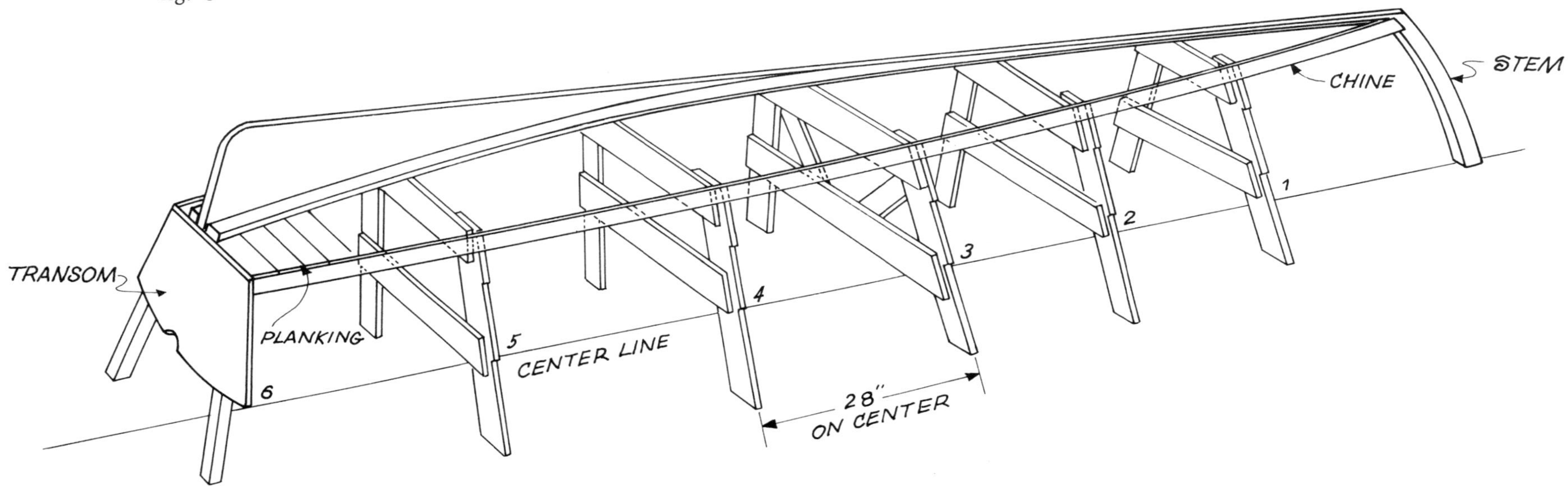

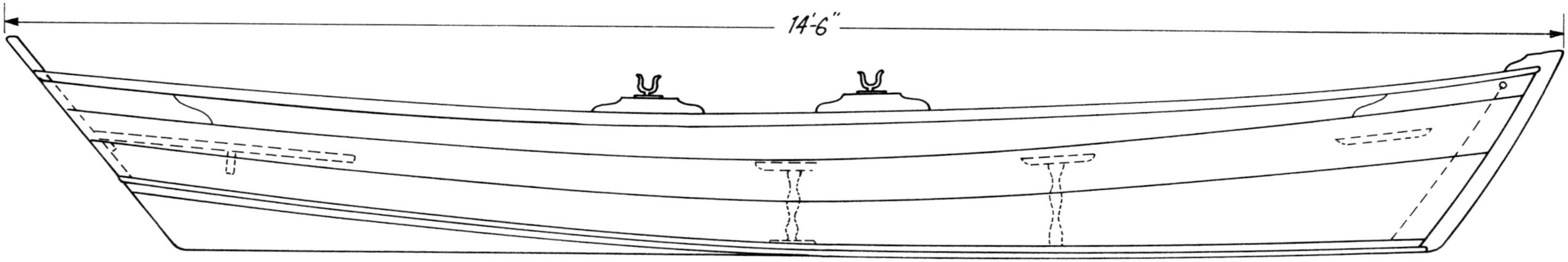

LENGTH: 14'-6"
WIDTH: 4'-6" AT WIDEST POINT

fig. 4

closer the grain parallels the cut the better. Because accuracy of measurements is so essential if a boat is to be seaworthy, templates or patterns should be made for the main parts — like the stem and transom. Captain Culler's are generally of soft wood, $1/4''$ to $3/8''$ thick, outlined on the piece of wood that is actually to be used for the stem or transom. In cutting the final stem piece, rabbet carefully so that the side planking will fit tightly into it (Fig. 4). Use a chisel for rabbeting.

4. When the stem, transom, and other molds are erected, and are perfectly square and upright, it is time to "try out" the curves that the side planking will take with the use of battens — long, narrow strips of white pine. Several of these should be used, bent from transom to middle mold to stem and lightly nailed to these pieces with small nails (both interior molds and battens will later be removed so they need not be firmly attached, but at this stage in building, they will not only assure you that your layout is "fair," which means that it makes a true curve for the side planking — but will

also hold the molds in place while you build the boat around them).

5. Chine pieces, $3/4''$ x $3''$ wide oak or fir, a wood that takes nails well, should next be put in place, fastened to the stem in two places with $1''$ bronze screws or ring nails. The chine pieces (Fig. 5) are to nail the boat where the side and bottom planking come together and the boat is likely to get hard knocks. In attaching them, bear in mind, Captain Culler warns, that holes must be bored for fastenings before they are inserted so as not to split the wood. This procedure should be followed whenever a fastening is to go into a boat. The holes drilled should be almost the length of the fastening inserted but a trifle smaller in diameter. As the chine pieces go from stem to transom they, like the battens, should be temporarily fastened to the molds with nails.

6. When the chine pieces are in place on both sides, the first planks should go in place outside them. No. 2 Everdur screws are good for attaching

them, using three on each side at each end (though Captain Culler is not inclined to divulge a great deal about fastenings, remarking that "You've got to have a little judgment about where they should go and how long they should be. Be sensible about it. Obviously, the length of a fastening depends on the thickness of the stock being used. There's an old saying among boat builders, and it's the best advice I know for the amateur : 'Nail where you can; screw where you must, and bolt where you have to' ").

7. In attaching planks to each other, copper clinch nails used every $3''$ are suggested for joining the planks in lapstrake fashion. Bear in mind that the side planks should be beveled on both ends and that each plank put in position should overlap the preceding plank by $1''$ (Figs. 4, 6). When Captain Culler is doing his planking, he attaches only one chine piece and one plank to each side and then proceeds with bottom planking, but if you wish, the entire side planking may be done first, so long as you go from side to side of the boat in doing it. Always be sure when a plank is attached

fig. 5

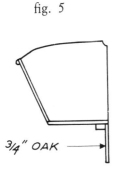

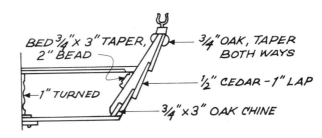

3/4" OAK

BED 3/4" x 3" TAPER, 2" BEAD

1" TURNED

3/4" OAK, TAPER BOTH WAYS

1/2" CEDAR - 1" LAP

3/4" x 3" OAK CHINE

fig. 6 *The side lapstrake*

fig. 7 *The shore and bracing of a Culler centerboard skiff, built by Bob Kelley*
(Tom Cocroft)

to one side that the comparable plank is attached to the other.

8. When you are ready to do the bottom planking (Fig. 1), Captain Culler suggests using cedar or pine (not oak because it is heavy and shrinks and swells too much). He starts by laying planks up forward (in a flat-bottomed boat, lay your planks all the way across the bottom). "Be sure," Captain Culler says, "that the wood you use is air-dried, not kiln-dried. Air-drying, after all, is Nature's way, and a boat is going to play with Nature, isn't it?" Use planks of about ¾" thickness and 4" in width for bottom planking. Because of the likelihood of swelling and shrinking, each plank's growth rings should curve in the opposite direction from those on the plank you lay beside it. After you have laid several planks at the bow, move to the stern, measure there, and lay several more, working all the time toward the middle. Toward the end of this operation, it will be necessary to plane a board down to fit a specific area amidships. But there

is no need for that to cause dismay. In laying planks, fit them together as tightly as possible. As he works, Captain Culler holds the boat down "like a patient." He extends a shore (a 2' x 4' of fir) between an overhead beam and the bottom of the boat in the midsection (when he is working indoors) (Fig. 7). Outdoors, he uses a heavy stone for the same purpose. To attach the bottom planks, use boat nails or bronze or galvanized screws. All boat fastenings should be countersunk and the holes filled later with wood dough or putty.

9. The keel, a width of oak tapering from bow to stern (see Fig. 1), should next be screwed down the center of the bottom planking with bronze ring nails or galvanized boat nails. The screwing should be done from the inside out.

10. Framing comes next, and the boat should be righted for this procedure. Frames are usually placed midway between the molds (Fig. 8). They should be about 16" apart and made from ¾" oak. Use a template to ascertain their shape. It will be necessary, to assure a proper fit, to put them in place against the inside of the boat and reshape and refit them if they are not precisely correct (Fig. 8). Hold them in place with clamps while they are being screwed in from the outside. Ideally, some of these supports should be made from tree limbs — knees. "They're stronger than steel, those knees," Pete Culler says. "Man never could learn to glue like the Lord can." And under Captain Culler's workbenches clusters of them — oak, cherry, elm, and apple — can be seen. He usually uses two knees at the stern, one at the bow, and two at the rowing thwart — one on each side. Although Captain Culler makes use of glue for additional support in his craft, he disparages it in general as overused, dead, and dormant. "And a boat isn't dead, it's alive," he stresses.

fig. 8   *Fitting the frames between the molds*

11. When the frames have been screwed into place, the clamps that hold up the seats should be nailed or screwed to the frames. They should be of cedar and about the same thickness as the chine pieces (Fig. 9).

12. Now it is time to put the thwarts in the stern of the skiff. A 17"-wide, 30"-long plank ¾" thick should be used (see Fig. 1 for complete dimensions). They should be rested on the clamps and fastened to them.

13. Finally, make the gunwale that will go all along the top of the boat. Use ¾" or 1" pine, rounded. The gunwale should be flush with the top plank and screwed into it along the outside with 1½"-long flathead wood screws set about 10" apart.

14. When the gunwale is in place, except for preparing the oak blocks for the oarlocks, drilling holes in them, fastening them in place with screws, and painting, the boat is done. Captain Culler generally uses red bottom paint. The rest of the boat can be painted with any good marine paint. As for caulking, Captain Culler says simply, "The better carpenter you are, the less caulking you need."

Although boat designing and building are Pete Culler's first loves, they are by no means the only crafts he pursues. He also makes his own tools and murmurs that "people nowadays tend to go overboard on power machinery. I have a minimum. You become a slave to it. It's no good unless it runs and is sharp." He also designs oars and canoe paddles and fashions blocks and quarterboards and sternboards.

As he sighs about motorized tools, so he sighs a little about the abundance of motorized boats.

"I like to build rowboats for the sheer pleasure of rowing," he says, and polishes his gold-rimmed glasses. "But people will always ask you if you won't put a motor in them. I go out rowing just for the enjoyment of it, but most people hate physical exercise nowadays. I know all the clams and quahogs and they put their horns up when I row by. But most people — I think sometimes my cat's got more sense than modern man!"

Pete Culler's boat shed door opens (his neighbors are always welcome) and a dentist friend comes in for advice on a boat he is building with his grandson. When he leaves, there is a visitor with an inquiry about sails.

"It's a heck of a life," Pete Culler says as he turns back to his tools, "not to be doing what you want to do. It makes ulcers and shortens your life. I'm doing what I want to do with the material with which I want to do it!" And his gray eyes gleam happily. "I love wood — and wood is available. Man should remember that. If you leave wood alone — if you keep the developers away — it's the one resource that is relatively quickly self-renewing."

fig. 9   *The clamps hold up the seats*

Not far above the alewife run in Damariscotta Mills, Maine, in a white house built in 1740, a dark-eyed, dark-haired housewife carves wooden dolls. Most are fashioned after old *Godey's Lady's Book* pictures and *Harper's Magazine* illustrations. A few are copies of the doll Hornbook used before 1800 in American schoolhouses. These are jumping-jack-like flat figures two feet tall with ABC's carved on their arms and legs and torsos.

The Eastern white pine ladies with their corkscrew curls and pink and white complexions and the bearded men perch elegantly on antique chests in Renie Taylor's parlor or sit on the mantelpiece above a spinning wheel that is broken and awaiting Mrs. Taylor's ministrations. The more rapscallion Hornbook dolls that can be manipulated by strings are likely to dangle from doorknobs, where the eight- and ten-year-old Taylor boys, John and James, tug at them.

Irene Taylor made her first doll in 1953 from a pattern in *McCall's Needlework & Crafts Magazine*. It was to be a birthday gift for her ten-year-old sister, but when the magazine offered $5 if the doll made from their pattern was good enough, its creator quickly made half a dozen more, photographed them, and sent the picture in. She not only won the $5 but began getting requests for dolls from all over. "Kansas, Michigan, Sweden, Australia. I couldn't believe it." Today, she has almost more requests than she can fill.

The dolls she makes are quite different, Mrs. Taylor emphasizes, from the penny dolls of the same period, the nineteenth century. Those had joints that often failed to work, but they were cheap (the reason for the name) and popular with children.

Taylor dolls are pretty dolls, though their expressions may vary as they reflect their carver's moods. "My mother warned me a long time ago to be certain I was in a happy frame of mind before I picked up my chisels," she remarks, pointing out some dolls with animated, cheerful expressions on their faces, others that look wistful, still others with a touch of coquetry in their ruby red lips, and a few with tight, sullen mouths.

Since she makes all her own clothes, and many of her husband's and sons', dressing her dolls in the fashion of their day has never been a problem. "I like to sew and knit and crochet and stencil. I love all kinds of craft work," she explains one afternoon in her old-fashioned

· 9 ·

FROM PINE BOARDS
INTO DOLLS

parlor. "I like to see the results from anything that I do. I've made more than three hundred dolls now."

Since Renie Taylor's husband, Colin, is a retired lumber buyer, and she is the daughter of a lumberman, getting wood to work with has never been a problem, though she does say wistfully that there was a time when her husband had a whole field full of pine boards eighteen inches wide, but he sold them. "And I sure could use that lumber now. I don't throw away any piece of wood ever," she says. "Whenever I have a piece of something left over, I'll make something out of it. From even the tiniest piece I'll make a head to use someday, or a pair of arms, or legs."

Diminutive, bright-eyed, and energetic, when Mrs. Taylor is not carving or sewing or keeping house, she is likely to be making use of spare moments reading history. And, with textbooklike detail, she will recount, at a breakneck pace, the history of her house, or of Damariscotta Mills, or the church up the hill.

She likes to tell how the house she now lives in was a general store about 1784, went into private hands as a home for about a century, and then, more recently, was used as a summer retreat for nuns.

The church up the hill, St. Patrick's, is the oldest Catholic church north of Saint Augustine, Florida, she points out. "It was built in eighteen-o-eight. There used to be one that was earlier that stood in Boston, but it burned down."

She and her husband discovered their home on a lumber-scouting trip to Maine from New Hampshire. "We often came here to look at different people's logs, and buy them at wholesale, then have them taken to the mill to be sawed into boards, and then down to the railroad to be shipped out. There were a lot of shipyards here in the early eighteen hundreds, I understand. The Great Salt Bay below our house was lined with them. They had to float the ships they built down our rapids at high tide, but they managed to."

The Taylors saw the old house and made an offer on it, but after thinking it over, "it looked so bad we took back our offer. One more big storm and it would have been a pancake." On their next visit to Damariscotta Mills they looked at it again, reconsidered, lowered their original price, and bought the house on the condition that they would restore it. Their restoration is still going on, and it is being done with care.

In an old house down the road, Mrs. Taylor discovered that there were eighteenth-century stencils of urns edging the ceiling. She copied them. A cobalt blue stencil borders the doors and the pine mantel in the parlor. "I've thought about sending a copy of that urn stencil to the Society of New England Antiquities," she says, "because I think it might be one of Moses Eaton's designs. He was among the most famous of the stencilers. He came down from New Hampshire with all of his patterns and traveled all over New England decorating houses in the late eighteenth century."

The four old fireplaces in the Taylor home are also being repaired, and a long-unused Dutch oven has been uncovered. Long ago, a log fort, 100 feet square with walls seven inches thick, stood across the road, and Mrs. Taylor says sadly she wishes it still were standing as a companion piece to her house. But it was torn down in 1812.

With the same historical enthusiasm, she likes to tell about Hornbook dolls, and how, when they were actually used in schoolrooms, they had a three-sided frame on their chests into which a piece of parchment protected by transparent animal horn was placed. On it was the day's lesson. "It might be the Lord's Prayer, the alphabet, the ten digits — any one of them might be there."

But it is the dolls that she dresses of which she is fondest. For them, Renie Taylor selects white pine that is without any streaks of pitch or knotholes. "And you want to seek a straight grain," she emphasizes.

Materials Needed

You will need a white pine block 1½″ x 1½″ x 6¼″ for the body, a pine piece ½″ x 2″ x 4″ for the lower legs, a piece ⅜″ x 1½″ x 3″ for the lower arms, two pieces of ½″ dowel 3¾″ long for the upper legs, two pieces of ⅜″ dowel 2¼″ long for the upper arms, one piece of ⅜″ dowel 2⅜″ long for the shoulder piece, and a 3/16″ dowel (or wooden Q-tips) for pegs. You will also need flat white paint; oil or poster paints in white, black, red, yellow, and blue; a small brush for painting the body; a fine sable brush for the features; and shellac.

1. To make a 12″ doll, take a piece of 1½″ square white pine and trace the body pattern (Fig. 1) onto it.

2. With two or three table-saw blades put together, or with a coping saw, cut mortises in the lower end of the block for the legs. So that the legs can swing up in front and the doll sit down, the cut should be 1″ deep in front, sloping downward to ¼″ deep in the back.

3. Drill a ⅜″ hole through the side of the pine block at the location that will be the doll's shoulder line (which will receive the shoulder piece) 2¾″ down from the top of the block of wood (Fig. 2).

4. Draw a circle on top of the wood block to suggest the size of the head. In a 1½″ block, there will be approximately ¼″ of wood to be cut away outside the circle.

5. Mark four lines on the face of the block where you would like the level of the eyes, nose, mouth, and chin.

6. Also draw a line to indicate the center of the doll's face. As you chisel, keep replacing the line so that the face is always properly centered.

7. Begin by chiseling the excess wood away from the body, carving first on the neck and waist and making straight cuts to begin with. Shape the body, turning it often, to keep its rounding even. Later, you may use curved chisels. "You kind of have to experiment and find your way," Mrs. Taylor says. "Be sure you cut with the grain."

8. Complete the shaping of the body, narrowing the waist, using a jigsaw or a hand saw to go around the curves if you wish. Carve the head and face, keeping the eyes well down on the face.

9. From a ½″ dowel, cut two pieces 3¾″ long for the upper legs (Fig. 1). Make the tenon on the upper end 1″ long in front and ½″ long in back.

10. Cut out two lower legs from ½″-thick wood; 4″ long (Fig. 1). Make tenons on the upper end, ½″ long in front, 1″ long in back; carve and shape, making slipperlike feet.

11. Fit the lower legs into mortises in the upper legs. Hold them in place and drill a 3/16″ hole for a peg all the way through. Remove the lower legs and round the ends of the tenons. Reassemble and gently tap the wooden pegs (Q-tips) through the holes. Cut off the ends sticking out. No glue is needed, for the pegs will be held by paint.

MAKING A WOODEN DOLL

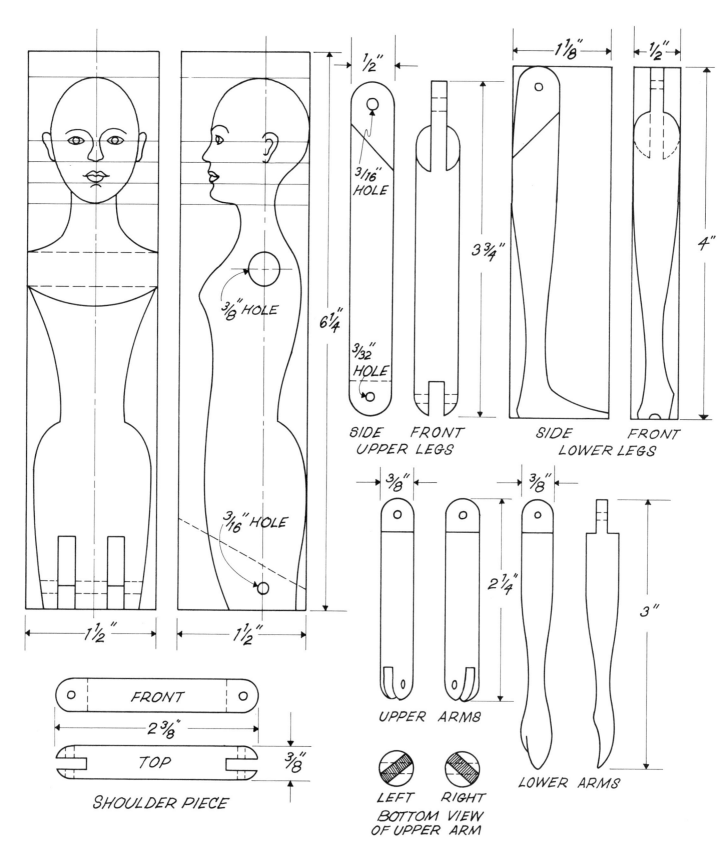

3/16" HOLE

3/8" HOLE

3/16" HOLE

1/2"

6 1/4"

3/16" HOLE

3/32" HOLE

SIDE   FRONT
UPPER LEGS

1 1/8"

1/2"

3 3/4"

4"

SIDE   FRONT
LOWER LEGS

3/8"

3/8"

2 1/4"

3"

UPPER ARMS

LOWER ARMS

LEFT   RIGHT
BOTTOM VIEW
OF UPPER ARM

1 1/2"

1 1/2"

FRONT

2 3/8"

TOP

3/8"

SHOULDER PIECE

fig. 1

12. Insert the tenons of the upper legs into mortises on the body. Hold the tenons in place. Drill a 3/16″ hole for a peg through the hip line ¼″ from the bottom of the torso. Take apart and round the ends of the tenons. Reassemble and tap the wooden peg through the hole. Cut off the ends if they stick out.

13. To make the shoulder piece, take a ⅜″ dowel and cut it 2⅜″ long. Mortise both ends ⅜″ deep so that the upper arms can be received (Fig. 1). Be sure the shoulder extends ⅜″ beyond the body.

14. Cut out two upper arm segments from a ⅜″ dowel 2¼″ long (Fig. 1). Cut a ⅜″ deep tenon straight across the top of the upper arm pieces to fit into the shoulder mortises. Cut a ⅜″ deep mortise in the lower end of the upper arm pieces, at an angle, not straight with the tenon. Fit the tenons into the shoulder piece. Drill a 3/16″ hole for the peg. Take the pieces apart; round the ends of the tenons and the shoulder piece. Reassemble the body and tap the pegs into the holes. Cut off the ends sticking out.

fig. 2 *A pine block with the shoulder hole drilled*

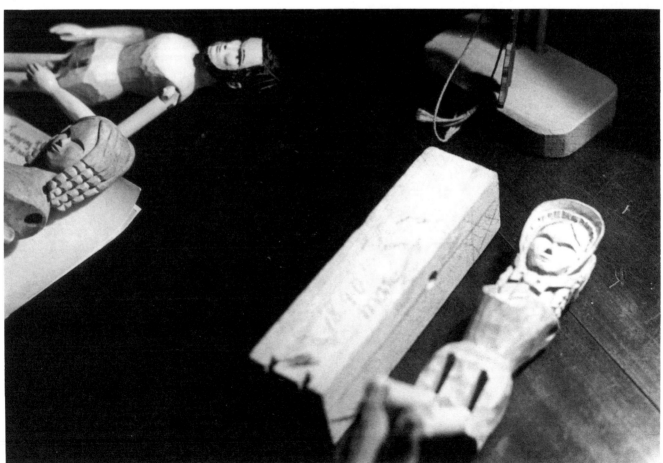

15. Cut out two lower arm pieces from ⅜″ thick wood 3″ long. Cut the tenons on the upper end straight across. Carve and shape, making spoonlike hands. Be sure to have right and left hands. Fit the lower pieces into the mortises of the upper arms. Drill holes for pegs. Take apart, round ends, reassemble, and peg (Fig. 3).

16. Sand the doll with fine sandpaper. If you are using oil paint, shellac the doll first before putting on the body color. If you use tempera or poster paint, shellac after the doll is completely painted. Paint the doll with flesh-colored paint (add a little red and yellow to flat white paint). When dry, paint again. While the second coat is still wet, add cheek color; add rosiness if desired. Paint eyes, lips, and hair. (If children are to play with the dolls, be sure there is no lead in the paint.) Dress as desired (Fig. 4).

fig. 3 *Pegging and joining a doll's arm*

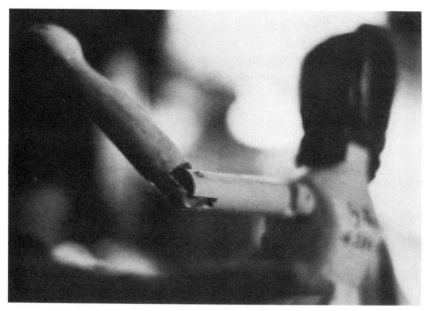

fig. 4   *A completed and dressed doll*

Only seven families live in Quaker City, New Hampshire, at the end of a rutted road, among maples and birches and oaks and hemlocks — where yellow-shafted woodpeckers tap at wild cherry trunks, catbirds call, hawks sweep low over the hills, and grouse scurry among the spruces.

Quaker City residents — craftsmen and nursery workers, a waitress, a mechanic — are all in their twenties and thirties, living in cabins that they have built themselves or old houses that they have restored. In 1820, there was a full-fledged settlement of Friends in Quaker City, and the nut brown meeting house still stands at the start of the rutted road.

Stanley McCumber is one of the village's residents. He is a bearded twenty-six-year-old from Glastonbury, Connecticut, who moved to the New Hampshire village when he grew tired of Tufts College. Now he prunes apple trees for orchardists of the region and makes lightweight, spruce-rail apple-picking ladders — open-topped to reach high into the trees, or pointed to fit the crotches where the tree limbs rise. He works only four to five months a year but says, "I have everything I want in the way of food and shelter. My house is only ten by ten, so it only cost a few hundred dollars, and I built it myself." It is just one room, heated by a wood stove. Gradually, however, Mr. McCumber expects to enlarge it. He shares it with his girl friend and her five-year-old daughter, and together, when they are not busy with apples, they tend their half-acre vegetable garden and preserve and can.

"Up until January, there's always canning to do, and brush to be burned, land to clear, vehicles to repair, gardens to expand and improve; there are books to be read, and sometimes we take a trip somewhere. Then from January to May, I prune apple trees, and in May and June there's the garden to work and ladders to make. There's not enough time for everything I want to do!" Stanley McCumber says.

His older sister discovered Quaker City and he moved there soon afterward. "She and her husband made a conscious decision to live out in the country, and found this place and stayed," he explains. She has become a dressmaker and her husband does leather work, and they are supporting a first child with their craft.

"In crafts, the secret is to find something that has a market," Mr.

• 10 •
APPLE LADDERS
FOR ORCHARDISTS

McCumber advises. "There's always a market among orchardists for my ladders, for example. You can buy manufactured ones of basswood or aluminum, it's true, but a lot of people just like something handmade."

Mr. McCumber starts from the very beginning with his ladders, cutting down his own trees.

"A ladder is made of rungs of hardwood such as oak for strength and durability. The rails are made from soft wood for lightness and ease in handling. It's not a difficult article to construct," he adds, as he offers the following directions:

MAKING A 12'-LONG APPLE-PICKING LADDER

1. For the rungs, look for a 50'- to 60'-foot-tall, fairly straight oak 12" to 18" in diameter. Cut the tree down and saw a suitably long chunk off the butt end. Split the chunk into rungs with a froe. The rungs should be approximately 1" square; then shave them smooth with a drawknife until they are about 7/8" square with the corners shaved off.

2. For the rails, a spruce is preferable, Mr. McCumber says, "because it is the straightest tree. Get the straightest ones you can find, four or five inches in diameter and about thirty feet tall." Mr. McCumber always goes after his spruces in the spring, "because the bark peels off easily then."

3. Cut down the tree; then peel off the bark, using a small knife to start. Saw off the knots so you can run your hand down the surface and not catch it.

4. Saw the tree in half. Mr. McCumber uses a power saw. "But that's the only place I use a power tool. I saw the tree down the middle by eye. You can't split it because the grain of a spruce twists in a spiral." Dry the rails for about six weeks, clamping them to a flat surface their whole length; otherwise, the spiral grain of spruce will make the ends twist.

5. Once the tree is cut in half and dry, use a draw shave to shave it smooth. The rails should taper from about 3½" thick at the bottom to 1⅞" at the top.

6. Clamp the two rails together. Drill holes through them while they are in this position. The holes should be 1" apart. Be sure that you drill with the rails level or the rungs will end up slanted. To be sure that the rails are level, lay them on level sawhorses and clamp them securely to the sawhorses. Hold the drill at a right angle to the rails and drill with a bit brace from the top one through the bottom one. A 12' ladder will have 11 rungs, so drill 11 holes. The top six holes should be 5/8" in diameter; the lower holes 3/4". The smaller holes at the top are necessary because the rails are thinner at the top than the bottom.

7. Turn the ends of the rungs in a lathe or with a spoke auger. Make tenons to fit into the rail holes you have drilled. The tenons should be the same size as the homes they will

enter. "The spruce will give a little to allow them to enter, but you want to be sure they're a tight fit. You may have trouble if you make them too big, though, and have to take them back to the lathe or the chisel. Don't make them so tight that they split the spruce," Mr. McCumber warns, and provides the following measurements for rungs of a 12' ladder.

Rung Number from Top	Rung Length	Tenon Length	Tenon Diameter
1	11 "	1½"	⅝"
2	12 "	1½"	⅝"
3	13 "	1½"	⅝"
4	14 "	1½"	⅝"
5	15 "	1½"	⅝"
6	15½"	1½"	⅝"
7	16 "	1½"	¾"
8	16½"	1½"	¾"
9	17 "	1½"	¾"
10	18½"	2 "	¾"
11	19 "	2 "	¾"

8. To insert the rungs, Mr. McCumber lays one rail on the grass. He fits the rungs into that rail all the way up. Then he lays the other rail on the ground and pounds it and the rest of the ladder together with a small mallet. Some rungs, he notes, will always protrude through the rails. "Just cut those off and shave them flush with the rail."

9. Nail the rungs on each side from the top of the rail to the bottom. Use a nail set so the nail does not protrude.

10. If you like, make the ladder water-resistant with linseed oil or varnish.

Two apple-picking ladders: a pointed one to fit the crotches where the tree limbs rise and an open-topped one to reach high into the trees

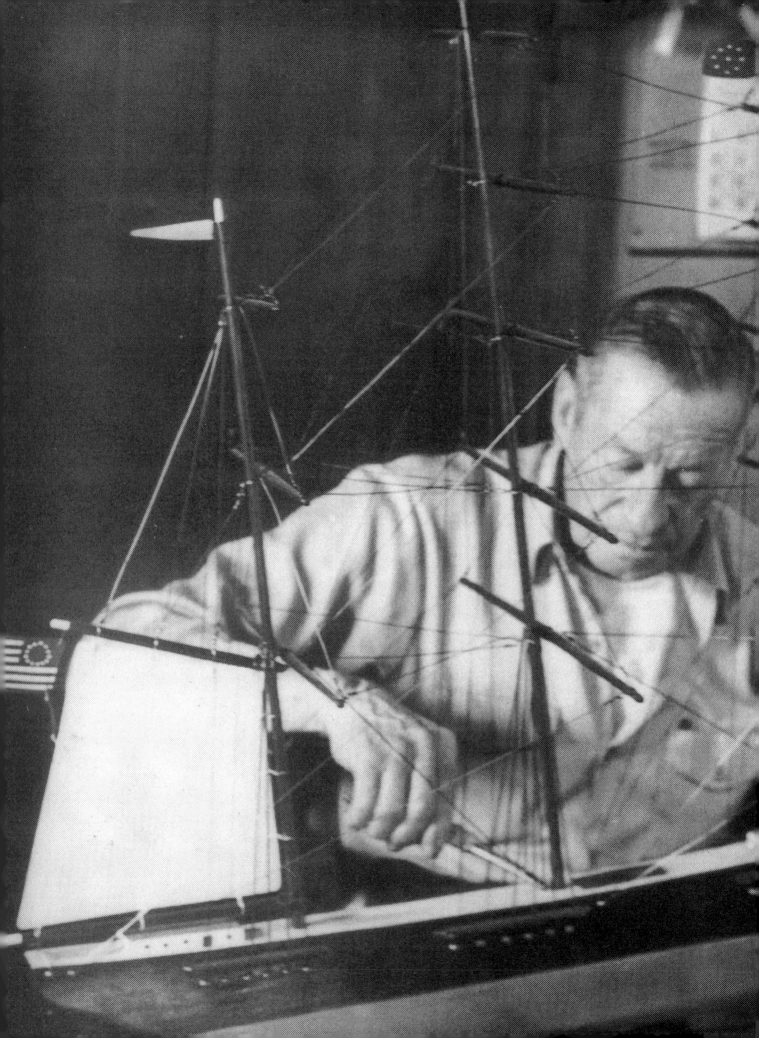

A century ago, on many a rooftop in a New England seacoast village, a weathervane of a sailing ship headed up into the wind. Sometimes she carried a full set of sails; sometimes only the spanker was up. In ice storms, her rigging glistened. A skipper home from the sea and nostalgic for it would reminisce as he looked up at his barn ridgepole at the sight of a two- or three-master pivoting there.

Here and there today, one still finds ship weathervanes fashioned from patterns handed down through the generations, but they are not a common sight. The fashioning of them is time-consuming. The balancing of masts and the stretching of shrouds are painstaking tasks calling not only for a skilled, but a patient, craftsman. But in Yarmouth, Maine, J. Warren Raynes, a former cabinetmaker and a former patternmaker for foundries still stretches and twists the wires for them, saws profiles of hulls from white cedar, and cuts spars of Honduras mahogany.

Warren Raynes is a tall, rugged man with bright blue eyes and a wide, shy smile. He began making weathervanes when he inherited his Grandfather Allen's white clapboard house and barn on Prince's Point Road and found a hull for a weathervane in the barn. Its discovery sent him back in memory over the years to his boyhood, when he used to visit his grandfather George Allen, an interior decorator and painter of landscapes (several of his oils of tragedy and heroism at sea decorate the Raynes's walls today). Grandfather Allen liked to make ship weathervanes as a hobby.

"I used to watch him rigging them with fishline," Warren Raynes recalls, "and I always wondered how he knew what went where. There were still quite a few sea captains going out of Yarmouth then, and there were big homes and servants and the like of that, and he used to give his weathervanes away to wealthy clients. How I admired his handiwork!" He adds a shovelful of coal to the potbellied stove in his workshed on this winter morning and remarks that the fire "either goes like the Old Scratch or it goes out — that was a great expression of my Gramps."

Between the time he admired his grandfather's threading of rigging from spar to spar and the time he inherited his grandfather's Yarmouth house thirty years ago, Warren Raynes operated his own woodworking shop, building skiffs

· 11 ·

ROOFTOP SAILING VESSELS

and rowboats and V-bottom boats and repairing and refinishing antiques; owned his own concern making the components for portable sawmills; and was one of the engineers working with the Hudson Motor Company when the Hudson station wagon was designed in 1941.

"They were pretty stout," he recalls proudly — "a larger model than the others." And he chuckles over the mystery that surrounded the unveiling of the design.

The first wagon was designed and constructed in Waterloo, New York. "When it was finished," he remembers, "I drove it to Buffalo and put it on one of the boats for an overnight trip to Detroit. When I got to the other side, company representatives met me with a van. They were so anxious not to have anyone see the model that they covered it up and hid it in the van to take it to the factory. All the big brass were assembled on the top floor to examine it. They put it on the turntable and everyone sat around on plush seats and looked at it. Within three weeks after that trip to Detroit to discuss it, it was in production."

But at the end of seven years, Warren Raynes says, rolling up the crackling-fresh sleeves of his khaki shirt as he sets to work on a weathervane, "I figured I'd had enough of assembly lines." So he returned home to Maine, and to woodworking. "I used to take a great deal of interest in manual training when I was in school. I always had a little workbench to come flying home to. I like wood. It makes clean dirt. It isn't like getting into an automobile engine."

When he discovered the old weathervane hull, he went to the library and supplied himself well with books on seagoing vessels and with home craftsmen's magazines so he could find out where the rigging went and how to attach it. It took a while, but eventually his Grandfather Allen's weathervane was heading up into the breeze again on Prince's Point Road.

Then Warren Raynes decided to try his hand at making a clipper ship weathervane from scratch. He scaled off the plan for the hull of *The Flying Cloud* from a picture in one of the library books and set to work. He chose a clipper ship "because George Raynes, who was one of my ancestors, used to build clipper ships in Portsmouth, New Hampshire, from about eighteen fifty or eighteen fifty-five to eighteen sixty. He built quite a few of them. Through research, I got a list of some of the ones he'd launched. One got lost in ice off Cape Horn, I remember, and another was boarded by pirates in the China Sea. There was quite a bit about his yard in a history of shipbuilding along the Northeast coast that I found."

He makes his ships in several sizes, but here is the plan for a thirty-seven inch one. "Don't hurry," Mr. Raynes advises. "Patience, perseverance, and nimble fingers will be rewarding. Read all the instructions at least twice before you start, and study the drawings as you read."

1. Cut a profile of the hull from white cedar "because it's light." Use a band saw or jig-saw to cut the profile from 1⅝" thick cedar. The boat should be 37⅞" long from bow to stern along the deck. At the bottom of the keel, it should be 34" long, exclusive of the rudder (Fig. 1).

2. Before doing any finish carving of the shape, drill three holes 2" deep for the mizzen-, main-, and foremasts directly into the deck. The holes should be made with a 7/16" drill and there should be a 3-degree angle after the rake. The hole for the mizzenmast should be 8½" from the stern; for the mainmast 9" forward of the mizzen. The hole for the fore-mast should be drilled 10⅝" forward of the mainmast, and when the crew's quarters are in place, the foremast should go through them too. (These measurements are all to the cen-ter of the hole being drilled.)

3. Drill a 21/32" hole 2" forward of the mainmast hole and directly through the boat's hull from the deck to the keel for the ⅝" copper tube into which the main supporting staff for the weathervane will be inserted. Just below the deck, enlarge the hole enough so that it will accept a ⅝" ball bearing.

4. Drill a ¼" hole at the base of the stern above the water line to insert the rudder stock.

5. Cut out the spars from ¼" to ⅜" square Honduras mahogany in the proper lengths (Fig. 1). Plane them with a small block plane and file to a taper at the ends. Or, if you prefer, use dowels of appro-priate thickness, planing and filing them. Cut the masts from 7/16" to ½" square cedar or pine. When they are done, the edges should be knocked off, but the 7/16" diameter re-tained. Masts should not fit so tightly into the mast holes that there is no room for glue. They should slide reasonably easily. The mainmast is 32 3/16" long, the foremast 29" long, and the mizzenmast 24½" long (2" go below the deck on all three masts). All three masts taper toward the top. Stain the masts with two coats of light oak and finish them with one coat of spar varnish. Stain the spars with dark mahogany, and finish them with spar varnish.

6. From cedar, cut a bow-sprit 3¾" long by ½" in diameter, tapering it toward the bow. Insert a small screw eye in the top of the forward end. From mahogany, cut a dolphin striker 3¼" long by ¼" across. Cut a jib boom 13⅛" long from ½"-inch-thick Honduras mahogany and a 6¾"-long gaff for the spanker sail and an 11"-long boom from the same material. Cut a ½" recess in the mast-end of the gaff and a ½" recess in the mast-end of the boom to receive the mast. They should all taper away from the mast. Stain the bowsprit with two coats of light oak and finish it with one coat of spar varnish so that it is like the masts. Stain the dolphin striker, jib boom, gaff, and boom with dark mahogany and finish with varnish as before.

7. From aluminum or zinc sheeting, cut the spanker (Fig. 1) with tin snips. Drill or punch three holes at the top, three at the bottom, and three at the mast-side, where it will be attached to the mizzenmast, gaff, and boom.

8. Cut the rudder from ¼"-thick cedar stock (Fig. 2).

MAKING A CLIPPER SHIP WEATHERVANE

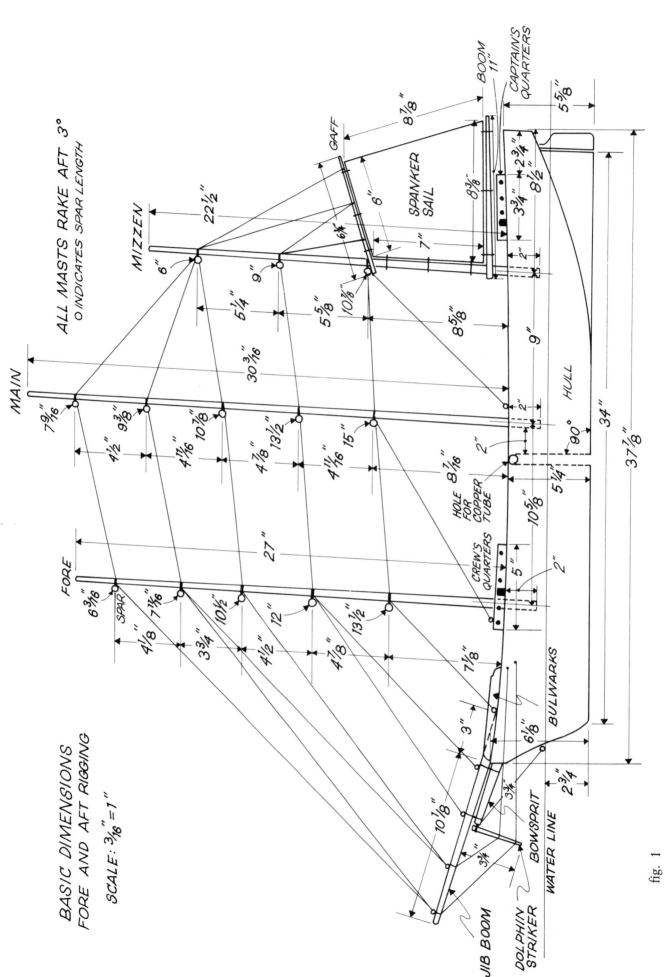

fig. 1

9. Cut the deckhouses from ½″-thick pine board. The crew quarters to go up forward should be 5″ long x 1 1/16″ wide, slightly bigger than the captain's quarters, which will go at the stern and be 3¾″ long. Insert four or five copper tacks on each side of the quarters. Prime the wood. Paint the tack heads black with outdoor gloss so they will simulate portholes. Paint the doors black. Paint the rest of the quarters white. Cut two bulwarks (Fig. 1) from ½″-square cedar and glue and brad them to the bow with good waterproof glue. After drying, carve the bulwarks to accept the jib boom and shape to the outside of the hull. Shape the channels and glue them to the hull (Fig. 3), four 5⅜″ long x ⅜″ wide for the foremast and mainmast rigging and two 4⅝″ long x ⅜″ wide for the mizzenmast rigging.

10. Paint the spanker with a base coat of thinned outside white paint. Let it dry, sand the paint smooth, and give it a final coat of flat white, and when it, the gaff, boom, and mizzenmast are dry, attach the spanker to them by threading No. 18 copper wire through the holes you have drilled in the spanker and then wind them around the gaff, boom, and mizzenmast. To hold the spanker securely in place and keep it from flapping, you can use two strands of No. 22 copper wire. Twist the strands tightly together around the aft end of the boom. Each wire should be secured on either side of the hull ¼″ below the deck with a small roundhead screw. Then secure the spanker gaff to the mast.

11. Around the ends of each spar, place a double-ended loop of 22-gauge copper wire (Fig. 4). Make a large loop of No. 18 copper wire for the middle of the spars, into which they will be inserted (Fig. 4). This will also secure the spars to the masts. After these are twisted around the masts, the ends should be long enough so that you can make other loops to receive the fore and aft wires and rigging. Attach the garnet clews (Fig. 3) from the masts to the loops of wire at the ends of the spars. Do not attempt to put this assembly of masts and spars aboard the boat yet, however.

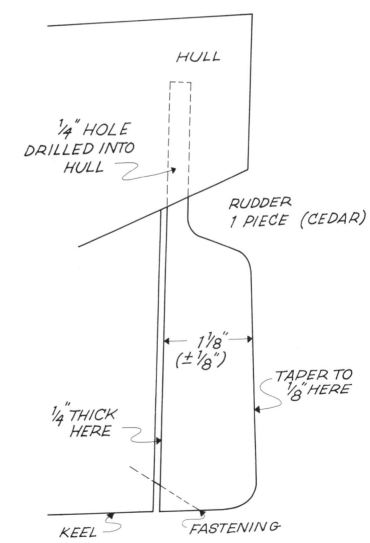

HULL

¼″ HOLE DRILLED INTO HULL

RUDDER 1 PIECE (CEDAR)

1⅛″ (±⅛″)

TAPER TO ⅛″ HERE

¼″ THICK HERE

KEEL

FASTENING

fig. 2

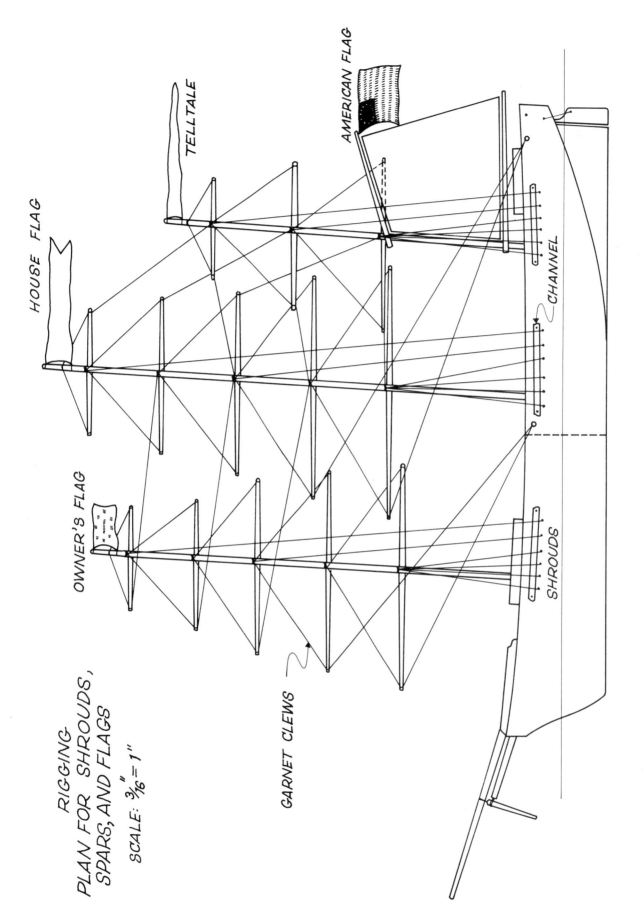

RIGGING
PLAN FOR SHROUDS,
SPARS, AND FLAGS

SCALE: $\frac{3}{16}'' = 1''$

HOUSE FLAG

TELLTALE

AMERICAN FLAG

OWNER'S FLAG

GARNET CLEWS

SHROUDS

CHANNEL

fig. 3

12. Finish carving the hull. Carve so, amidships, it is 1⅝" wide. At the forward end, shape the deck so it is 1" across. At the stern, it should be 1½" across. From the deck to the bottom of keel, the vessel should be 5¼" at the mainmast, gradually increasing to 6⅛" at the bow and 5⅝" at the stern.

13. Attach the rudder. Secure as shown (Fig. 2).

14. Seal the hull with orange shellac or white outside primer, except the areas where the cabins, bowsprit, and the jib boom will be glued (glue will not stick to a painted surface). When the hull is dry, paint the deck with semigloss light tan outdoor paint. The body of the boat is black in Mr. Raynes's design; the bottom is painted with bronze paint since the old clipper ships were sheathed in copper. To make sure his water line is even, Mr. Raynes covers the bottom with masking tape while he paints above it; then he spray-paints the bottom with the bronze paint after remasking the black hull at the water-line level.

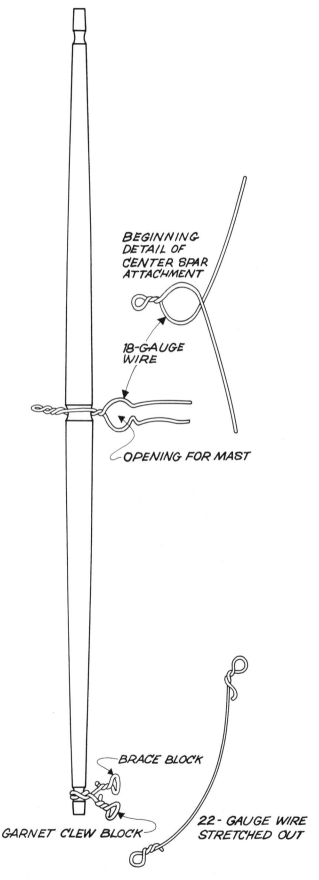

fig. 4

15. When the paint is dry, attach the bowsprit (Fig. 5). The end of the bowsprit should be flat so that it fits snugly against the flat bow of the vessel. Glue. Then take a No. 16 brad 1″ long, cut its head off, and insert it into the bowsprit near the end of it closest to the hull and drive it into the hull to "pin" the bowsprit in place. Attach the dolphin striker to the bowsprit (Fig. 6) by inserting the top end of the striker through a screw eye driven into the forward end of the bowsprit. Glue the jib boom in between the bulwarks (Fig. 5) and screw it onto the deck with two brass screws.

16. Glue the cabins in place with waterproof glue and reinforce by driving a few brads from the tops of the quarters into the deck. The captain's quarters should be 2¾″ from the stern and the crew's 8½″ from the bow.

17. After the hull has been completely painted and the cabins are in place, step the masts to which you have already attached the spars, including the gaff, boom, and spanker sail. Attach all the fore and aft rigging (Fig. 1). Begin at the stern, with the lowest rigging. Go from the after end of the stern forward, and continue moving from stern to bow and bottom to top, following the rigging pattern. Rigging is made of No. 22 copper wire and attached by the garnet clews from the ends of the spars to the masts (Figs. 1, 3, 4).

18. Attach the shrouds. Mr. Raynes suggests using 22-gauge solid hookup wire with a black plastic covering that is available in any radio and TV shop. "It's fairly limber and easy to work with. It also looks as if it had been tarred." Attach the shrouds to the masts and then to the sides of the vessel just below the channels. Use six No. 4 roundheaded brass screws ⅝″ long for each set of shrouds on each side. Wind the wire around the screws from right to left with your fingers. The screws should protrude about ⅛″ from the sides of the hull, and the wire is wound around under the head of the screw. Then, as the screw is seated, the shrouds will be tightened.

19. A ½″-in-diameter steel rod about 14″ long will be needed as the staff for the weathervane. Grease it with hard grease. Also grease the interior of the ⅝″ copper tube that has been inserted from the keel to the deck. Insert a ball bearing into the tube. When the staff is inserted, the ball bearing should rest on top of it but with only a very small contact point. Make a hatch cover of copper, and cover the ball bearing. Mr. Raynes flattens a copper bar to ⅛″ thickness in his vise, smoothing it on his anvil, but a small rectangle of sheet brass can be used in place of the copper. It should be 1″ wide and 2½″ long. Screw it in place with small brass screws.

20. Since he has his own metalworking shop, as well as his own woodworking tools, Mr. Raynes is able to fashion his own cardinal points and the staff on which they are set quickly and easily, but the cardinal points can also be cut from ⅛″ aluminum or copper or brass with tin snips and inserted into slits made at the ends of the crossarms. These are made of ¾″-thick white pine. There are two of them, 20″ long, 1¾″ wide at the center, tapering to 1″ wide at the ends. A hole should be drilled in the center of the crossarm to receive the steel staff. Prepare the crossarm by fitting the two pieces of pine together and joining them with a lap joint where they cross.

fig. 5   *The bowsprit attached*
(Charles R. Brown)

fig. 6   *The dolphin striker attached*
(Charles R. Brown)

Reinforce the joint top and bottom with 6"-long, ¼"-thick pine strips. The hole for the staff goes through these (Fig. 7). When the weathervane is put in position, there should be about 6" of rod between the hull and the crosspiece and another 2" to 3" between the crosspiece and the roof. About 6½" of rod should go into the roof.

This is the method of mounting a weathervane employed by Lawrence Winterbottom of Vineyard Haven, Massachusetts, who makes schooner weathervanes in his cellar workshop. Mr. Winterbottom, a retired carpenter, contractor, and home builder, follows a design originated by the late Frank Adams of West Tisbury. Mr. Winterbottom's vessels, with one- to three-foot-long white pine hulls, carry full sets of zinc sails and have melted lead inserted forward of the foremast for balance. Their bowsprits are of fir because he likes its strength, and his masts are of hard pine to withstand the wind.

Mr. Winterbottom, a stocky man with gentle brown eyes, moved to Martha's Vineyard from New Bedford as a young man and married the daughter of a state sena-

tor. He was never without his jack-knife and was soon known island-wide for his whittling abilities. When Frank Adams, who had established a reputation for his weathervanes throughout New England, died in 1944, his widow asked Mr. Winterbottom to complete his unfinished orders. When those were filled, Mr. Winterbottom accepted more, and he has been twisting copper wire (he uses picture wire rather than electrical wire) for rigging, soldering stays to hulls and whittling out cabins and dories and booms and gaffs and masts on and off ever since.

Properly made, the schooner weathervanes of Martha's Vineyard and the clipper ship weathervanes of Yarmouth, Maine, are sturdy vessels, able to ride out any rooftop wind.

fig. 7   *A Winterbottom weathervane on its staff*

Lawrence Winterbottom with the beginnings of a weathervane

In winter, when northeast storms buffet Cape Cod and tug shingles from the rooftops, most residents stay indoors, but Jan and John and Geof Newton put on their slickers and set out shingle-hunting in South Chatham, Massachusetts, for they are in the business of making shingled dollhouses.

The dollhouses that they make are like the houses that they pass — narrow eighteenth-century half houses with just two windows and a door in front, or three-quarter houses with three windows, or full Cape houses with four, and the shingles are pewter gray from the salt in the air.

Jan Newton comes from old Cape Cod stock. Although she grew up in Manchester, Connecticut, and went to college in Marietta, Ohio (where she met John), she spent summers in the family homestead in Harwich. She likes talking about Cape Cod architecture — especially the earliest houses that were only a story and a half. "And the upper garret was little better than a barn, usually unheated. The fireplaces in the beginning were just open hearths; then they evolved into massive brick structures. They were always directly on a line with the front door and the chimney broke through the roof precisely in the center of the ridge. It was always a broad and low chimney, usually plastered, and the dark red cedar shingles they used on the roofs contrasted strongly."

She has done considerable research into Cape Cod architecture and will go on to tell how "the front of the house always faced south and contained the best room — the parlor. The door was traditionally on the west side of the house front and could either be solid or Christian paneled, in a cross design, with windows. This is the kind of house they built between about seventeen fifty and eighteen twenty." And it is the kind of house the Newtons like building in dollhouse size.

When John Newton finished service in the marines in 1960 and was thinking about where to settle, Jan proposed Cape Cod.

"I told him how quiet and peaceful it was," she remembers, "and how pretty the dunes and the beaches were, and what a fun place it would be for Geof to grow up. We found the Mid-Cape Lumber Company in South Dennis needed a general manager, and so we came down."

As she talks, Jan Newton stirs sand into paint to give a plastered

SHINGLES MAKE DOLLHOUSES

effect to dollhouse chimneys or mixes paints in the kitchen of Wee Three, the name they have given the shop where they sell their houses ("There are three of us and we make wee things"). Or she kneels by Geof's aquarium and points out miniature sea robins and baby scallops to young visitors to the shop.

Wee Three is housed in a cottage just off the main road through South Chatham. When the Newtons first moved to Cape Cod, this site was their home, but once dollhouse making became a business for them, they turned their living room into a display room for their wares and bought another house in town. In the basement of that house, John Newton splits weathered shingles and saws plywood on his table saw, in the few periods he is not at his Mid-Cape job. When the splitting and sawing is done, and the dollhouses assembled, Jan Newton begins painting them. She has always enjoyed dollhouses, but it wasn't until Geof and Jan both caught the flu at vacation time one year that the Newtons thought of dollhouse building as a part-time occupation.

"We were supposed to be going away for two weeks," freckle-faced Jan recounts, "and we just couldn't do it. There was poor J. going nutsy with nothing to do except look after a sick wife and child. Once he'd made a dollhouse for one of our baby-sitters, so I said how about making another — a Cape Cod house, and he did. I'd already started drawing houses for people's Christmas cards soon after we got here."

It wasn't a far cry from those pencil portraits of houses to reproducing them in miniature as dollhouses. Today, if a customer wishes his own house reproduced, the Newtons will happily oblige. "We visit a house and look it over and take photographs and come home and build it," Jan explains. "Sometimes people even come to us with old shingles from their houses and ask us to use them on the dollhouse, or maybe they'll bring the paint they used on their own house."

The Newtons, not long ago, were commissioned to do reproductions of the Old Sturbridge Village houses. Today, there are samples of their Cape Cod half houses, three-quarter houses, and full-Cape houses as far away as Saudi Arabia and England.

Meanwhile, Wee Three has expanded to include birdhouses, which Geof nails together from wood his father saws out, sea-gull and lobster marionettes, and whales on wheels. And there are also gingerbread houses and one brick house under construction. "We tried making our own miniature clay bricks for it, but they were too heavy and made the house simply immovable," Jan Newton says. "J. likes the real McCoy and not using real bricks almost broke his heart."

Although the Newtons' houses have meticulously constructed exteriors, they keep the interiors rustic and unfinished because they believe, "people have their own tastes to such a great extent in interior decoration." Since the houses they are producing, too, come from an era that predated bathrooms and electricity, they feel no need to introduce these elements. Sometimes they build staircases and chimneys, sometimes not.

It is the preparation of the shingles that is the most complex part of the Newtons' operation, and John Newton solemnly warns, with a shake of his red head, that it is inadvisable for the amateur to use his sawing technique, so he provides an alternate method below. His own method, however, is to use the butt end of the shingle that is thick and exposed and naturally gray, and rip it into thicknesses of 1/16" with the use of a carbide tip blade and universal guide. Then he cross-cuts the thinned shingles into 1" strips with the fence of his table saw set 1" from the blade. He uses a plywood or fine-tooth blade so as not to chew up the shingle.

He likes this method because it enables him to make use of the weathered end of the shingle, but he notes that the other end, or a new shingle, can be stained a light gray with stain available from hardware stores (use a darker gray for roof shingles). "Or some of our customers have reported good results from dipping the shingles in bleach, then in saltwater, and drying them outside in the sun for a week."

MAKING A HALF-CAPE DOLLHOUSE

Materials Needed

a. One piece of ¼" AC plywood (2' x 4') for the walls, floor, and roof

b. One piece of ⅜" AC plywood (16" x 18") for the base

c. Six feet of 1⅜" x ¼" lattice or 18' of ⅜" x ¼" basswood for trim

d. Fifteen 5"-wide red cedar shingles or some other dark wood for roof shingles

e. Twenty 5"-wide white cedar shingles or some other light wood for siding

f. Ten to twelve Popsicle sticks for door panels

g. Used kitchen matchsticks or four pieces of 1/16" square x 3' long balsa wood for window grills and for the shingling starter course

h. One 2" x 4" x 2" block of pine for the chimney

i. ½" brads

j. 1" brads

k. Nontoxic white glue (Elmer's, Elmco)

l. Nontoxic white and green paint, flat finish

m. Pair of ¼" brass butt hinges (available at hobby and craft shops) for the door

n. Drill, hammer, ruler or square, X-acto knife or razor-blade knife, hand saw or other cross-cut saw, coping or saber saw, table saw if available, but the latter is not essential

1. From the ¼" plywood, cut one front piece 12" x 6", two side pieces 14" x 16", a front roof 13" x 12½", a back roof 12½" x 3", and a second floor 12" x 10" (Fig. 1). Mark the sides for the roof peak (gable) and cut. From ⅜" plywood cut a base piece 16" x 18".

John Newton with a three-quarter dollhouse

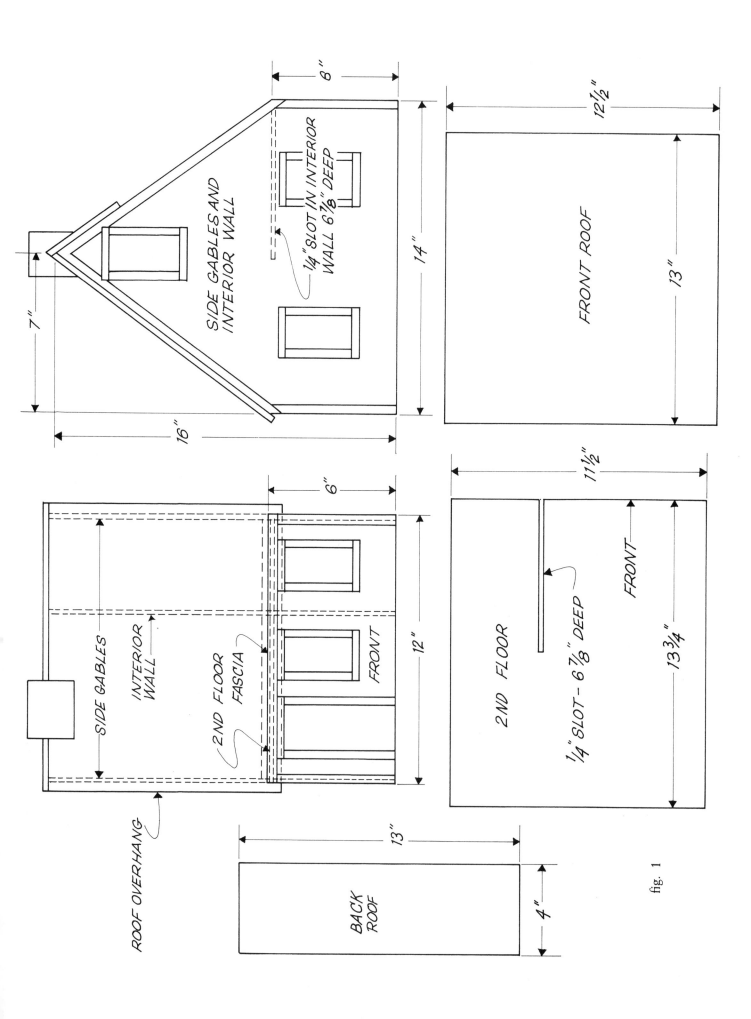

8"

¼" SLOT IN INTERIOR WALL 6⅛" DEEP

SIDE GABLES AND INTERIOR WALL

7"

16"

14"

12½"

FRONT ROOF

13"

11½"

2ND FLOOR

¼" SLOT - 6⅛" DEEP

FRONT

13¾"

6"

SIDE GABLES

INTERIOR WALL

2ND FLOOR FASCIA

FRONT

12"

ROOF OVERHANG

13"

BACK ROOF

4"

fig. 1

2. To begin assembly, attach the side pieces to the ends of the front piece, using glue and reinforcing with ½″ brads. (Brads help to hold the structure together while the glue dries.) The overall front dimension is now 12½″.

3. Prepare to install the second floor by drawing a line on the inside of the gable ends 8″ above the bottom and parallel to it. (An 8″ ceiling height will allow properly, for 1″ equals 1′ in scaled miniatures.) Glue and nail with ½″ brads the second floor into place (Fig. 2), fitting the ceiling side of the floor piece along the lines you have drawn. (Mr. Newton points out that if the plywood appears warped, it may be necessary to use more than four brads per side to attach the floor piece. If it is not warped, however, four should prove sufficient.)

4. Glue and nail with ½″ brads the front roof piece to the sides and the front. If necessary, you can use ½″ brads driven through the roof and into the second floor to hold the roof on in front, but it is better not to, since the wood into which you will be driving the brads is so thin. Glue and nail the back roof piece in place, making it flush with the front roof at its peak.

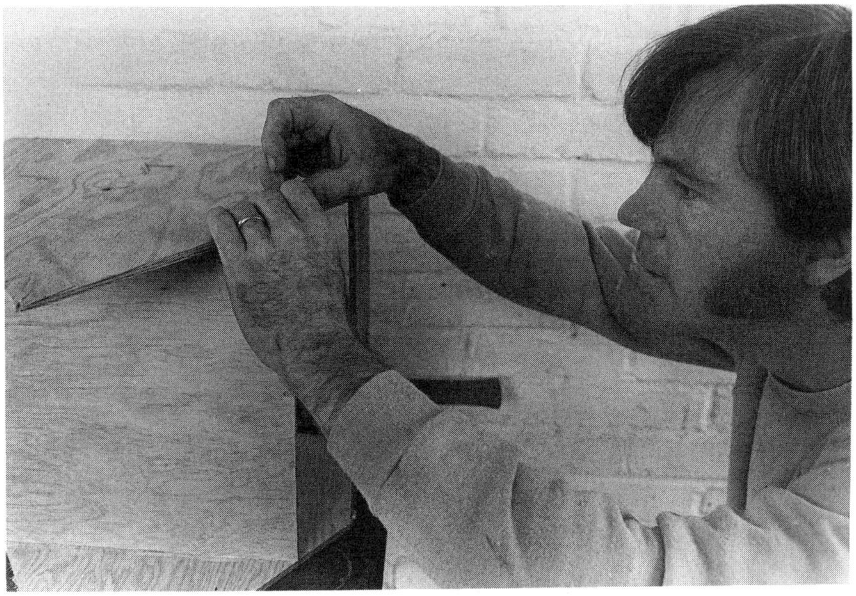

5. Rip the lattice into ⅜″ strips for trim. (If you do not have a table saw to rip it, basswood may be substituted as noted above. It is available at most hobby shops. Do not use balsa wood, however, for it is too soft.)

6. Apply the fascia trim piece on the face of the house just underneath the roof. This is a 12½″-long piece cut from the lattice you have ripped. Cut two pieces of trim 6″ long for the front corner boards. These may need a little trimming at the bottom after they are glued in place.

7. For the rake trim (along the rake of the roof), you will need two 13″ pieces of trim and two 3″ pieces for the rear partial rake trim.

8. Now apply the side corner trim. Cut four 7½″ pieces (two for each side). These must be cut at an angle so that they join tightly with the rake trim. Mark the angle of each piece and cut. (The corner trim that goes on the front of the house will abut the side corner board trim that you have already glued in place.) Trim any excess off the side corner trim at the bottom and glue.

fig. 2 *Nailing the second floor into place*
(Peter Vandermark)

fig. 3 *Drawing the window locations*
(Peter Vandermark)

fig. 4 *Drilling the window openings*
(Peter Vandermark)

fig. 5 *Sawing out the windows*
(Peter Vandermark)

9. For each window, you will need two pieces of trim 2¼" long for the top and bottom of the window and two pieces 3⅛" long for the sides. On the plywood front of the house (and on the sides) draw the window locations (Fig. 3). Then glue the frame pieces on. If you do not wish to wait for the glue to set, you can tack the frame pieces on with ½" brads, which can later be removed with pliers.

10. Cut the door trim. Two pieces 5½" long are needed for the sides and one 2¾" piece is needed for the top. Draw the door location on the front of the house and glue the trim in place. Trim the excess trim from the bottom.

11. Now cut out the window openings by drilling a hole in the center of each window location (Fig. 4). Using a coping or saber saw, insert the blade in the hole drilled and saw out the opening (Fig. 5). Saw out the door in one piece and set it aside, marked "door," for future use.

12. Before proceeding with construction, it is advisable to sand the exposed edges of the plywood. File or sand through the insides of the windows. Fine-sand the window frames.

13. Fitting the window grills in place will be easier if you begin by making four light marks equidistant from both ends of the window on the side frames. These will help you to place the five horizontal grills (Fig. 6). Note that one horizontal is doubled. For the grills themselves, use matchsticks or 1/16″-square balsa wood. First, using an X-acto knife or a razor-blade knife, cut the horizontal grills to fit inside the window frames. (You will notice here that the windows of this period and style are "nine over six" — nine panes in the top sash and six in the bottom — all panes of equal size.) Glue the pieces in place and allow them to dry. Then cut the vertical grill pieces to fit between the horizontal pieces, gluing them in place from top to bottom.

14. Center the house on the base piece and attach with glue inside and 1″ brads underneath by inverting the house onto its peak and hammering from the reverse side of the base.

15. Cut a roof peak notch in the 2″ x 4″ x 2″ pine block. Glue it in place on the peak directly in line with the front door. When the chimney is in place and the glue is set, measure the distance from the notch to the gables on each side and cut four pieces of trim to fit as ridge trim, two for the front and two for the back. Glue and nail both sets of pieces together to form a V. Then place and glue them over the peak itself.

The ½″ brads may be used to hold them if necessary.

16. Fine-sand the trim. Paint all the trim and window grills white. This is only the first of two coats. (The paint of this period, Jan Newton says, was heavy in lime and was therefore chalky. Using a flat white paint will give the same illusion but not the mess.) Either buy sand paint or mix fine sand with white paint and apply it to the chimney block. A small black rectangle painted on the top may be added to represent the chimney flue.

17. Prepare for shingling by cutting the thin end of the shingles into five 1″ strips with an X-acto knife or razor-blade knife. Then break them into strips or cut them with the knife into random shingle widths (Fig. 7).

9 OVER 6 WINDOW

CHRISTIAN DOOR

fig. 6

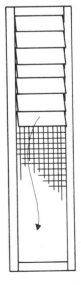

HALF-CAPE SHUTTER

fig. 7 *Preparing the shingles*
(Peter Vandermark)

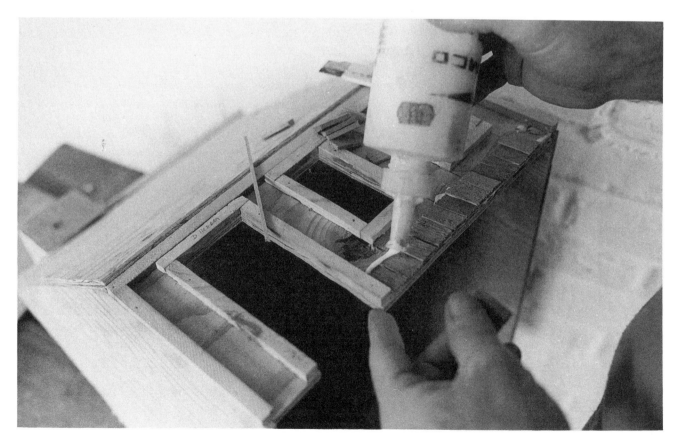

fig. 8 *Gluing the shingles*
(Peter Vandermark)

18. If you wish, draw guidelines for the placement of the shingle courses on the house. The lines should be 7/8″ apart. To set the first row of shingles, cut pieces of 1/16″-square balsa wood or matchsticks. These pieces, glued at the bottom of the walls (and over the window frames), simulate a starter course of shingles.

19. Apply plenty of glue along the starter pieces and along the face of the house in a line 7/8″ from the bottom. Glue the shingles in a straight line, touching the base with this first course, varying the shingle widths (Fig. 8). Repeat, applying a glue line along the top 1/8″ of the first course and attaching the second and so on. These lineations allow for a 7/8″ exposure and 1/8″ overlap on each course. Continue in this manner, trimming individual shingles for fitting around windows and under the roof line. (Jan Newton explains that you must be sure the glue is always completely set before you turn the house to shingle another side. Otherwise the glue will drip down through the courses, messing up the trim, finish, and work surfaces.) Don't forget those starter pieces on the roof edges.

20. Prepare a six-panel Christian door with the Popsicle sticks cut to fit the plywood door piece you saved earlier. The top and bottom pieces should fit inside the side pieces (Fig. 6). After all the strips are applied on both sides, paint with a first coat of flat white. Shave the door piece to fit the opening on the front of the house loosely and hang the door with 1/2″ hinges mounted on the door edge and on the inside of the door frame. The door should open out. Paint the base piece for the house with two coats of green paint. Put a second coat of white on all the trim, window grills, and both sides of door.

21. Paint or wallpaper the interior of the house. Stencil designs both on walls and floors were very common from 1750 to 1820. The Newtons advise visits to houses of this type in museum villages or consulting books on Colonial architecture if you wish to make your interior exactly as it was.

22. Shutters are the most popular "extra" the Newtons attach to their houses. Instructions follow for constructing a single shutter. Multiply by the number of shutters you want.

a. Materials you will need are graph paper (3/4″ x 3″) for each shutter

b. Two 1/4″ x 1/32″ x 5″ coffee stirrers for each shutter

c. One 8″ long x 1/16″-square strip of balsa wood for each shutter

d. Glue and a knife

e. On the piece of graph paper, place and glue two 3″ side pieces of balsa wood. Cut two 5/8″ pieces for the top and bottom to fit inside the side pieces and glue. Cut 5/8″ slats from the coffee stirrers. Cover the remaining exposed paper (Fig. 6) with glue and place the first slat slightly overlapping the top edge. Overlap the next slats and proceed in this manner to the bottom, using 16 slats. (Since the shutters have a tendency to warp, the Newtons advise putting a weight on them as they dry; a brick serves well.) After the glue is dry, paint the shutters with two coats of black paint, preferably a flat finish. Then glue the shutters onto the house with the shutter overlapping the window trim 1/8″. Nail at the corners, inside the balsa-wood frame of the shutter, with 1/2″ brads.

Thetford Center is a quiet little hamlet in the undulating hills of eastern Vermont. Most travelers come to its white frame farmhouses, sturdy red brick buildings, and a sprinkling of trailers through a forest of soft white pines and regal spruces and across a covered bridge. Once there were mills in the township, but they are all gone now, and most serious farming has ended. Just fifteen miles away in neighboring New Hampshire is the campus of Dartmouth College, and a goodly number of commuters come from the busier New Hampshire community to the peaceable Vermont one. Thetford Center's population, however, stays steady at about 200.

In the summer of 1973, Ron and Susan Voake, two young Pomona College graduates from California, moved to Thetford Center when Susan Voake got a fourth-grade teaching job. For several years, the Voakes had sought to leave the smoke and smog of Etiwanda, California, where a curtain of black from a steel plant conceals the mountains. Clean air, bubbling streams where trout jumped, and the melodies of birds attracted them to Vermont.

Ron Voake had been a student of philosophy, both in California and later at the University of Toronto, where he did graduate work in existentialism. Like his wife, he taught for a time, but now he has given up both philosophy and teaching. Instead, every morning, he puts on his wide-brimmed ranch hat, walks across the yard, and swings open his heavy barn door. But he is not preparing to milk the cows or feed the horses. In a workshop where every child who peers in is breathless with delight, Ron Voake makes wooden railroad trains for young riders, moving vans that open to transport doll furniture, doll cribs and toy wagons and trucks and buses.

Ron explains, "For me, this is a lot more creative than attacking the problem of 'Is God dead?' or being hassled in a teaching situation. Kids come by to see what I'm doing, and they stop and play and check out my toys. They'll tell me the propellers on my helicopter should be longer, or that I've put the seat in the wrong place on my train. And they understand what I'm doing when I exaggerate things — when I make a Diesel stack that's bigger than a Diesel stack really is, or put ladders on my fire truck that are out of proportion. That's what makes a toy fun — exaggerating the details so you want to touch a ladder or a stack or you want to bat a mud flap around."

• 13 •

FROM PHILOSOPHY TO TOY WAGONS

MAKING A TOY WAGON

Ron Voake is tall and slender and shy. He indulges his sense of humor by trimming the outside of his barn with his handiwork. Over its door a five-car railroad train chugs. Above a frame window, a bus is ready to roll.

Woodworking was never a craft Ron Voake had dreamed of entering. But his wife asked him to make a few toys for her classroom. "And I got hooked on it. The only time I'd ever done anything with wood before was in the seventh grade, and I had such bad hay fever I couldn't be around shavings. I never imagined I'd someday have woodworking as a livelihood!"

The first toy he designed was a trailer truck, which he followed with a fire engine, then a bus. "When I was a child, I always used to like buses," he recalls. "I was even going to be a bus driver, but I didn't turn out to be a good driver, among other things."

Ron Voake's toys are simple because he thinks toys should be, and they are unpainted because he likes a fresh look. The only finishing he does is with a lead-free urethane stain or linseed oil to keep the wood clean. Here are his directions for a twenty-one-inch wagon.

Materials Needed

1. For the bottom, you will need 1½' of 1" x 8" kiln-dried pine. ("Try to find lumber that is not green and sappy," Ron Voake says, "because green wood is more likely to warp. It may look better green; the grain may be prettier, but it will gum up your tools.")

2. For the sides and wheels, buy 6' of 1" x 4" kiln-dried pine.

3. For the axle blocks, you will need a little more than 1' of 2" x 4" kiln-dried pine which must be ripped to a narrower size. Rip the 2" x 4" down to 2¼" width.

4. For the tongue of the wagon, you will need a half foot of 5/4" x 4" pine that must be ripped down to 3" wide.

5. Buy one standard 3' length of 1" dowel, 5/8" dowel, 7/16" dowel, and 3/16" dowel.

6. Sixteen screwhole buttons, ⅜" size, can be used if you wish to cover the 16 1"-long No. 8 roundhead wood screws you will use in construction. If these are not available, you may use 16 1½"-long flathead No. 8 screws and countersink them.

7. No. 400 sandpaper and polyurethane or some other lead-free stain will be needed for the finish.

Construction

1. Cut the bottom and side pieces square with a radial arm saw, skill saw, or hand saw.

2. Cut a 1″ x 8″ bottom piece to a 16″ length, and cut the ends equal to the width of the 1″ x 8″ piece (this is usually 7¼″). From the 1″ by 4″ piece, cut the sides to 17½″.

3. For axle blocks, once the 2″ x 4″ is ripped, cut two pieces 6″ long. Cut the ripped tongue piece to a 5¼″ length.

4. For the handle, cut the 1″ dowel to a piece 12″ long. The handle crosspiece is made from the 5⁄8″ dowel cut to a 3¾″ length.

5. Cut the 7/16″ dowel into two lengths, each 8½″ long. Also cut a 4″-long piece as the hinge for the handle.

6. Cut four 3″-in-diameter wheels with a hole saw from what remains of the 1″ x 4″ board. The wheels may also be 2½″ if no 3″ hole saw is available.

7. For pegs, cut the 3/16″ dowel into six 1¼″-long pieces. (If a power saw is used for this work, Ron Voake warns, eye protection should also be worn, for the pegs might "shoot off like bullets.")

Drilling and Sanding

1. Drill four holes in the top of the wagon bottom in which to sink the screw heads that will go into the axle blocks. To sink roundhead screws, drill 3⁄8″ holes 3⁄8″ deep 2¼″ from the ends of the bottom pieces and 2″ in from the sides (Fig. 1). Also drill 3⁄8″ holes in the sides and ends for sinking the screwheads. All of these four holes should be 3⁄8″ from the bottom edges. The holes in the side pieces should be 4″ from the ends of the piece, and the holes in the end pieces should be 2″ from the end of the piece (Fig. 1). Two 3⁄8″ holes should also be drilled halfway down the sides and ½″ from the ends of the side pieces.

2. On the bottom of the tongue, drill a pair of 3⁄8″ holes 1″ from the inside ends and 1″ from the sides. They should be 5⁄8″ deep. Drill a hole all the way through the side of the tongue slightly larger than 7/16″ (Fig. 1). Drill from both sides to avoid splitting out. The hole center should be 5⁄8″ from the end of the tongue to avoid splitting.

3. With the same bit, drill a hole through the 1″ dowel 5⁄8″ from one end. Using a block (Fig. 2), put the opposite end of the 1″ dowel in the groove and drill a 5⁄8″ hole 1″ from the opposite end. This hole should be parallel to the other hole running through the dowel. Drill one more hole in the 1″ dowel. This should be a 3⁄8″ hole centered in the very top end of the handle. This 3⁄8″ hole should only be ¼″ deep.

4. In the axle blocks, drill a ½″ hole through the blocks (with the grain). The holes should be near the one edge but not so close that they will cause splitting (the center of the ½″ hole should be ½″ from the edge of the block). Drill slowly and carefully so that the bit goes straight down.

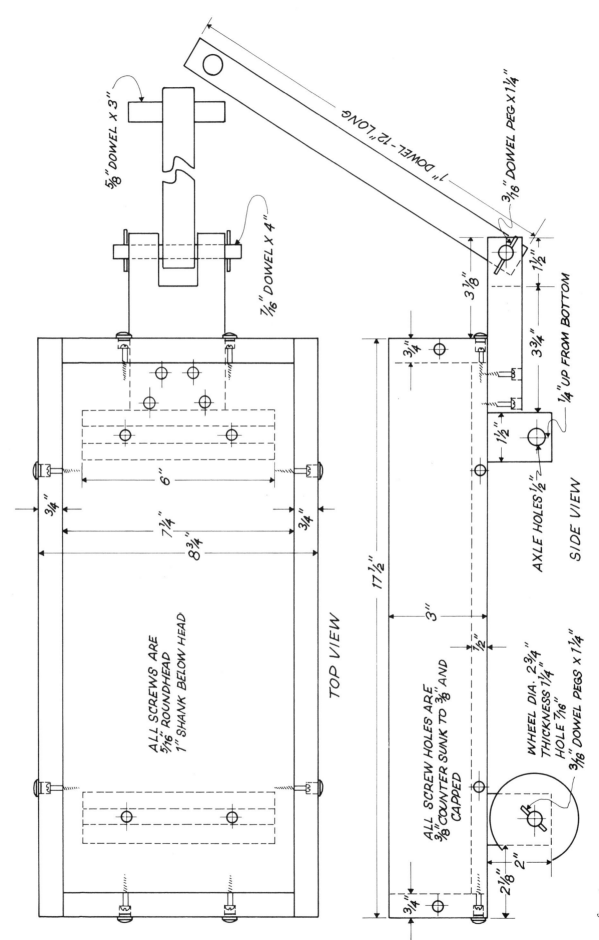

5⁄8" DOWEL X 3"

7⁄16" DOWEL X 4"

1" DOWEL - 12" LONG

3⁄16" DOWEL PEG X 1¼"

ALL SCREWS ARE
5⁄16" ROUNDHEAD
1" SHANK BELOW HEAD

6"

3⁄4"

3⁄4"

7¼"

8¾"

TOP VIEW

3⅛"

1½"

3¾"

¼" UP FROM BOTTOM

1½"

AXLE HOLES ½"

SIDE VIEW

3⁄4"

17½"

3"

½"

ALL SCREW HOLES ARE
3⁄8" COUNTER SUNK TO 3⁄8" AND
CAPPED

WHEEL DIA. 2¾"
THICKNESS 1¼"
HOLE 7⁄16"
3⁄16" DOWEL PEGS X 1¼"

2⅛"

2"

3⁄4"

fig. 1

Drill halfway through the axle block and then drill halfway through from the other side to prevent splitting.

5. Drill holes in the centers of the wheels slightly larger than 7/16". Then test them to see if they are large enough by slipping the wheel on the axle to see if it spins freely.

6. Using the block (Fig. 2) again, put 7/16" dowels into the groove and drill 3/16" holes close to both ends of the three pieces of dowel. In the top of the tongue, drill two 5/16" holes 1" in from each side and 1½" in from the front. This is to allow for the cutting out of space to fit in the handle. To cut this space, use either a jigsaw, saber saw, or hand coping saw. Draw a line along the outside edge of the holes (holes allow you room to turn the blade 90 degrees and cut perpendicular — without holes, you cannot make the cross-cut).

7. Now sand all the parts with either a hand or an electric sander using fine sandpaper. Since a child will be using the wagon, be sure that it is smoothed everywhere. Don't forget to sand the ends of the long side pieces, the front, and the inside of the tongue.

8. After sanding the dowels, use a 3/16" drill again on the three pieces of 7/16" dowel. Using the wooden block (Fig. 2), run the drill through the holes again, this time wiggling the dowels slightly to enlarge the hole. If you fail to do this, these dowels may split when you are ready to fit pegs into them.

9. Sand the wheels. There will be a sharp ridge on them that you must sand off. Also sand the rims round.

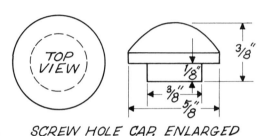

SCREW HOLE CAP, ENLARGED

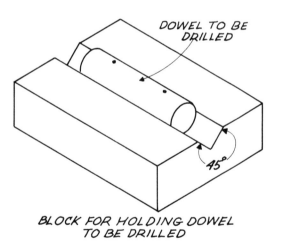

BLOCK FOR HOLDING DOWEL
TO BE DRILLED

fig. 2

Assembling

1. Begin by attaching the end pieces to the wagon bottom. You will use a 9/64″ drill bit to drill your pilot holes for the No. 8 screws. Take the end pieces of the wagon, and butt each against the back and the front of the bottom piece, squaring the edges. Drill through the centers of the ⅜″ holes and into the ends of the bottom piece for pilot holes. After the pilot holes are drilled, put a light to moderate coat of hide glue on both the bottom and end pieces where they will be joined. Then join the ends to the bottom with the wood screws. Repeat this process joining the sides to the bottom and ends. When you are through, you will have an open box.

2. Turn the wagon over and center the axle blocks over the predrilled holes in the bottom of the wagon, squaring the blocks with the edge of the wagon (Fig. 1). Drill pilot holes from the top of the wagon into the axle box, taking care not to drill too deep. If glue gets into the axle box, the wheels will not turn. Apply glue 1″ wide where the axle boxes and the wagon will join.

3. Attach the tongue to the bottom of the wagon, centering it and butting it against the front axle block (Fig. 1). Drill pilot holes through the centers of predrilled ⅜″ holes. Be careful not to drill through the bottom of the wagon. Apply glue to the areas where the tongue joins the axle block and wagon, and screw in the screws.

4. Turn the wagon over and put the crosspiece in the end of the handle. It should fit snugly. Start it into the 1″ dowel, turning it as you go, and it will fit more easily.

When it is close to being centered, run a thin line of glue around the ⅝″ dowel piece that is sticking out and continue to turn. Wipe off any extra glue remaining on the crosspiece. Drill another pilot hole through the ⅜″ hole in the end of the handle and put a wood screw in to hold the crosspiece more securely.

5. Attach the handle to the tongue by sliding a 4″-long, 7/16″ dowel through the tongue and handle. (It should move easily and not bind.) Start the 3/16″ dowels into the 7/16″ dowel by hand. Open up a pair of pliers and gently drive the pegs into the holes so that they fit snugly.

6. To attach the wheels, run 7/16″ axles through the axle blocks and wheels. The wheels should turn freely. Put in pegs as you did before.

7. Wipe the wagon clean of sawdust and apply a first coat of finish. Allow it to dry overnight. Then sand lightly with No. 400 sandpaper. Wipe clean. Apply another coat of finish. Use a glossy finish, not a satiny one for a rich look, Ron Voake advises. A satiny finish turns a dull yellow.

A completed Voake wagon waits to be pulled

On a country road west of Boston stands a mailbox marked "S. Coffin." An arrow on it points up a long drive to a cluster of weathered farm buildings. Mrs. Coffin's geese hiss. A pheasant darts across the drive. A collie barks. At one time, the farm at the end of the road was a thriving nursery, but when the Coffins bought it a decade ago, it had been abandoned. They have put it to work again, using organic farming methods. But when winter comes, and food and fuel have been brought in, Stewart Coffin retires to a small building attached to one of the greenhouses to design wooden geometric puzzles.

There are shelves of them in the little building and rows of them in the greenhouse, and Mr. Coffin, a sandy-haired, blue-eyed man just past forty, readily and agreeably shows them off as he talks of the wood that he uses and of how captivated he is with it.

Stewart T. Coffin has come to farming and woodworking from a varied background. He is a former staff member of the Massachusetts Institute of Technology Digital Computer Laboratory; has been in the industrial electronics business; has designed, made, and sold fiberglass canoes, kayaks, and paddles; and has compiled the Appalachian Mountain Club's New England Canoeing Guide.

"I never used to know anything about wood at all," he says, "but now, look at these," and he heads toward his woodpile. "That bright yellow wood is Osage orange. It's used for fence posts in the Mississippi Valley. And the bright purple is purple-heart. It's a hobby wood from Brazil. And here's some pau rosa — that's an Argentine rosewood — with all of those lovely streaks. "And that beautiful red wood," he continues, "is from a breadfruit tree."

Mr. Coffin has three table saws that he has modified for his puzzle-making purposes, a band saw which he says results in much less waste and makes a finer cut than a table saw, and a sander. He has also designed a special, high-speed abrasive jumbler which rounds and polishes wood scraps like jewels. His thirteen-year-old daughter, Abbie, has begun a bead business using these scraps and the jumbler, and twelve-year-old Tammy is doing the same with wooden buttons. A few years ago, the youngest Coffin girl, Margie, then eight, started a miniature puzzle-making business of her own making use of the scraps.

· *14* ·

RARE WOODS
FOR MYSTIFYING PUZZLES

As he passes his saws and the sawdust on them strikes his nostrils, Stewart Coffin is likely to comment that whenever he isn't sure what a wood is, he simply smells it, for one can distinguish hundreds of different woods that way.

Because he is an orderly man, he likes to keep his puzzles in groups so he can readily explain, and point out, how his basic design was conceived from the principles of polyhedral symmetry (many-surfaced symmetry) and how it has been modified again and again to make new creations. A few of these have been sent to manufacturers and are now available in plastic, but Mr. Coffin continues to produce his favorites only in wood.

His most elaborate puzzle, which he describes as a "dissected castellated triacontahdron," is made of sixty separate pieces of wood glued in five places to make twelve identical puzzle pieces.

"The complex symmetries in this design present a challenging production problem," he comments, for, to produce the effect he wants, he must use six woods with contrasting colors or grains. One of his favorites of this kind is made of canarywood (green); zebra-wood (striped), rosewood (dark), breadnut (red), primavera (light), and walnut (brown) and sells for $25. Mr. Coffin never uses stains and all woods have a natural finish. Only beeswax, which is colorless, is used as a polish.

One of the best woods for puzzle-making, he maintains, is teak since it will not warp and a good puzzle must fit together perfectly (though not so perfectly, of course, that it will not come apart once its mystery has been solved).

Stewart Coffin first started making puzzles — jigsaw puzzles — when he was a boy of ten growing up in Amherst. Anyone can make jigsaw puzzles, he says, though he admits that it helps if you have a power jigsaw with a fine blade. As a boy, his work was done by hand with a coping saw.

After that, for a time, he was interested in three-dimensional jigsaw puzzles made from balsa-wood blocks, and then he used some Epoxy left over from his paddle-making to fashion some puzzle pieces for fun. "And the next thing I knew, we were in the puzzle business." About six years ago, he began trying his hand at symmetrical interlocking puzzles.

Another kind of puzzle he finds interesting is the topological one. People often ask him for wood samples, so, to satisfy their request, and also supply them with a puzzle, he has devised a topological puzzle (such puzzles involve sticks or boards with holes, strings, and beads — the problem they pose is to remove the cord or move the bead). His topological puzzle is simply a stick of wood with a hole at one end and a loop of string through it. "You put it on someone's buttonhole and try to get it off. Some of our parents knew of this as the Idiot Stick. It's an old gag that's been around for years. No one knows who invented it." This, Mr. Coffin says, is true of most puzzles.

Puzzle-making is, he believes, one of the oldest of the folk arts. Puzzles are found everywhere in the world, made of materials as varied as ivory and machine screws.

As far as he is concerned, a good puzzle is not necessarily one that is hard to solve. "All you have to do to make a difficult puzzle, after all, is to drop a jar on the floor," he says. "Now there's something that's hard to put back together again! But a really good puzzle has to have something novel and intriguing about it. You shouldn't expect the final shape from the parts — that's an important directive to bear in mind in puzzle-making."

For the beginner who wishes to make interlocking puzzles, Mr. Coffin advises making those requiring only right-angle cuts. "The most familiar of these are probably the so-called 'burr' or notched-stick puzzles, usually with six pieces. The small and very inexpensive ones of this kind have long been referred to as Chinese puzzles. With a little ingenuity, the amateur puzzle-maker can invent his own version of one."

One of the more interesting of the "burr" puzzles for an amateur to try, if he is not ready to invent his own, is the twelve-piece burr puzzle that William Altekruse patented in 1890 but that is now in the public domain.

The only tool needed for it, he says, is a saw; a power saw with a dado blade is best. A belt sander is also very useful in finishing. Any type of well-seasoned wood will do for this puzzle, but, preferably, it should be kiln-dried.

For his experimental puzzles, Mr. Coffin is likely to use birch wood because it is easy to work with and available. Maple, however, will make a longer-lasting puzzle. "Walnut is another excellent wood to work and takes a beautiful finish. So does cherry."

In making his own puzzles, Stewart Coffin has his lumber planed to a precise thickness. "I then rip it to the desired shape and size with either my table saw or my band saw with a very fine blade. If you have access to a thickness planer and/or jointer, you can produce very accurately the square stock you need," he says. But he emphasizes that, at all times, measurements of a puzzle should be checked with a vernier caliper and maintained as closely as possible. He tries to keep his measurements to within plus or minus five thousandths of an inch. "This is as close as you can work in most woods," he points out, "because the change in humidity can cause much variation."

For the amateur puzzle-maker, here are Mr. Coffin's directions for constructing the twelve-piece Altekruse burr puzzle.

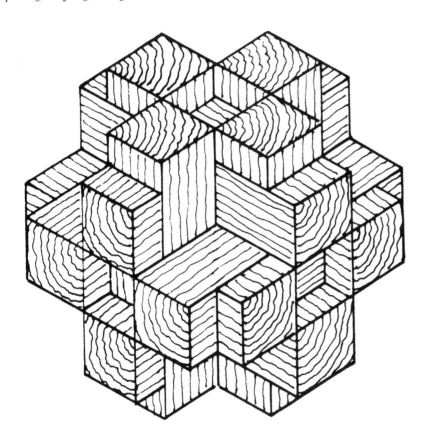

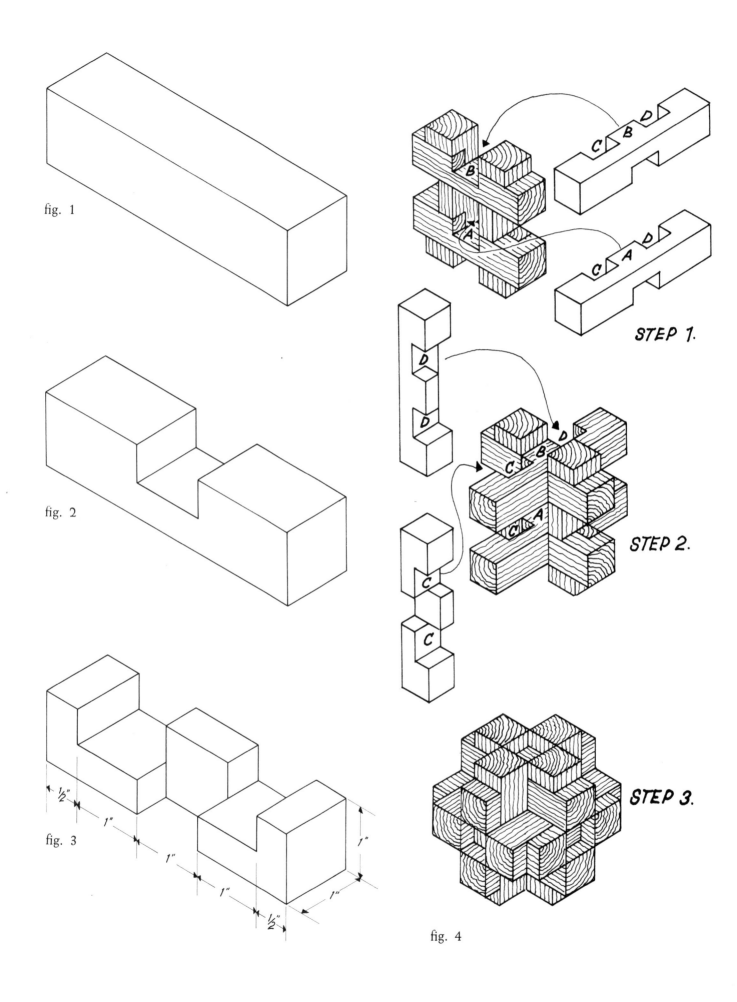

fig. 1

fig. 2

fig. 3

½"
1"
1"
1"
½"
1"
1"

STEP 1.

STEP 2.

STEP 3.

fig. 4

MAKING THE ALTEKRUSE PUZZLE

1. Start with uniform square stock of any desired size — 1″ square, for example. Use almost any wood of your choice except pine. It gums up tools.

2. Saw from the stock fourteen pieces 4″ long, or longer if desired, but all exactly the same length (Fig. 1).

3. Saw a notch exactly in the center of each piece (Fig. 2), 1″ wide and ½″ deep. The advantage of using a dado blade for this, rather than multiple saw cuts, is not so much that it is faster — which it is — but that the width is controlled precisely. Similar notches should be made on either side of the center notch, with the pieces rotated one-quarter turn (Fig. 3). All of these cuts should be made by using some sort of mechanical stop on the saw to position the pieces accurately rather than by using pencil marks.

4. Now you should be able to fit any four pieces together, using the outer notches, to form a square ring. Test all the pieces for fit, and sand any that are too tight.

5. Drop two additional pieces horizontally into the spaces shown in step 1 of Fig. 4.

6. Then slide two vertical pieces into the exposed slots of the last two, as shown in step 2, thus, in effect, constructing another four-piece square ring at right angles to the first. Construct another four-piece square ring, this one horizontally, by fitting the four remaining pieces into slots around the puzzle. The result will be Step 3. Try with twelve pieces first. There are several different solutions. In one of them, the most difficult, the puzzle will come apart in any one of three different directions.

"This particular design is the second in an infinite family," according to Mr. Coffin. "The smallest member is a simple six-piece version, with two notches in each piece. The third is a twenty-four-piece puzzle, with four notches in each piece. Next comes a beautiful thirty-six-piece design, five notches per piece. It has a thirty-eight-piece relative. I haven't gone beyond that."

A shelf filled with Coffin puzzles

In New England when you talk about woodcarving, the name of John Upton is sure to be heard. When President Dwight D. Eisenhower visited Maine, Jack Upton was asked to carve the state's gift. He had less than a week in which to transform a block of native white pine into a gilded eagle with a two-foot wing spread.

Informed of the honor that had been bestowed upon him — and the task he had to accomplish — Jack Upton took both calmly, marched into the kitchen to his wife, Eleanor, an accomplice for more than fifty years in his multifarious escapades, and explained, "Look, Babe, that was the governor's secretary. Ed Muskie has ordered an eagle from me for the President of the United States. I propose that I shall get up at half-past five every morning this week and work until dark until I get that carving done, and no one is to know who it is for, or what I am doing. If you will help me keep people away, I will be greatly obliged."

"Will you want your meals?" Eleanor Upton matter-of-factly inquired.

"Yes, that would be fine."

Jack Upton, now seventy-seven but still hearty, erect, and hardworking, chuckles as he recalls that incident of two decades ago. "Eleanor — I couldn't do without Eleanor — did just as I asked. She warned everybody who came to the house looking for me that I was not to be disturbed, that they had better stay away from the barn where I was working or they'd find something sharp thrown at them and they'd probably be hit. I'm a good marksman, you know.

"Well, I got that bird character done, and I made a special crate for him so all the padding could be easily removed and examined by the Secret Service, and when the governor opened it, and Ike saw it — why, he grinned that wonderful grin of his and said he would hang the eagle at his Gettysburg farm. And *The New York Times* took a picture of him and my eagle that they put on page one. It's a helluva lot of fun to think that you're awfully good," Jack Upton says in the booming voice that served him well with the Naval Reserve in two World Wars. In World War II, he was a lieutenant commander in charge of convoy control in the port of New York and, later, was in the port director's office at Pearl Harbor.

"And it's good to look back on your life and appraise it and be able to say that you've had one of

· 15 ·
HOPE CHESTS
MADE TO ORDER

the most interesting lives you can imagine. In nineteen fourteen, I quit high school for the Massachusetts nautical school ship *Ranger*, and later I signed on board a full-rigged ship sailing to Buenos Aires. She was the *Timandra*, one hundred and eighty-one feet long and weighed one thousand, four hundred and ninety-two tons. I set the main sky sail — that was my particular rag — and I squeezed a lot of my fingerprints into that top gallant mast! Oh, God, that was a marvelous experience, sailing on one of those full-rigged ships surging against the seas.

"And after the First World War, I decided I wanted to see the Blue Ridge Mountains, so I bought me a horse and a saddle and bridle — the horse was a buckskin wilder than Hell, and I rode from Warrenton, Virginia, to Tyron, North Carolina. I had more fun on that trip than any man has had before or since.

"Some guy with a shotgun held me up and said he wanted my horse. I told him that was nonsense, the horse was no good, and just rode on. And a little farther on, because I had an army surplus saddle and U.S. on my stirrups, I was picked up by a sheriff in Virginia who didn't like the cut of my jib and thought I was a deserter. And when I wrote my name in the ledger of one hotel and they couldn't read it, they thought I was a forger. Oh, Jesus, that was fun!"

Jack Upton will reminisce in the neat workshop that adjoins his barn in Damariscotta, Maine, or upstairs in the study where he has written two books about carving (the latest *A Woodcarver's Primer*), or downstairs among the antiques and hooked rugs and ginger jars that his wife has collected. Down here too is much Upton handiwork — Martha Washington chairs, corner cupboards, coffee tables, hutches, chests, and the seal of the United States ("That says something to me, doesn't it to you?").

If it is winter, there is a bright fire in the fireplace and flickering tongues of light and shadow across the pine-board floors, while the wind rattles the windows and the snow mounds in drifts in the yard.

Jack Upton moved to Maine from Wayland, Massachusetts, a Boston suburb, after World War II. He had been doing research in engineering for a Cambridge firm. "But one day I said to myself, 'What the hell am I doing here? I don't want to do this. I want to repair furniture and antiques. I want to start to work for a fella named Upton!'"

The first few years were arduous ones, with more income resulting from Jack Upton's green thumb at raising Boston Market lettuce than from his woodworking. But in 1951, five years after his move to Maine, he decided he had had enough of crossbreeding vegetables and placed the ad "Woodcarvings Made to Order" in *The New Yorker*.

"The first order was for a breadboard, and the female who asked for it wanted 'Give Us This Day Our Daily Bread' carved on it in French. I don't know a word of French, but, thanks to Eleanor, I made out."

Since then, Jack Upton has produced more than 400 carvings on order. Their prices range from $150 to $3000.

With characteristic gusto, he comments as he shakes a wood shaving out of his grizzled crew cut that woodcarving is "without exception, the most rewarding and wonderful business in the world. Everything you do is a pleasure to do and to make, and people write to you and they say things like 'Enduring admiration for your carved eagle over our doorway prompts us to write this letter and ask if you will design a war memorial for our town.' Or you make a hope chest for a young woman for her wedding day, and twenty years later, she asks you to carve one for her daughter."

Jack Upton thinks he was three or four when he first cut his finger with a jackknife. He made up his mind, then, that he would never do it again, and he almost never has. He is as careful with his tools — both in the way he looks after them and the way he uses them — as he was aboard ship. Improperly caring for and handling tools can be every bit as dangerous as being lackadaisical in a storm at sea, he maintains. Since a blunt tool can actually cause more harm than a sharp one, he makes sure that his are sharpened regularly.

At the same time, he insists that anyone can carve "if he has an idea in his head and heart that he wants to express in wood, and he has patience, and a certain amount of skill with his hands."

He taught himself to carve, and in private lessons, as well as in his books, has taught others. "If you really like to work in wood, and are willing to take time, you'll find nothing is a problem — or the things that are problems will be fun to solve. You know, it doesn't matter whether it's mermaids for the bow of a yacht I'm making, or teak dolphins or a rosewood seahorse, or a Salem eagle, I love to work as long as I have a knife or a gouge in my hand and a good piece of wood before me.

"Say, do you know about Salem eagles?" he is inclined to ask any visitor to his shop who is bound to notice the photographs and drawings of eagles of all sorts above the orderly array of jelly glasses filled with nails on his shelves.

"You see, before and just after the Revolution, there were a great many people emigrating from Massachusetts to Maine. Most of them preferred to come up by vessel rather than by ox cart, which was doing it the hard way, after all. Of course, a lot of them couldn't read or write, so the shipmasters of Marblehead and Salem, where most of the vessels sailed from, used a replica of an eagle to show they had coasting schooners going Down East. You know what

Down East means, don't you? When those fellas from Massachusetts were coming this way, they said they were going Down East because the prevailing winds here are southwest, so they were heading east before the wind when they came up to the province of Maine. Maine, of course, was a Massachusetts province till eighteen twenty.

"Anyway, those eagles were strong, stern, sturdy-looking creatures with their wings down. Even though they were roughly done, they had a look about them that made it clear any schooner having that eagle's sign would have a good, safe journey. Those were the first eagles I ever carved. I couldn't think of a better name for them than Salem eagles.

"I've always loved eagles, ever since I was knee-high to a hop toad. I think the eagle is the most magnificent bird on earth. They're cruel, of course, but they're not like men, slaughtering just to slaughter. An eagle won't slaughter unless he's hungry."

Nowadays, Jack Upton is in and out of his workshop, for he is writing a tongue-in-cheek book on old age. But he is still there most afternoons, ready to offer advice and counsel to the would-be carver. Here is a sample of some of his counsel, as well as directions for the making of a hope chest, a project he feels is a less difficult task for a beginner than carving an eagle.

Especially important for a woodcarver is the selection of the wood he will use. "A lot of people like to work in basswood," Jack Upton says, but he warns against it. "It's too gritty and spoils your tools. And beware of any contrary wood with warps and checks, hidden blemishes and knots that are buried. You want to be sure to have a wood that works honestly. It doesn't matter if it's hard, but it must not have characteristics that you come upon unexpectedly." His own favorite carving wood is second-growth white pine — lumber cut from trees about 100 years old. "Nothing is more annoying than to have a carving three-quarters done and then run into a pitch pocket whose presence in the stock was not foreseen."

Mr. Upton again reminds the would-be carver to keep his tools sharp. He makes the general suggestion that long cuts are best made with the run of the grain of the wood; short sweeps can be made diagonally across the grain.

The tools that he uses most often in carving are a 3/8" No. 13 gouge, a 1/2" No. 41 parting tool, a 3/4" No. 5 straight gouge, and a 1" No. 4 straight gouge. A mallet, preferably of lignum vitae, is also necessary for driving the gouges. Other helpful tools are a backsaw, hand saw, straightedge, dividers, scroll saw, jointing plane, hand drill, hand screwdriver, fractional drills, a wood rasp, a spokeshave, and a drawshave.

1. Select stock, being sure that you have more than enough on hand. Look for well-marked, straight-grained Northern white pine. You will know how much you need and where you are going if, in the very beginning, you make a full-scale drawing of the chest's front, side piece, and top. Show all pertinent dimensions on these drawings.

2. Make a list or schedule of all the pieces required, giving the exact dimensions for each piece or pair of pieces. Here is Mr. Upton's suggested form for this. He emphasizes that both end panels should be made with the grain of the wood in the vertical position. For all the other panels, the grain should be horizontal.

BUILDING AND CARVING
A HOPE CHEST

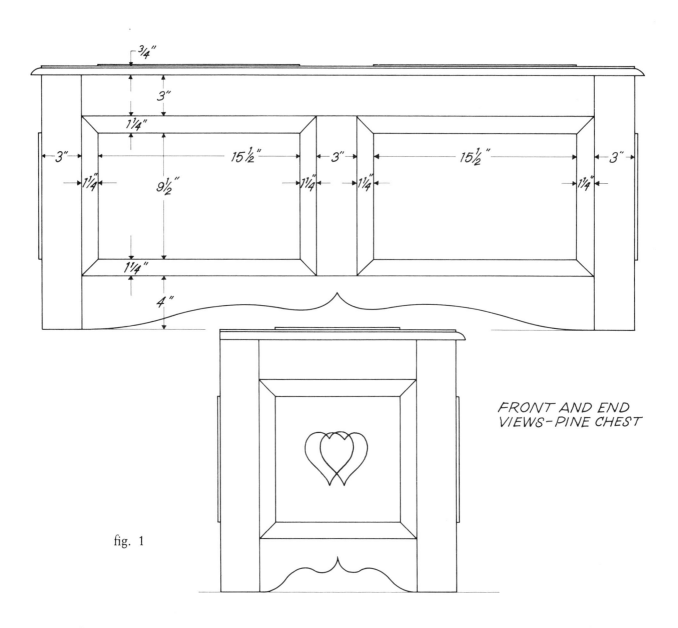

FRONT AND END
VIEWS – PINE CHEST

fig. 1

Schedule of Pieces
(See Figs. 1, 2)
End panels, two, 13" wide, 12½" long
Front and top panels, four, 19" long, 13" wide (all six panels will have chamfered edges with raised centers — all chamfering will be done to the same dimensions) (Fig. 3)
End stiles, two for each panel, 3¾" wide x 13" long, including tenons on each end, i.e., overall length
Front stiles, two 3" wide x 19" long and one 3" wide by 13" long

Top stiles, two 3¾" wide x 13" long for the ends of the top and one 3" wide x 13" long for the division in the center for the panels
Rails for the front, one 3" wide x 40" long and one 4" wide x 40" long
Rails for the top, one 4" wide x 46½" long and one 3" wide x 45" long
Rails for the ends, four (two for each end), one 4" wide x 13" long and one 3" wide x 13" long

Back of the chest, rails, two 3" x 46½"; stiles, two 3" x 19"; back panel of quarter-inch plywood, pine, good on two faces, 13" x 40"
Bottom, quarter-inch pine plywood stock, good on two faces, approximately 18" wide x 45" long. To determine this piece's dimensions, assemble the whole chest and make it to fit. Also be sure to check the squareness of the assembled chest before you cut this piece out.

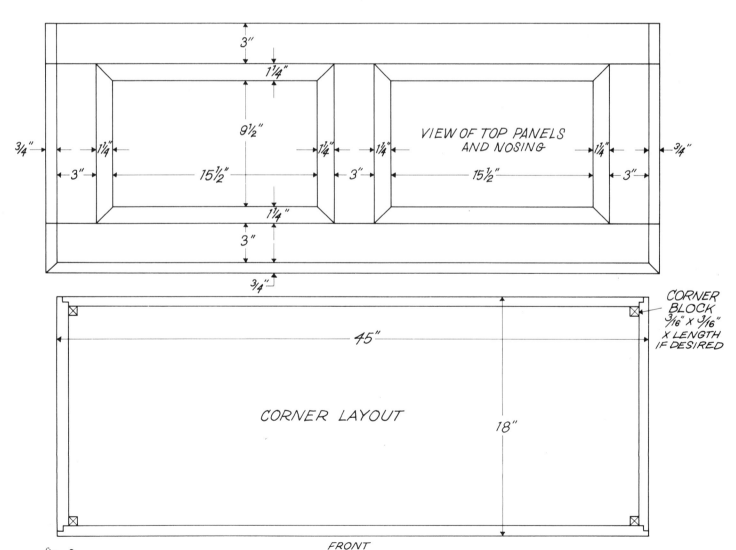

VIEW OF TOP PANELS AND NOSING

CORNER LAYOUT

CORNER BLOCK ³⁄₁₆" X ³⁄₁₆" X LENGTH IF DESIRED

FRONT

fig. 2

fig. 3 *The start of the second chamfer cut on the waste stock*
(Jack Upton)

fig. 4 *Using a saw, jack, and clamp to make the top and bottom rails the exact lengths*
(Jack Upton)

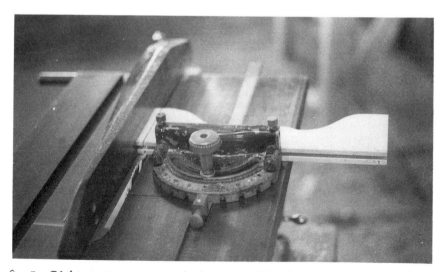

fig. 5 *Making a tenon cut on the bottom rail for the chest ends*
(Jack Upton)

General Directions

1. In selecting stock from which the panels, stiles, and rails are to be made, try to get material wide enough for all the panels and long enough for all the stiles and rails. If stock wide enough for the panels is not available, cut stock roughly to the panel's two dimensions, length and width, and glue the pieces together for these parts.

2. Square up one end of each piece of stock to be used. Then lay out each piece to its proper length, scribe stock, and then clip each piece to the length. The ends must be perfectly square as the fit of tenons and other joints will depend upon this (Figs. 4, 5).

All tenons used will be ½″ long and cut to fit the mortises or grooves exactly. Mortise and tenon joints will be used where necessary. The grooves for the panels and, in some cases, stiles will be made with the dado cutters. All tenons will be blind, i.e., they will be stopped ½″ from the outside edge of the stock so as to be invisible when assembled (Fig. 6). To make tenons, set

fig. 6 *Starting a blind end cut to develop the groove on the stiles as required.*
The pencil mark shows where the cuts with dado cutters begin.
This is the start of a blind mortise on the tenon joint
(Jack Upton)

fig. 7 *Squaring up the end of the blind groove*
(Jack Upton)

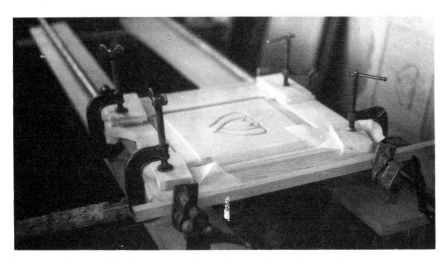

fig. 8 *The completed end panels are clamped in stiles and rails to
complete assembly of these parts.*
Apply glue only to the grooves
(Jack Upton)

the rip-fence over from the outside of the saw blade 1/2″. Run the saw blade down to make a cut 1/4″ deep. Use the cut-off guide to make a cut on the face of the stock with the end placed hard up on the side of the rip fence. Make cuts on both sides. Next, do not change the position of the fence or blade. With the face of the stock on the tabletop, end parallel with the fence, pass the stock across the saw so that the blade will remove the waste stock little by little. Take care you do not get too close to the saw blade with your hands. Hold the stock firmly down on the tabletop. Complete cuts on both faces.

To develop the tenon blind, make a cut with the rip fence left in the existing position, but run the saw blade up 1/2″ above the tabletop. Use the cut-off guide to make this cut accurately. Place the end of the tenon against the fence, hold the stock on its edge, grooved side up, not its face, and pass the stock across the saw blade carefully. The result will be the removal of the stock from the edge of the tenon (Figs. 6, 7).

3. Set either the bar or pipe clamps so that they will function properly. Lay paper underneath the places where the glued-up joint will come in contact with the surface of the clamp. To simplify the description of his method, Mr. Upton describes the routine for the end panels (Fig. 8) shown in the clamps.

4. Apply liquid glue, Elmer's glue, or a comparable glue to the sides of the mortises on the stile. Then apply the glue to the face of the tenon on the rail that will be inserted into the mortise — it does not matter which end is inserted first. Next, insert the tenon into the mortise and so join these two parts. Using care, apply glue to the inside of the grooves, but apply it sparingly for if too much is used it will be difficult to get it off the sides and the face of the parts. Then apply glue to the tenon and mortise and the groove on another part, preferably the top rail. Finally, apply glue to the last piece, the stile. Slip the edge of the panel into the groove of the two parts already put together. Next, slide the top rail partially into place, being sure the tenon is set in properly and the edge of the panel is properly fitted into the groove. Last, ease the last stile into place. If you will start the top rail tenon into the mortise on the end of the stile into which the edge of the panel has already been inserted, you will be able to set it to the opposite stile that is already in place.

5. Position all the stiles and rails so the outside edges are flush at the joints. Place the panel assembly on the pipe (or bar) clamps, and slip scraps of ⅛″ hardboard between the clamps and panel (this avoids marring the panel).

Slip scraps of paper between the hardboard and the panel to prevent gluing the panel to the hardboard. Place scraps of wood between the clamp jaws and the panel to prevent marring the surface.

6. Tighten the pipe (bar) clamps to pull the assembly snug-tight. Wipe off the excess glue. Put scraps of paper, then waste wood blocks, over all four joints. Clamp snug-tight with four C-clamps. The assembly should look like Fig. 8. Now, but not until now, fully tighten both bar clamps and all C-clamps.

7. The inside corners of the chests Mr. Upton makes are always fitted with a piece of stock squared up, usually ¾″ on each face. Then he drills and countersinks holes for 1¼″ No. 8 flathead wood screws with which these stays are held hard up against the insides of the corners (Fig. 9). Half-joints, or rabbet joints, are made on the edges of all the stiles, the overlaps of the face or chest from half-joints making the front perfectly smooth by having the corresponding but opposite half-joints made on the edges of the stiles of the end panels (Fig. 10). The back, the top, the front, and the ends of the chest are all assembled in the manner described.

fig. 9   *A detail of the corner stay. The stay is glued to the abutting faces of the ends and side stiles. Then 1¼″ No. 8 flathead screws are run in* (Jack Upton)

8. The bottom of the chest must be made after the rest is assembled because the probability is that there will be some slight degree of "out-of-square" involved in the final assembly, so — Mr. Upton says — measure and then fit the bottom in place. Use ¼"-thick pine plywood, good on both faces, for both the back panels and the bottom of the chest.

9. Mr. Upton uses fillets about ¾" square to support the bottom panel in place. He applies these fillets so the top surface on which the chest bottom will rest is about 4" above the bottom of the chest frame, i.e., where the chest will rest on the floor. Glue these fillets in place.

10. Mr. Upton says that he finds, too, if he dresses up the inside of the chest with ¼" squares where the sides and the bottom board of the chest come together, "the final piece looks as if the maker had taken some degree of pride in his workmanship, which, of course, he should."

11. The top of the chest should overhang the front and sides by about ⅜". This makes it easier to open. Mr. Upton generally rounds off the front and side edges of the top and frequently, if not always, uses four butt hinges gained into the top edge of the back of the chest and the underside of the chest top as well. Use ⅝" brass screws when you apply the hinge to the top and ¾"-long screws for the opposite side of the hinges.

12. Once assembled, use sandpaper No. 120 or No. 150 grit, as you prefer, and sand off to a very small radius all the corners and edges of the chest frame. Then, if you desire, apply a very light oil stain.

13. Shellac the chest inside with clear or white shellac to finish that surface off properly.

14. "Shaping the edges of the bottom frames for the chest is an optional feature," says Mr. Upton. "I do so in place of making feet or the like." Fig. 11 shows the completed chest.

fig. 10 *The completed chest, without top.*
Note the corner stays, 3/4" square, with inside edge chamfered
(Jack Upton)

fig. 11 *The completed chest*
(Jack Upton)

There are not more than a dozen people in America today making wooden pitchforks, the New England practitioners of that ancient craft maintain. The founder of the movement is a soft-spoken former mechanical engineer named David Sawyer, whose eyes smile behind gold-rimmed glasses and who recounts, in his green New Hampshire fields, how it was a Mennonite in Pennsylvania who taught him to make pitchforks. He, in turn, passed on the knowledge to others — among them Timothy Gastler, a fellow inhabitant of the hills of Quaker City, New Hampshire, and to George Havell, who lives a few hours away in southwestern Vermont.

None of these pitchfork makers is, as might be expected of craftsmen of such old-time objects, a grizzled farmer who has fashioned his own pitchforks, of necessity, since childhood. David Sawyer is a slender, bearded 1958 graduate of the Massachusetts Institute of Technology. Timothy Gastler is a young man who likes to spend his springs — wooden pitchfork in hand — helping his father in Connecticut prepare his pansies for market. George Havell is a forty-three-year-old Princeton graduate who reads German fluently, has a fondness for rare books and prints, earned a master's degree in forestry, but, in 1954, before other people were doing it, adopted a simple, rustic "alternative" lifestyle.

George Havell lives alone, miles down a wooded road that is icy in winter and muddy in spring. His only companions are two cats, fifty chickens, and two hives of bees, so he welcomes the chance to talk to a passer-by about his craft. He likes fork-making because he can earn about $6 an hour at it without leaving home, and it leaves him free to garden, tend his bees, and cut wood in the warmer months. Fork-making elicits a warm response in many people, and he finds it satisfying to be proficient in an almost forgotten craft. He also likes being self-sufficient.

"One of my basic principles," he says in a Yankee twang, "is not to buy anything I can make, scrounge, or grow. I grow about seventy-five percent of my own food. I moved here to the country because I like country living, though I'm not one of those roots and berries and outdoor bathroom types. I'm not interested in roughing it, and I've found farming is hard to do. But now you can make a living at crafts, and I'm all for it!"

· *16* ·

"WOODEN PITCHFORKS ARE A PLEASURE TO USE"

In blue jeans, an Icelandic fisherman's sweater, and a gray knitted cap, he talks in the shop above his garage one harsh March afternoon of how he came to the making of pitchforks.

Perched on a sawhorse, George tells how his mother and his father, who was in the publishing business, in 1937 bought the farm where he now lives "for the price then of a good used car. It was our summer place." In the winter, the Havells lived in New York, New Jersey, and Connecticut. When George Havell's service in the Korean conflict was over, he moved to the farm to live year-round.

"I have one hundred and ten acres and half a million feet of timber on the property, and so I decided I could operate a sawmill part-time, and that and the pitchforks are what I do for money, basically, now." For a while, because he had had some experience cross-country skiing and was good mechanically, the proprietor of a resort ski shop hired him.

fig. 1

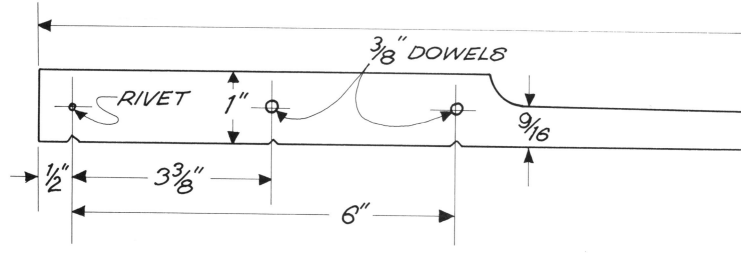

TINE TEMPLATE – THIN WOOD STOCK

NOTCHES ON LOWER EDGE LOCATE DOWEL AND RIVET HOLE.

He can talk extensively not only of skis but of the merits of various snowshoe designs, and his snowshoes hang outside the garage ready to be donned when he goes to feed the chickens or sets out after maple sap.

"I've sugared most seasons for the past fifteen years," he says. "Two years ago was the best year. Then, with a full-time helper, I made sixty gallons of Grade A and Grade B syrup, as well as another ten gallons below grade that was perfectly usable. But of course that's only work that lasts about four weeks."

He also has supplemented his income with the honey from his bees. "If I could have my druthers, I'd have a couple of dozen colonies of them, but I've had some trouble with them."

Mr. Havell lives twelve miles from the nearest town and goes into it infrequently because pitchforks and farm work keep him too busy. For his farm activities, he keeps "a small and elderly tractor that I've had for twenty years," and his blue eyes light with an interior laughter as he talks affectionately of it and his Model A Ford dump truck.

He began making pitchforks in 1971 and has made more than 300. He knows that he could have made a good many more than that if he had devoted himself to it full-time.

Wooden pitchforks, he admits, are not superior in any way but aesthetically to metal-pronged ones. Indeed, he doubts that the pitchforks he makes are as durable as their iron counterparts. "But they're handier and they're pleasant to use." They sell well at crafts fairs, where he goes and shows how he makes them, and at antiques and crafts shops.

George Havell's introduction to pitchfork-making came at a time when the financial going in rural Vermont was tough for him. "But I knew I wanted to stay. I'd known that ever since I was in my teens and had read William Vogt's *Road to Survival*, a book that made quite a splash when it was published but has been surprisingly forgotten. I've been pretty violent on all this environmental stuff ever since." When his old friend David Sawyer proposed pitchfork-making as a means of supporting himself in the country, he apprenticed himself with alacrity.

He makes four styles of pitchforks — two-tine forks for stable bedding and stirring up litter in the hen house; five-tine manure or compost forks, four-tine hay or grass forks, and three-tine general hay forks. He does all of his pitchfork-making with hand tools — "the same tools as those used way back when."

As he warms his hands over the wood stove (above it, ears of seed corn hang out of the way of marauding mice), he says he is sorry to admit that he uses a power saw for cutting down the trees for his forks and a propane torch for hardening the wood and making the bends in the forks permanent.

But here are his directions for what, otherwise, is an entirely hand-done pitchfork, which he sells for $12.

"Before I enter on this exposition though," he emphasizes, "let me offer a caveat. While making a wooden pitchfork is not so difficult as one might suppose from an examination of the finished product, it is fairly complex and involves the use of some now rather obscure skills. There is a fair risk of breakage without a gentle touch. I think it unlikely that a person inexperienced in the hand-woodworking techniques involved can successfully complete a fork working from written instructions — but here goes!"

20 ¾"

7/16"

MAKING A HANDMADE PITCHFORK

1. Material Needed

a. A green log of white oak, hickory, red oak, or white ash 5' to 5'6" long (these woods are listed, roughly, in order of preference)

b. Dowel stock prepared from any of these woods from which will come roughly squared or octagonal pins, approximately ½" x 5" and ½" x 9" to be driven through a dowel-sizing plate — there should be one pin of each size

c. One 16- or 20-penny common nail, with an appropriate size washer, to form the rivet

d. Six ¾" or ⅞" channel nails or fine, headless brads

2. Tools used, in order of use

a. Ax and felling saw, power or otherwise

b. Steel maul and splitting wedges

c. Froe and froe club

d. Cross-cut hand saw, preferably one with 10 to 12 points to an inch

e. Shaving horse and draw-knife (or drawknives — one is sufficient if it has a reasonably narrow blade, 10" wide or near 10")

f. Tine template and marking pencil (medium copying pencil marks well on green wood) (Fig. 1).

g. Straight and concave spokeshaves (concave optional but handy)

h. Hand ripsaw

i. Bit brace and ⅜" auger bit

j. Hand drill and appropriate size twist drill to drill for 16- or 20-penny common nail (the fit should be close — the nail should have to be driven in)

k. Dowel-sizing plate (Fig. 2) and heavy wooden mallet — do not use a steel mallet or a hammer for sizing the dowel

l. Steel hammer and anvil surface

m. Tapered wooden wedge for spreading tines (Fig. 11)

n. Loop of strong twine to stretch 12"

o. Bending form (Fig. 5)

(All of the less common tools referred to above may be obtained from Woodcraft Supply Corporation at 313 Montauk Avenue, Woburn, Massachusetts, or in "junk shops and odd, rare corners," according to George Havell.

fig. 2 *The dowel-sizing plate*

He also advises the potential pitchfork-maker to examine Eric Sloane's *A Museum of Early American Tools* and Henry Mercer's *Ancient Carpenter's Tools* for discussions and explanations of old tools.

3. Making the fork must be done in three stages, with considerable intervals between the second and third to allow time for drying.

4. To prepare your material, cut a 5' to 5'6" log of one of the suggested varieties from the butt end of a freshly felled tree. The log should have a minimum top diameter of about 6" and be reasonably free of knots and irregular grain. It should not have more than about eight growth rings to the inch or it is likely to prove brittle in bending. It should not include the "swell" just above the roots.

5. Using the maul and wedges, split the logs into halves, again into quarters, and, in the case of a larger log, into eighths, each time as equally as possible. Reject any pieces with large knots or irregular grain.

6. Mark with indelible pencil the lower end of the section as shown in Fig. 3. Make the first split with the froe at *a*, the second split at *b*, then if the outer section ("2", "3") is wide enough to divide into two pieces 2" each in width, split again at *c*. Parts

1, 2, and 3, if free from irregularities, should be suitable for fork stock; 4 is waste. For a three-tined fork, your stock should be, at the head end (nearest the butt of the tree) about 2" wide x 1½" thick (Fig. 4). It is important that the split tangent to the annual rings continue between the same rings the width of the stock.

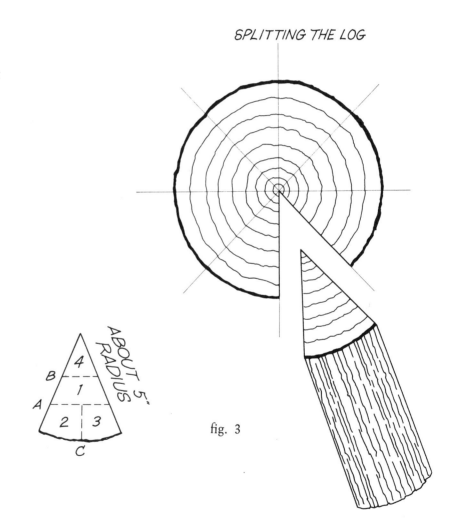

SPLITTING THE LOG

fig. 3

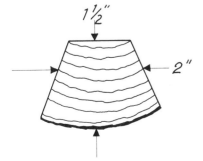

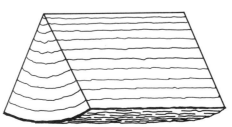

fig. 4

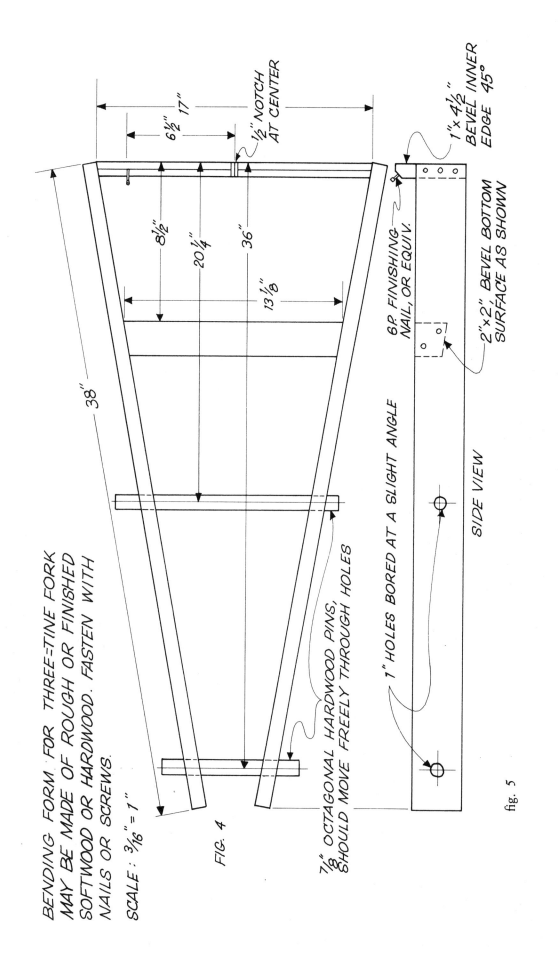

BENDING FORM FOR THREE-TINE FORK
MAY BE MADE OF ROUGH OR FINISHED
SOFTWOOD OR HARDWOOD. FASTEN WITH
NAILS OR SCREWS.

SCALE : 3/16" = 1"

FIG. 4

7/8" OCTAGONAL HARDWOOD PINS,
SHOULD MOVE FREELY THROUGH HOLES

17"

6½"

½" NOTCH
AT CENTER

8½"

20¼"

36"

13⅛"

38"

1" HOLES BORED AT A SLIGHT ANGLE

1"x 4½"
BEVEL INNER
EDGE 45°

6P. FINISHING
NAIL, OR EQUIV.

2"x 2", BEVEL BOTTOM
SURFACE AS SHOWN

SIDE VIEW

fig. 5

7. Now it is time to prepare two pins of straight-grained wood. They should be finished with a froe and drawknife so that they are ½″ square (or octagonal) ; one is 5″ long and the other 9″. They should be pointed at one end. Keep them in water until you are ready to use them. Similarly, keep the fork stock in water after you have cut it if you do not plan to use it within a couple of days.

8. Shaping and bending the fork

a. First, trim both ends of the stock square with the hand saw, removing an inch or less from each end. Then, using the shaving horse and draw-knife, shave the outer (widest) surface flat and true, being careful not to cut across the annual rings, especially on the lower end, which will form the tines. In the case of stock with bark on, remove both bark and the cambium layer completely. You will use this side as the underside of the fork, and it is the point of reference.

b. Next, shave the sides perpendicular to the underside until the width of the tine to be is 1⅝″ to 1¾″ across. Shave to a point 21″ above the lower end of the stock. From here upward, the sides may taper in to about 1″ width at the top.

When you have shaved to this width to make the tines, you will have three ½″ tines plus two 1/16″ saw cuts equaling your 1⅝″ altogether. (Measurements need not be absolutely exact — 1¾″ is quite all right.)

c. Take the tine template (Fig. 1) with the straight edge aligned with the bottom surface of the fork and trace the outline of the template top edge on both sides of the stock, marking the location of the two dowel holes and the rivet hole (Fig. 6). Shave the top surface down to conform with the widest part of the template, working down from slightly above the rivet location toward the tine end. Then cut out the

fig. 6 *Marking for the rivet*

fig. 7   *Sawing the tine sections into equal thirds*

wood above the lower part of the tines. (In the concave areas, it is best to use a draw-knife upside-down, beveled side down.)

d. Next, shave down the top side toward the handle end, level with the tine part. Then, starting just above the rivet location on the underside, shave out the lower surface toward the handle end, removing about 1/8″. Do the same on the sides.

e. Shave the handle section to an octagonal shape, and finish with a drawknife and spokeshave to a slightly flat-tened oval cross section, taper-ing a little toward the handle end.

f. Locking the tine end in the shaving horse, strain the thinned portion of the tines to produce an upward curvature. Do this carefully, varying the pressure point. Nearly a 90-degree arc should be achieved. In this and other stress bending to follow, it will be helpful to soak the fork in very hot water prior to bending, although this is not always necessary. Next, strain to produce a downward curvature of the handle just above the rivet point.

g. Mark the top of the tine section, dividing it into equal thirds lengthwise from the rivet location to the end of the tines; then saw along the marks (Fig. 7) from the end upward to just beyond (1/8″ or less) the rivet location, finishing with the saw vertical to the work.

Check the lower surface while working to avoid drifting off.

h. Just above the upper dowel location, shave the sides inward and slightly concave so that the thickness of the outer tine at the rivet point is half or slightly more than that distance from the dowel to the lower end.

i. Locking the head of the fork in the shaving horse between rivet and upper dowel location, strain each outer tine to produce outward curvature between the rivet and the upper dowel. Again, vary the pressure point while doing this.

j. Clamp work vertically in the vise, tines up. Clamp the tines together with a C-clamp between the dowel marks. Bore the dowel holes with a ⅜″ auger bit; reverse and bore from the opposite side when the lead screw emerges. Drill a rivet hole with the appropriate size twist drill (Fig. 8).

k. Form ⅜″ dowels by driving green wooden pins that you have cut to 9″ and 5″ lengths through ½″ and ⅜″ holes of the dowel plate successively. Bend the pins to approximate the curve shown in the photograph of the finished fork. (Again, soaking with hot water will make the pins more pliable.) Wax the dowels with block paraffin.

fig. 8   *Drilling the rivet hole*

fig. 9 *Two dowels driven through the dowel holes*

fig. 10 *Spreading the tines with a wooden wedge*

l. Rivet the fork at the upper end of the tines, using a 16- or 20-penny nail and a washer. Draw the head of the nail and washer well into the wood. This is done by boring a hole for the rivet, inserting the nail, and pounding till the top is flush with the wood. On the opposite end, cut off the nail, but leave enough to peen over the washer. Pound until that rivet end is squashed into wood too.

m. Drive the dowels through the dowel holes and through the middle of the center tine (Fig. 9). The shorter dowel goes nearest the rivet. Drive the channel nails or brads through the center tine from underneath straight through the dowel. Start the nails from underneath in the outer tines where the dowels cross them, but do not drive them into dowels yet.

n. Slide the hammer handle down between the tines toward the lower dowel to spread the tines slightly. Insert wooden wedge (Fig. 11) behind the lower dowel and drive it until the top is flush with the tines (Fig. 10). Now drive the nails home in the spread tine. Repeat the procedure on the other outside tine.

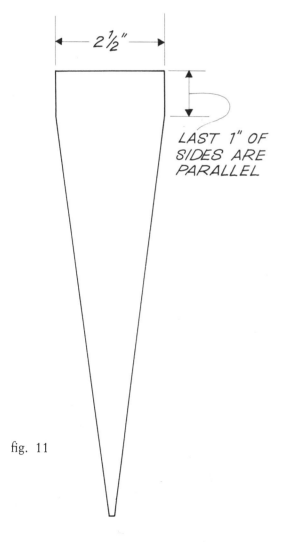

← 2½" →

LAST 1" OF SIDES ARE PARALLEL

fig. 11

WEDGE FOR SPREADING TINES, ¾" HARDWOOD, ABOUT 10" LONG, CHAMFER SIDES ABOUT ⅛" TO BACK

fig. 12 *Looping the cord over the tines before tine trimming*

fig. 13   Tapering and rounding the tine ends

o. Now flex the outer tines inward until the ends can touch the center tine, or nearly so. Avoid placing a strain on the dowel points. Fit a loop of cord over the ends of the outer tines to hold them in (Fig. 12). Then mark the center tine for cutting at or slightly outside the line of cord. Trim the center tine and dowel ends.

p. Using a shaving horse, drawknife, and spokeshave, taper the tine ends from the sides and bottom and around the edges of the tines (Fig. 13). Check again to make sure the dowels are trimmed flush with the tine sides.

q. Bend the fork in the bending form (Fig. 14), inserting the longer pin under the handle and the shorter pin over it. Allow it to dry several days (or longer) until the handle places little pressure on the upper pin.

9. Finishing

a. After drying, char the curved portion of the tine on the bottom side with a propane torch (Fig. 15) rubbing with a lump of rosin while it is still hot so the rosin penetrates the wood. Remove the fork from the frame. Char the underside of the handle just above the rivet for 4″ to 6″.

b. Scrape, sand, and oil the fork. Stain it with a mixture of half linseed oil and half thinner or turpentine with a little burnt umber stirred in.

fig. 14 *Bending the fork in the bending form*

fig. 15 *Charring the fork*

It used to be in New England that any man who went duck hunting carved his own decoys, not quite trusting the way some other hunter would carve the tilt of a head or the flare of tail feathers. But today most of them take a chance on the handiwork of George Soule of Freeport, Maine, who's been fashioning ducks of white pine, cedar, and cork on the evergreen-lined shore of Casco Bay for more than a quarter of a century.

For his first decade as a decoy-carver, George Soule wouldn't have thought of using a machine tool, but the demand for his ducks became so great that fifteen years ago he installed a carving machine to rough-cut his birds in the red wooden shed he calls the Decoy Shop. There, the bodies of twelve ducks at a time are produced and then hand-finished and painted by Mr. Soule and his crew of six men. But there are still decorative decoys that he handmakes on order for collectors.

George Soule began making decoys to sell — canvasbacks, scaup, golden-eyes, mallards and widgeons, black ducks and pintails, eiders and brant — thirty-five years ago when he was a hunting partner of the late L. L. Bean, founder of the sporting goods store.

Mr. Soule is a gentle, gray-haired man who recalls how the decoys Mr. Bean was using were not especially good, "so I got some cork from a refrigerator plant — at that time they insulated with cork board — and I made him a set of decoys. And when he saw them, he said, 'George, I've got room in my shop for decoys.' Now I make not only working decoys and decorative ones, but decoy lamps and bookends and wall plaques and gun-rack heads. It's become a very popular hobby, collecting decoys. Some of the decoys you run into from the old makers can cost as much as four or five thousand dollars."

Mr. Soule looks out the window onto the glistening waters of Casco Bay. "Look there," he says, and his eyes — blue as the bay — squint as he peers out. "Look out there. See those black ducks," — he nods toward dots bobbing in the distance. "They're typical of Maine, and this area carries a good population of them. They're probably the choicest duck there is. And they fly all up and down here. Casco goes from Cape Elizabeth to Cape Small Point. They used to say, you know, that there were three hundred and sixty-five islands in the bay — one for every

• 17 •
DECOYS AND MORE DECOYS

day in the year. But I'm not sure that's really so. Seven of us own Lane's Island out there" — and he nods again toward the ducks. We bought it around World War Two for the hunting. We never shoot ducks along our shore here. We go over there. We've got one of the best sand beaches in the bay and the sea moss harvesters used to bring their moss in there to dry it. I guess they don't use that moss for puddings anymore, for we never see them nowadays."

Mr. Soule affectionately ruffles the red brown fur of his water spaniel, Chief, who snoozes at his feet, and remarks that he was a first-rate hunting dog. His daughter's blond Labrador, Bunny, eager for attention, too, leaps off a day bed and ambles, tail wagging, toward his mistress, who is sitting at a tableful of decoys, painting feathers.

Toby Soule, a jolly, dark-haired, outspoken young woman, gave up teaching five years ago to come home and join the family decoy operation as a painter.

"This isn't just an area for ducks," George Soule continues. "Used to be quite a place for Indians too. There was an old Indian burial ground on our island, and once when I was walking up along the shore here I saw an Indian skull coming out of the bank. You could pretty well identify it without even

checking because of the high cheekbones, but we sent it into the museum in Portland all the same. They said we were right. Indians used to congregate at these points along the bay and dig clams and mussels. The Means Massacre was at Flying Point just a step across from here. They came down from the north, the Indians did, and massacred half the Means family here. They took one of the daughters back to Canada, where they came from, as I remember it, but she escaped with a brother and came back."

Not only Indians have contributed to the legendary lore of Casco Bay's sun-silvered waters, wooded islets, and moon-white beaches. Longfellow wrote "The Wreck of the Hesperus" about a schooner wrecked on the rocks of Peak's Island, and it has long been said that mermaids and mermen swim in the bay's depths. George Soule, a practical man, doesn't talk of them, for he has been too busy with hunting and wood-carving to take much stock in such imaginary matters.

When he was first lured into decoy-making by L. L. Bean he was not long out of school and had gone to work with his father as a woodworker. In those early days, he did fly-tying too. "So much more, in those days, could be hand-done," he says, taking off his cap and smoothing his hair.

"Handwork, of course, is the way to do anything for fine detail," he explains, "but you just can't afford it that way now, especially with all the demand there is for decoys and decoy-decorated objects.

"Of course, the idea continues to be to duplicate as close as possible a real duck — but it's in terms of the way they sit more than the way they look." He stops to pick up two oversize cork decoys from the floor beside him.

"These two," he says, "are about twice the size of a real bird, but they work better than a real-sized bird would, and you can get by with nine of these decoys in a spread whereas if you use the smaller ones you might want to start with a dozen. You're limited, of course, in how many you use by how many you can carry. We use a typical laundry basket for ours — a woven ash basket that I think was made by the Indians. We take our decoys down and set them in the boat and take them out. But other people may use carrying bags or carrying vests.

"If you're setting out decoys for puddling ducks — mallards and blacks and pintails — you put in a loose formation of decoys. For diving birds — scaup and golden-eyes and redheads — you use a lot of them — one hundred and fifty or two hundred they used to use, and you have some with their heads carved high and some low to look real.

"You know, if they made a decoy the exact shape of a bird, though, it would probably be the poorest in the world because it would have to be round-bottomed, which a duck is, but a duck has feet to keep it steady. You don't want to have a decoy that skitters from side to side. You usually make your decoy extra wide, too, for the same reason — for stability.

"Ducks aren't stupid, you know," Mr. Soule continues, examining the painting job that had been done on an oversized hen mallard decoy. "As a matter of fact, I think they're getting smarter and smarter every year. You just can't get them with a decoy that doesn't sit like a duck. Even if the feathers aren't quite right that's not nearly so important as how a duck sits and the way it's colored.

"That's the way things are now, but years ago they used to decoy black ducks with any old decoy chopped out with a hatchet. And they used to decoy snow geese with pieces of newspaper stuck all over the ground. But that doesn't work nowadays. I claim every fall when you hunt it's the stupidist ducks you get first. This leaves the smarter ones to breed and gradually we've produced a smarter breed of ducks. Just the foolish ones get shot off, and the rest are on the alert."

CARVING A FLAT-BOTTOM MALLARD DECOY

1. Since cork is hard to obtain, use two pieces of white pine or cedar 18″ to 19″ long, 3″ thick each, and 7″ to 8″ wide for the decoy body.

2. Cut from a piece of white pine 7″ x 7″ x 2″ for a head.

3. Tack the two body pieces on top of each other.

4. Draw the rough shape of the decoy 18″ long from the breast to the end of the tail, 15″ long on the bottom, 7¼″ (at the widest part of the back) on the side and bottom (Fig. 1).

5. Take the pieces apart. Hollow out the center of each piece with a chisel, leaving a ½″ thickness all around the edges. ("Eighty percent of decoys are solid," George Soule says, "but if you want to make a really nice decoy, hollow it out.")

6. Cut the body pieces out on a band saw or coping saw (Fig. 2). Glue the pieces on top of each other with waterproof glue. Sand.

7. Draw a rough shape of the head (6½″ from the end of the bill to the neck, 3″ thick at the highest point of the head. (This is a duck with its head held low.)

8. Cut the head on a band saw or coping saw (Fig. 3). Sand.

9. Drill a hole for a ⅝″ dowel in the neck end of the head. Insert the ⅝″ dowel point into the hole. (To find the correct spot for drilling your hole, find the center of the neck end of the head and mark it with an X.)

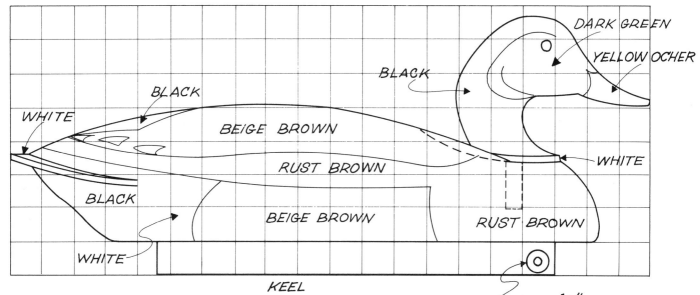

DARK GREEN

YELLOW OCHER

BLACK

WHITE

BLACK

BLACK

WHITE

WHITE

BEIGE BROWN

RUST BROWN

WHITE

RUST BROWN

BEIGE BROWN

KEEL

HOLE ¼" WIDE
COUNTERSUNK
FOR ANCHOR LINE

BEIGE BROWN

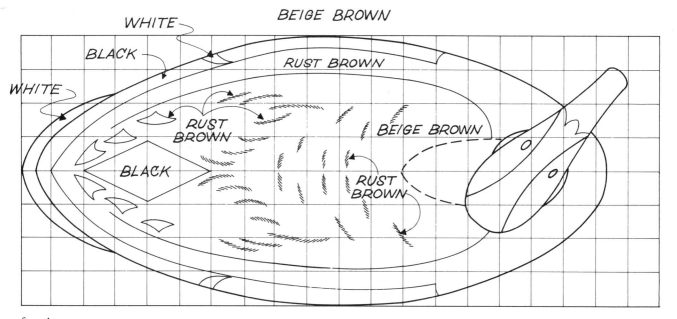

WHITE

BLACK

WHITE

RUST BROWN

RUST
BROWN

BLACK

BEIGE BROWN

RUST
BROWN

fig. 1

10. Move the head about on the neck area of the body until it fits properly and its head is centered. Push the head with the dowel point in it down onto the neck area of the body and the dowel point will mark where the hole should be drilled in the body for the correct placement of the head. Then drill a ⅝″ hole in the body's neck area for continuation of the head's dowel. Remove the dowel point from the head and substitute an actual dowel. Place the head with the dowel in it on the body where the dowel hole has been drilled.

The dowel should be long enough to extend ½″ to ¾″ into the body. The head and body should be fitted firmly together. If you have carved and fitted well, there should not be a crack here through which water can seep.

11. Saw a keel of ¾″-thick pine, 1½″ wide. Drill a ¼″ hole in the bow of it for the anchor line (Fig. 1).

12. Attach the keel to the bottom of the decoy with Weldwood glue. (The keel should be centered and will

help the decoy to line up properly in a stiff breeze.) Reinforce the gluing by nailing the keel, too, with copper or brass tacks at the tail and bow.

13. If the decoy is to be used in a windy area, tack lead, either in the form of a strip or a flat piece, around or along the bottom of the keel. Flashing for a chimney can be used. Tack it in place with copper or brass tacks. For an 18″ decoy, use ¼ to ½ pound of lead.

14. Once the bird is completed to this point, insert the glass eyes, which you can purchase from a taxidermist.

fig. 2 *A decoy rough-carved*

These will come on long wire, which can be cut in two. The eyes are inserted as if they were tacks.

15. Float the bird in your bathtub to make sure it floats evenly. ("The duck might ride too high in the tail. Then you've got to add more lead there to bring it down," Mr. Soule comments. "Or if it's too high in the head, do the opposite.") If the head is slightly off center or turned too much in one direction, compensate for that by cutting a small half-egg-shaped piece of lead and affixing it where it seems required to counteract the excess head weight on one side or the other.

16. Paint the well-sanded, thoroughly dry decoy with flat, waterproof oil paint in two coats (Fig. 4). This can be obtained from L. L. Bean or from Herter's in Waseca, Minnesota. For a painting pattern, see Fig. 1 or any good color guide to water birds.

17. When the bird is painted and properly weighted ("Remember, the higher the decoy rides the farther away a duck can see it," Mr. Soule notes), you are ready to go hunting — that is, as soon as you have fashioned half a dozen, the minimum number of mallard decoys needed to attract their genuine counterpart.

If you are like George Soule, you will thrive on decoy-making. "It's been a good life," he says, and his eyes crinkle at the corners as he searches the bay again for a duck in that characteristic, almost unconscious way of the hunter. "I think I've probably enjoyed this as much as anything in the world that I could have done."

fig. 3 *A decoy head rough-carved*

fig. 4   *Toby Soule paints a decoy*

In Leslie Randall's basement workshop in North Dartmouth, Massachusetts, is the boat builder's tool chest that came home with him when he retired in 1968 as chief carpenter at the South Wharf of the Concordia Boatyard. Inside its lid is glued a color picture of Christ the Pilot guiding a boy at the wheel of a ship.

"Surely you know that hymn 'Jesus Savior, Pilot Me,'" Leslie Randall says, adding that it is one of his favorites, as he proudly shows off his tools, tenderly taking them, one after another, from his tool chest.

"This one's a slick for cutting the scarves when you're joining big timbers, and this is a spoon adz for hollowing out, and here's a boat builder's bevel. And this — this is just what it looks like — a door-knob. We used to use it to turn a bit when there wasn't enough room for a bitstock.

"Now, of course, they use electric tools for most ship-building jobs, and lots of them are better and easier to use. One thing I don't like, though, are electric screwdrivers. They're all right on production work, I suppose, but you don't get the feel of the screw tightening up the way you ought to. And I'll tell you another hand tool I wouldn't be without. I wouldn't be without my jack-knife."

But Leslie Randall isn't building boats anymore. Christ the Pilot on his tool chest is significant. In 1962, Waldo Howland, the Concordia yard's owner, was having his own yacht, *Integrity*, built, and asked Mr. Randall to make the wheel for her.

"Well, I'd never made a wheel before, but I said I'd try. A wheel, you know, is something that wants to be real good on a boat. It should be unusual — a conversation piece. Of course, what it is mostly is circles, and I figured I could make it without too much trouble."

And it was made so successfully that, ever since then, up and down the New England seacoast when a skipper wants a first-rate wheel made, he gets in touch with Leslie Randall. If he happens not to, Leslie Randall is likely to be in touch with him, for he simply doesn't like the idea of a good boat being equipped with a second-rate wheel.

They still chuckle on the island of Martha's Vineyard, for example, about how, when Vineyard captain Robert M. Douglas's revenue cutter replica, the *Shenandoah*,

HE MADE THE WHEEL
FOR THE *AMERICA*

was about to be launched from the shipyard where she had been built in Camden, Maine, Leslie Randall appeared, unexpectedly, at the launching — driving his little Volkswagen, with a carrier top, and a wheel four and a half feet in diameter sticking out on both sides of it.

"I'd read about the *Shenandoah*," Mr. Randall says simply, "and I'd said to Bob Douglas, 'A boat like yours deserves a good wheel.' He'd already made arrangements for one, but I just didn't like it. So there I was. We unlashed my wheel from the top of the car, carried it up alongside the vessel where she was on the ways, and fitted it into place. Oh, that was quite a launching! I burned a hole in my overcoat up against the cabin stove. There was a Scotch band and shrimp sandwiches. They were delicious. Yes, that was quite a launching!"

Mr. Randall remembers, too, the specifics of nearly every wheel he has made. He recalls how Mr. Howland wanted locust spokes and black walnut rims for the *Integrity*'s wheel. "And I had to talk him out of the locust. It's hard to get good locust so we used hickory instead."

The wheel for the *America II*, replica of the famous America's Cup winner of the last century, is another of which he is particularly proud.

"As a matter of fact, I made two for her — one for the first owner, another for the second because he wanted the first one in his living room. She was built in nineteen sixty-seven and had a tiller when she was launched because that's what the *America I* had and they were using her in a film. The original *America* was built in eighteen fifty-one, you know, and they weren't making wheels too much then. She had a great long tiller, but they soon found out a wheel is much handier.

"I remember how I first saw the *America I* when I was young. It was nineteen twenty-one and she was going from Boston down to Annapolis. She was being towed by a submarine chaser. I lived just up here in Padanaram right near the water then, and I went down to the South Wharf where she was tied up, her masts lashed onto her deck. Golly, I was excited! She was quite a famous boat, after all."

Leslie Randall is a jolly man with an enthusiasm for work that is infectious. He comes of old New England stock. "The first Randalls came over from England in sixteen thirty-four and landed near Providence. They were shipbuilders then, and farmers, and some went whaling. But my father, like me, was a woodworker. We had three and a half acres over in South Dartmouth, and a barn and workshop. It was a nice way to grow up."

When it came time for Leslie Randall to go to work, he started out in a picture frame shop, then a mill. Then his father proposed that he join him at New Bedford's F. C. Washburn Company, an old cabinet-making firm, and he did, for a time. "But I always liked boats when I was a kid. I always wanted to do some kind of boat work, so I changed to that. For six years, I

did repair work on yachts and fishing boats, but I never did like those stinking holds. When I was a boy, even, I didn't like the smell of fish. My mother couldn't get me to eat it. You know, a boatyard in the summertime can be a nice place or an awful place. Sometimes the sun pours down and the wind goes over the top of the wharf when the tide is low, and it can be pretty hot and rough." He was pleased to get away from repairing fishing boats to start work at Concordia as a yacht joiner and spar maker.

But he is happy now, too, as a cabinet-maker and wheel-builder, to be fashioning just the objects he enjoys making. In his living room, the sun gleams on the eagle mirror hung on the wall over his wife's favorite piece, a reproduction of a Governor Winthrop desk that he made for her. And the banjo clock in the room is his, too, and the end table.

The basement is largely devoted to cabinet and wheel-making and nostalgia of boats. On a wall bulletin board, yellowed newspaper clippings and photographs tell of old Fall River Line steamers and famous yachts of the past.

"That's the old *Palestine*," Leslie Randall remembers. "She was a beautiful schooner yacht built in nineteen-o-three by Carey Smith on Long Island. Padanaram was her home port, but she was wrecked in the thirty-eight hurricane. The stern was knocked off of her. They used her afterwards for a fishing boat, but she was lost off Noman's Land."

"In her heyday, they used to use her to sail to the Harvard-Yale races in Connecticut — the crew races, don't you know. She was a big vessel — one hundred feet long. Andrew G. Pierce, who owned cotton mills, I think, was her owner. One time they sailed down to the race and when it came time to head home, it was blowing a gale. Pierce didn't like the look of that at all, so he said to the skipper he'd take the train home and he could bring up the schooner later. Pierce couldn't believe his eyes when he got up the next morning and there was the vessel! They'd gotten under way right away that night as soon as he'd left. She was quite a boat!"

Lumber abounds in Mr. Randall's cellar, and he possessively points out an ebony log "that washed up and was rolling on the beach on the island of Cuttyhunk off Cape Cod. It came from a schooner wrecked fifty or sixty years ago, but ebony won't float, so every now and then when the tide is right after a storm, a log still washes in."

Leslie Randall also likes to tell the story of the black walnut he uses in his wheels.

"You see, I wanted some one day, and I heard that there was a woman in Tiverton, Rhode Island, who had a sawmill and some black walnut, so I went to her and asked her if she'd sell it. There were two hundred or three hundred feet, I guess. She said she'd think about it, but when I asked her again, she told me she thought she'd hold onto it. 'But I'll tell you where there's a black walnut tree that needs cutting,' she said. So I followed her directions and went to the man who owned it. It was nearly dead, but I still had to get the man's permission to cut it down, of course. 'How much is it worth to you?' he wanted to know.

" 'I'll tell you,' I said, 'I'll cut the tree and take the logs and have them sawed and figure how much that costs me, and then I'll pay you forty-five cents a foot minus my costs.' That was the going rate for black walnut then. Right away, the man wanted me to cut the tree down when I told him that. But it was the wrong time of year, and I explained that I'd come back in December when the sap was all down in the roots. For good lumber you don't want the sap in the wood.

"That wasn't the end of that story though. When I went to the sawmill, they wanted to be sure the tree hadn't come from the side of the road before they'd saw it up for me. They weren't taking any chances with nails from signs being in the wood somewhere and breaking their saws. I had quite a time with that sawing too. We had to use a chain saw, and when we started sawing, a whole family of brown and white mice came out of a hollow in the tree — the prettiest little things you ever saw."

Mr. Randall has equipped his cellar with a round table for his wheel-building, which he describes as a craft that just involves "thinking out." His round table is made from a wire rigging cable reel put on legs and topped with plywood. It is three and one-half feet in diameter. "When I need a bigger piece than that for a bigger wheel, I just cut a bigger circle of plywood out."

The work table is a wire-rigging wheel put on legs and topped with plywood (Leslie Randall)

To mark the center of the wheel, he has a one-inch bronze propeller shaft fastened into a three-quarters of an inch steel plate underneath the table. The table is about three and a half feet high.

"The correct height of a workbench is rump high," he says, illustrating his remark with a wiggling of his hips, "but I like my workbench a little higher."

One needs a good woodworking shop to make a ship's wheel but not too many tools, according to Mr. Randall. A band saw is needed to cut out the wheel felloes, a lathe is required for turning the spokes, a low angle block plane is best for fitting all the sections together.

"They don't chatter and jerk so. They make a better cut." Chisels are necessary, as are a router with a straight bit and a hand-shaper attachment for putting inlay in if one chooses to decorate one's wheel as Mr. Randall does.

He suggests that the amateur buy the bronze hub for his wheel from a foundry, for the making of a hub is complex.

He proposes making a 24″ wheel, using mahogany for the wheel. Teak and walnut also make fine wheels, he says. Whatever wood is used, the wheel-maker should be sure that the grain goes with the contour of the circle, Mr. Randall emphasizes.

HOW TO CONSTRUCT A 24″ WHEEL

1. Draw a 24″ circle on the round table's plywood surface. Draw the outside diameter (or extremities of the spokes) on the work surface of the table (Fig. 1).

2. Then draw in the inside and outside diameter of the felloes (see Fig. 4).

3. Use a pair of dividers and divide these circles into six equal parts. Draw lines from the center to each of these six points.

4. Turn the spokes in the lathe (see Fig. 2a for a possible pattern). Note that a surplus chunk of wood should be left unturned at the end of each spoke so the spokes can be hammered in place with a mallet. Fit the spokes into the hub (Fig. 2b). To do this, taper the inside end of each spoke to fit the tapered notches in the hub. This can be facilitated by marking up a cardboard template to match the template of the hub notch and using this to make a taper on the end of each spoke. Saw off excess wood on the taper with a small hand saw, leaving some excess for final fitting. Trim to a perfect fit with a block plane.

5. After the spokes are all fitted in place, lay ⅛″ plywood or cardboard 6″ x 12″ under two properly positioned spokes. Scribe two lines against inside of each spoke on this template. Using a radius arm (see Fig. 3) scribe the inside and the outside curves of the felloe on the template and the ends. Take the width of the felloe from your scale drawing of the wheel. For the felloe template, also see Fig. 1.

6. From here on, the radius arm is used to keep everything in a true circle. On its edge, in addition to the outside and the inside edge (or width) of the felloe, mark the width of the cap that goes on later (the template for the cap is shown in Fig. 3). Also mark the location of the screws so that they will be in a perfect circle. Make the template for the cap using the cross-section for width and using Fig. 1 for the shape. Now, using the cap and felloe templates, saw out the actual pieces on a band saw. Saw them larger than you need.

They will be square-edged coming off the band saw. Put on a shaper to round the two edges. They will still be too long, but, using the template, mark the correct length. Cut the ends on a band saw and fit with a block plane so each cap fits neatly together with the next cap, each felloe with the next felloe.

7. Once the felloes are in place, glue each end to the spokes, holding the felloes tightly to the spokes with a wooden block or cam (Fig. 3) screwed onto the table against the outer edge of the felloe.

8. Next, take radius arm and mark with a knife point on the spokes where the cap will go. The spokes are thicker than the felloe (Fig. 3) so cut a space in the spokes the width of the cap. Place the cap into this space.

fig. 1 *Finding the outside of the diameter on the work table*

fig. 2a

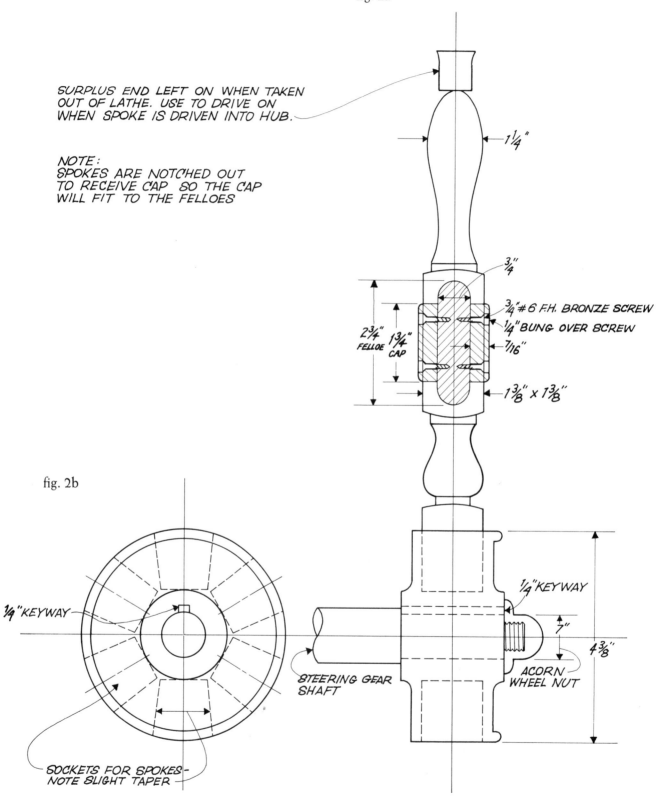

SURPLUS END LEFT ON WHEN TAKEN
OUT OF LATHE. USE TO DRIVE ON
WHEN SPOKE IS DRIVEN INTO HUB.

NOTE:
SPOKES ARE NOTCHED OUT
TO RECEIVE CAP SO THE CAP
WILL FIT TO THE FELLOES

1¼"

¾"

¾"#6 F.H. BRONZE SCREW

¼"BUNG OVER SCREW

7/16"

1⅜" x 1⅜"

2¾"
FELLOE

1¾"
CAP

fig. 2b

¼"KEYWAY

¼"KEYWAY

7"

4⅜"

STEERING GEAR
SHAFT

ACORN
WHEEL NUT

SOCKETS FOR SPOKES-
NOTE SLIGHT TAPER

fig. 3

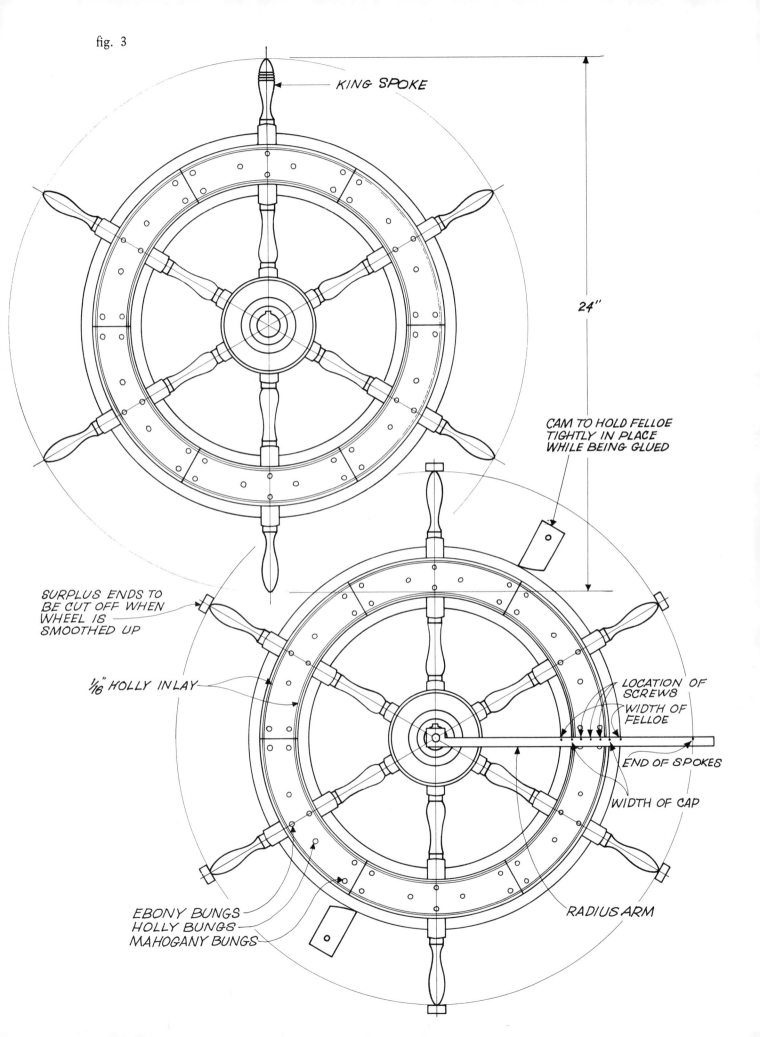

KING SPOKE

24"

CAM TO HOLD FELLOE
TIGHTLY IN PLACE
WHILE BEING GLUED

SURPLUS ENDS TO
BE CUT OFF WHEN
WHEEL IS
SMOOTHED UP

1/16" HOLLY INLAY

LOCATION OF
SCREWS
WIDTH OF
FELLOE

END OF SPOKES

WIDTH OF CAP

EBONY BUNGS
HOLLY BUNGS
MAHOGANY BUNGS

RADIUS ARM

9. Now divide the distance evenly between the spokes on the felloes, and, using the radius arm, mark across each felloe, and fit the first section of the cap between these marks, then glue and screw them into place, using two No. 6 screws into the spoke, two in each end, and one on either side of the spoke — eight screws in each piece. Then fit the next section of the cap to the one that is already fastened and glue and screw them into place as before, and so on until six sections are all fastened and ¼" bungs put in (Fig. 3). When drilling for these screws, use a drill that drills for the thread, for the shank, and for the bung that will be put in to cover each screw.

10. The cap is now completely glued and screwed in place. Smooth the outside and inside edge of the cap to a true circle with sandpaper and smooth the bungs and the surface. One side of the wheel is now complete. Cut off the knob at the end of the spokes. Remove the wheel from the center shaft, turn it over, and repeat the procedure on the other side.

11. Sand and give it four coats of varnish. Spar varnish is best.

Teak, walnut, and mahogany all make fine wheels, according to Mr. Randall, who further advises, however, that whatever wood is used, the wheel-maker should be sure the grain goes with the contour of the circle.

If you use mahogany for the wheel, you can make a good design for the bungs if you use ebony ones over the screws in the spokes, a holly bung on either side of each spoke, and mahogany bungs in the ends of each section of the cap. Weldwood is the glue Mr. Randall favors. To fashion a wheel that is still more handsome, use a router in the radial arm and cut a 1/16"-wide groove just inside and outside of the bungs. Lay a strip of holly inlay into these grooves, and glue as you have glued the bungs.

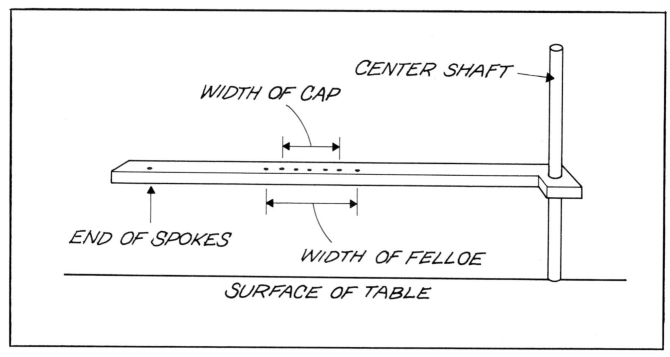

fig. 4

fig. 5 *Holly inlay and bungs*

Behind an old Maine captain's house with a view of Camden harbor, an exuberant thirty-six-year-old artist is making miniature furniture in a sunny workshop. He carves scrimshaw so minuscule it will fit on a dime, paints bud vases a half inch tall, and makes three-inch-high spinning wheels of fifty component parts, thirty-eight of them hand-turned.

An admirer describes Harry Smith's handiwork as "collector's items of the twenty-first century." And in the fifteen years that the tall, dark-haired Mr. Smith has been making miniatures, he has attracted more than 7000 collectors as customers. They have come from as far away as Paris to view him at work in his shop, manipulating dental probes and a surgeon's scalpel on postage-stamp-size bits of wood or turning two-inch-long Hitchcock chair legs on a jeweler's lathe. His prices range from fifty cents for a breadboard for a dollhouse kitchen table (his pieces are for adults' dollhouse collections, not children's) to $700 for a 7½″ japanned highboy made from pine and butternut, lacquered with black to correspond with museum examples and decorated with gold leaf.

The inlaid doors of Harry Smith's miniature cupboards are made of seven pieces of whatever wood his original full-scale model is made. He uses many layers of wood to assure that they will never warp and crack. His piecrust tabletops are made of two pieces of wood each laminated across the grain from the other to make sure one warps down while the other warps up so the lamination doesn't split.

Although he uses both kiln- and air-dried wood, his preference is for wood at least 100 years old, which will absorb little water and not change in shape. In the Smiths' backyard a spruce log 85 years old still has 15 years of drying-out ahead of it.

Almost all of his pieces, dovetailed and mortised as the originals were, take as long to make in his one-inch to one-foot scale as their models did. "At least they take as long to reproduce as any of those pieces produced in the early factories."

In the same way that the cabinet-maker of a century ago added a touch to his labors that was distinctly his own, so Mr. Smith, though copying genuine antiques with precision, adds a bit of himself from time to time.

"If I'm asked to make a miniature of a chair with a cabriole leg

• *19* •

THE ART OF MINIATURE FURNITURE

that I think is clunky, for example — if I have the feeling that the chair was made by a less qualified craftsman than I am — then I am likely to say to my customer that I'll reproduce the piece as he wants it, except that I'll make the leg a little more graceful." (Nowadays, all of Mr. Smith's work is made-to-order.)

"I can know what's graceful or graceless," he says, "because I have a background as a painter." A graduate of Washington University in St. Louis, Missouri, and the Chicago Academy of Fine Arts, Harry Smith was making his living as a painter of oils and acrylics and a designer long before he was making miniature furniture.

Glibly he comments that he has often described making miniatures as "an albatross that hangs around my neck. Each piece becomes a challenge and I insist that every one must be better than the last. You know, I can get three thousand dollars for a painting that takes me forty-eight hours to do, whereas a miniature lowboy that takes exactly the same amount of time I sell for one hundred and twenty-five dollars, but I just can't keep myself from doing the miniatures."

He began making miniature furniture, he tells the customers who find their way to his house at the foot of Camden's Mount Battie, when he was ill with the flu in his home city of Chicago. His wife gave him a kit from which he was supposed to make a scrapbook with a basswood cover. Instead of the cover, he carved a deacon's bench with a pocketknife and began thinking about making a miniature fireplace to go with it.

"We lived at that time in back of the Playboy Club, and in between the buildings was a place where we thought we could get some tiny flat stones." Smiling at this recollection, he continues, "There we were, crawling around on our hands and knees, and pretty soon some of the Bunnies got curious and came out to see what was going on. And then they were down on all fours, too, trying to help, with their little fluffy Bunny tails up in the air!"

Those first miniatures were sold to Marshall Field's department store, where his wife was working. Then F. A. O. Schwarz, the children's toy store, became a customer.

"You know," Harry Smith says, and grins, "I never even took a shop class." He recalls with amusement, too, how he had to set the first jigsaw he owned on an eighteen-inch-thick piece of foam rubber since, in those early days, he and his wife were still apartment dwellers.

But it is not only with her gift of the basswood kit that Marsha Smith has been important to her husband's work. An artist herself, she helps him in the assembling of pieces.

"It was art that brought us together," Harry Smith says, with a fond look at his long-haired young wife. "It was when I was a student at the Chicago Fine Arts Academy and she was a student at the Ray-Vogue Academy of Fine Arts that I saw a young girl on the beach and began to sketch her. It turned out that she was sketching me, too, and a month later we were married." They are now the parents of one son and one daughter. "And our daughter doesn't have a dollhouse," her father murmurs apologetically.

Before they moved to Maine three years ago, the Smiths had always lived in the Midwest — after Chicago, in St. Louis and Perrysville, Indiana, where Marsha Smith was born, and where, for a time, the Smiths operated a gift shop and built and operated a tourist ghost town that they made out of old barns.

They became New Englanders after Harry Smith was asked to prepare a show of winter pictures of the New England states for an exhibition at Sturbridge Village.

"I went home and said to Marsha, 'We're moving to Maine,'" Mr. Smith remembers. "I'd always wanted to live near the sea. When I was a child, I never wanted to grow up to live on a ranch. It was sailing I wanted. My studio in Indiana was filled with sextants."

"Camden has been just right," Harry Smith says. "I look out the window and there are the windjammers — Camden is the windjammer capital of the world. I can see them sailing in and sailing out. In the spring, the old oyster boat *Columbia* tows them up to Rockland for their annual overhaul. In summer, there's always a sail to be seen here."

And last year, to his delight, he was commissioned to make a two-inch model of the vessel *Constitution*. "What it is," he explains, "is a model of a three-foot fireplace model. Compared with the actual *Old Ironsides*, it's in a one one-thousandth of an inch scale, but like everything else I do, it's one inch equaling one foot in terms of the three-foot model. Its hull is carved from a piece of the *Constitution* — in nineteen twenty-seven when they were restoring it, apparently they gave away pieces of it, and a man who had one gave it to me. And the base of my miniature comes from a one hundred- to one-hundred-twenty-five-year-old piece of mahogany that we found in this house."

Miniatures appeal to almost everyone, Mr. Smith believes. "After all, the human ego has always cherished the idea of being big and being surrounded by little objects."

He likes to tell the story of the woman from Maryland who asked him one day to furnish the captain's house she was having done in miniature. "She said she even wanted miniature portraits of herself and her husband to hang on the walls. I went so far as to go down to Maryland to take their pictures, and I painted the portraits, and was about to send them off when she mailed me a photograph of her Pomeranian and asked if I would mind including him in her portrait, too — painting him on her lap!"

For the amateur craftsman who would like to make his own miniature, Mr. Smith provides the accompanying plans (Fig. 1) for a Shaker scholar's desk and stool.

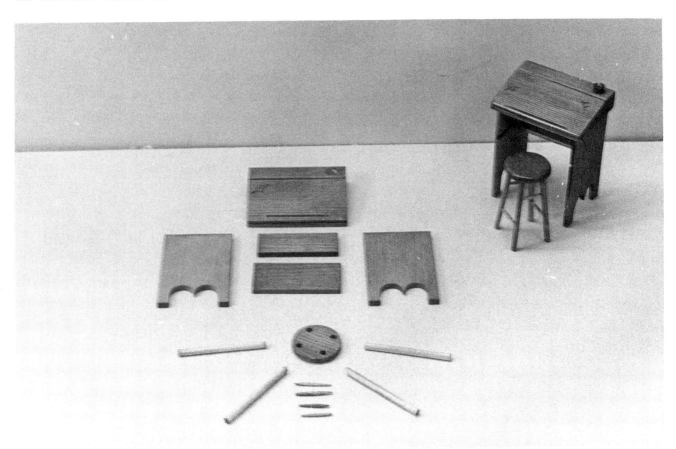

A shaker desk and stool apart and together

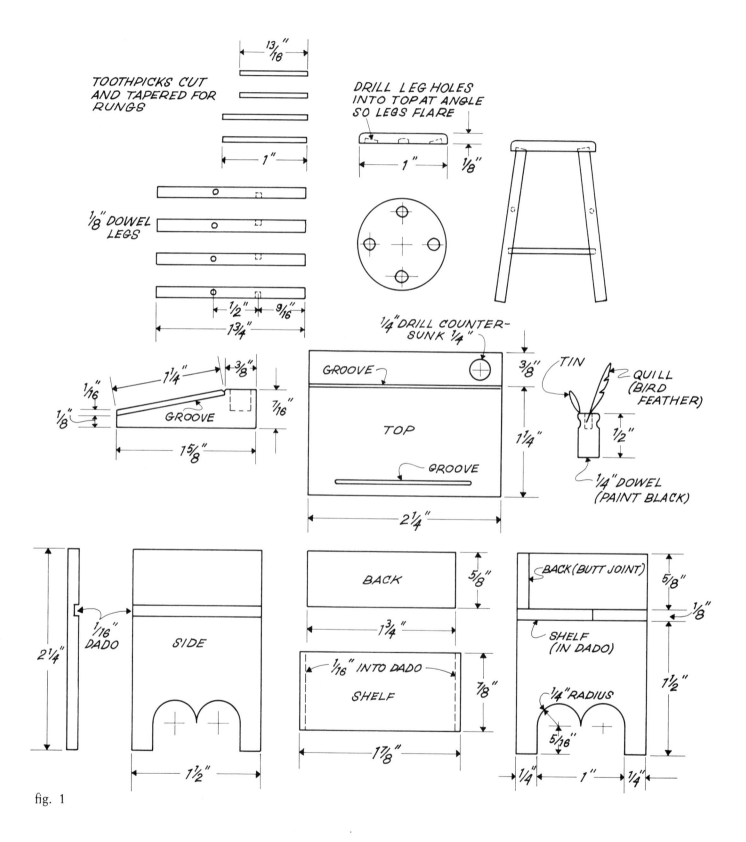

TOOTHPICKS CUT AND TAPERED FOR RUNGS

13/16"

1"

1/8" DOWEL LEGS

1/2"   9/16"

13/4"

DRILL LEG HOLES INTO TOP AT ANGLE SO LEGS FLARE

1"   1/8"

1/4" DRILL COUNTER-SUNK 1/4"

GROOVE

TOP

GROOVE

3/8"

1 1/4"

2 1/4"

3/8"

1/16"

1/8"

1 1/4"

GROOVE

7/16"

1 5/8"

TIN

QUILL (BIRD FEATHER)

1/2"

1/4" DOWEL (PAINT BLACK)

1/16" DADO

SIDE

2 1/4"

1 1/2"

BACK

1 3/4"

1/16" INTO DADO

SHELF

1 7/8"

7/8"

5/8"

BACK (BUTT JOINT)

SHELF (IN DADO)

1/4" RADIUS

5/16"

1/4"   1"   1/4"

5/8"

1/8"

1 1/2"

fig. 1

Except for ⅛″ dowels for the stool legs and toothpicks for the stretchers, the only materials needed are a 2″-wide, ⅛″-thick piece of native pine 1′ long, any white casein glue, stain, sandpaper, steel wool, and shellac. The pieces can, if necessary, be made entirely with a pocketknife, but Mr. Smith suggests using a hand fret saw or a jigsaw for cutting the pieces of stripped-down wood, an X-acto knife for making dadoes, and a drill to make the holes for the stool legs.

He emphasizes, however, that in ordering wood for this project, you should ask the lumberyard to strip the pine down slightly thicker than ⅛″ so that you can sand it smooth on both sides at home.

When the pieces of the stool and desk have been completely assembled and glued together (Fig. 2) from the accompanying plan, Mr. Smith suggests that they be sanded and sealed "with Sherwin Williams or anyone's sealer." Then allow them to dry and sand again.

After that, a fruitwood stain and shellac can be applied — though the shellac will give a dimension and a richness to them that the originals did not have. If you use shellac, three or four coats are needed, and you must sand after each coat has dried before applying the next coat. When the final coat has dried, touch up the pieces with No. 0000 steel wool, and put on a good grade of paste wax. For a less satiny finish, simply apply linseed oil after staining.

fig. 2

In Westbrook, Connecticut, is another maker of highly acclaimed miniature furniture. Edward G. Norton is crew-cut and heavy-set, with powerful hands accustomed, from many years as a plumber, to repairing kitchen and bathroom fixtures. But now the outsize thumbs dexterously attach brasses 1/5,000 of an inch thick to the drawers of his Queen Anne desks and affix thumbscrews from earrings to the pulls.

In a cellar workshop in a modest house that he built himself, he works ten to twelve hours a day with a magnifying glass on a crook-necked stem, whittling and piercing tiny pieces of wood and fitting them together.

"You have to overcome difficulties," forty-seven-year-old Ted Norton says, "and when my back went bad and I couldn't find work as a plumber anymore, I was pushed to do something. I'd made

Ted Norton makes a Queen Anne table
(John E. Méras)

a saltbox house and largely furnished it for my eldest daughter, Grace, in 1971, as a graduation present when she finished college. And when she liked it, and I liked doing it, I decided I'd try making miniature furniture full-time. I'd worked a little in wood when I was a boy."

The influence of his mother, eighty-three-year-old Lynda Stannard Norton (for whose family Westbrook's Stannard Hill was named) very likely helped to bring him back to woodworking too. Today, in the senior Nortons' shingled house just down the lane from the younger Nortons', she proudly displays Grace's dollhouse, keeps a guest book of all who visit it, lights up its tiny chandeliers for visitors, and chats with much vivacity about an inch-and-a-half-long footstool.

"I think it's wonderful that this dollhouse can give so much pleasure to people," she says. "There are well over two hundred visitors who've come here and put their names in Grace's book. I'm delighted that I have the privilege of looking after it." And while she talks, she points out some of her son's earliest efforts as a child at dollhouse furniture-making.

One of his more recent and most popular pieces she rather considers her own, for it was she who urged him to make it. "It's a rocking horse modeled after one that was my husband's when he was a child. Ted was asked to make three hundred and fifty of them as table favors not so long ago."

Mr. Norton's own favorites, however, are his Chippendale and Queen Anne pieces. "I can't say why exactly," he says self-consciously. "In the art books they say in those pieces that 'all the facets contribute to the whole,' but that's an arty way of looking at it. What I admire is the simplicity."

Mr. Norton, like Mr. Smith, uses a scale of one inch equals one foot. He copies either from actual pieces of furniture or from magazines like *Antiques*, old Sears Roebuck catalogues, or furniture books. He, too, is particular about the woods that he uses.

"Cherry, Southern maple, Honduras or African mahogany — these are all good woods."

Birch and maple are his favorites for his Windsor chairs, but they have seats of pine because the original Windsors did. Ash is used for chairs that have bent backs because it is a wood that bends easily.

"One of the things that I've found out doing this is that the early furniture-makers didn't select their woods for aesthetic reasons. They chose wood to suit their purpose."

One of the simplest of Mr. Norton's creations, he believes, and one that is attractive, too, is the drop-leaf Queen Anne table.

It begins, like most of his pieces of furniture, after he has bought wood 2" x 2" in a piece 18" long that is put out by specialty houses for turnings. This is enough wood for a dozen tables, since Mr. Norton saws it into 5/64" thicknesses with a table saw for his tabletops. But he likes this kind of wood, because "it is generally straighter and nicer in its grain than other wood." An alternative kind of wood is a carving block 6" x 6" x 2". The wood for this project should not cost more than $2.

A stage setting of miniature furniture at the Norton house (John E. Méras)

1. You will need 18″ of wood 5/64″ thick x 2″ wide. "If sawing is a problem, of course," Mr. Norton adds, "you can always buy ⅛″-thick mahogany or cherry, but then your finished product won't be to scale. If it's that thick on a miniature, it means the original it's fashioned after is 1½″ thick, and very few tables are. Most are ¾″ to 13/16″ in thickness.

2. Cut 2″ width down to 1⅞″ x 4″. You should get three 4″ pieces out of your original 18″ length.

3. Take an X-acto modeler's knife and make a cut with it 1/16″ wide, on a slant from the top of the wood down all the way around the center leaf and on the two ends and the outer edges of the outer leaves (Fig. 3). Finish up with a file and sandpaper to give the table leaves molded edges. What will be the inside part of the outer leaves will be cut on the opposite contour to make a rule joint.

4. Fasten the pieces together with tiny tapered U-1 hinges that are available from hobby shops. Lay these on what will be the underside of the table's center leaf 3/16″ from the two outer edges.

Where the pin part of the hinge is laid is important. It should be under the center section, not under the outer leaves. The edge of the hinge pin should be flush with the edge of the center section. After the hinge pin is in, trace around it with a pencil. Then remove it and carve out the area where it was laid to about 1/32″ deep.

5. Put a little Epoxy in the carved-out places but not anywhere near the edge of the hinge or the hinge itself or it will not work. It is best to do this work on a flat board. Let the hinges dry. Then put a little Epoxy over the tops, too, to hold the hinges more strongly. The hinges Mr. Norton uses are not an authentic shape, "but they're about as close to it as you can get," he says.

6. From his original piece of wood, Mr. Norton next cuts ⅜″-square x 2½″-long pieces to be used as the table's four legs.

7. For the frame that will go under the table to support the leaves, four other pieces are needed. For the two frame sides (Fig. 3) they should be ⅛″ x ½″ x 3″; for the two frame ends, they should be ⅛″ x ½″ x 1″ (Fig. 3). Each of the two 3″ pieces should be notched 1 7/16″ from one end and ⅛″ square (Fig. 3) to allow for a pull that will slide in and out and to allow the leaves to be out or to fall.

8. For the pull dividers and the pulls themselves, cut from your original 18″-long piece three pieces ⅛″ square x

MAKING A QUEEN ANNE TABLE

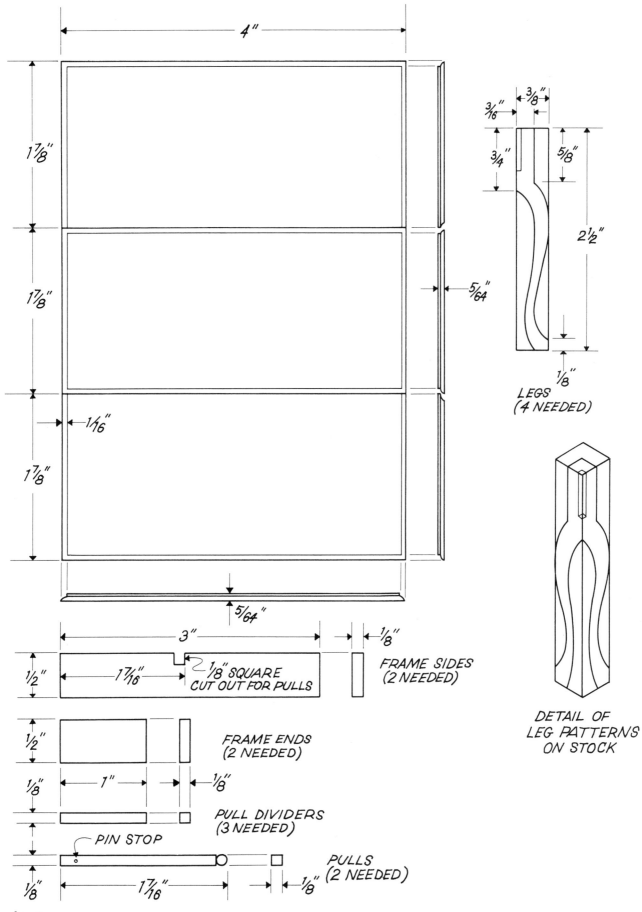

4"

1⅞"

1⅞"

1/16"

1⅞"

5/64"

3/16"   3/8"

3/4"   5/8"

5/64"

2½"

1/8"

LEGS
(4 NEEDED)

3"   1/8"

½"   1 7/16   1/8" SQUARE
CUT OUT FOR PULLS

FRAME SIDES
(2 NEEDED)

½"

FRAME ENDS
(2 NEEDED)

1/8"   1"   1/8"

PULL DIVIDERS
(3 NEEDED)

PIN STOP

1/8"   1 7/16"   1/8"

PULLS
(2 NEEDED)

DETAIL OF
LEG PATTERNS
ON STOCK

fig. 3

1″ long for the pull dividers that separate the pulls and two ⅛″ squares x 1 7/16″ long for the pulls (Fig. 3). Drill a little hole near the inside end of each pull and insert a tiny common pinhead or a brad cut 3/16″ long. Hold it in place by putting glue in the hole. This brad will serve as a stop for the pull (Fig. 3) and keep the pulls from pulling all the way out.

9. The legs, Mr. Norton believes, are the most difficult part of the table to make. He suggests that the beginner start by tracing a leg pattern on a scrap of wood. Each leg, when it is finished, should be ⅜″ square x 2½″ long (Fig. 3).

10. To draw the pattern properly, be sure to line up the straight top of the inside of the leg against the edge of the wood. Then turn the block of wood on which the tracing has been made a quarter of the way around and draw another contour so that there are two back to back. Mr. Norton uses a jigsaw to cut out his legs but warns that, in so doing, about ⅛″ of leg should be left uncut from the wood piece and cut out by hand.

11. Cut a 1/16″ square in the back corner of the straight edge part of each leg and a 1/16″ notch in the ends of the 3″ frame sides for the legs to fit into them (Fig. 4). Mr. Norton glues the legs into the notches with Elmer's glue but warns that it should be used with the utmost care because it seals the wood and keeps stain from taking. Glue the legs carefully into the long frame pieces and let them dry. Then align the end pieces of the frame by eye and glue in place.

12. For staining, use boiled linseed oil and walnut stain. The boiled oil will help to give the wood a hard finish.

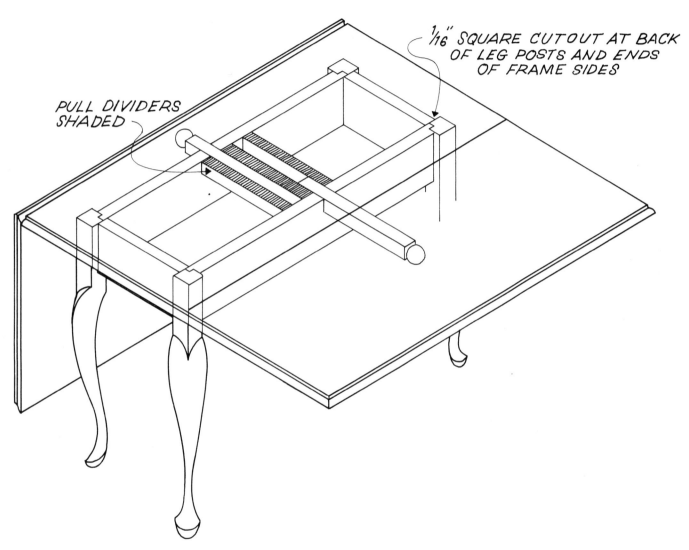

PULL DIVIDERS
SHADED

¹⁄₁₆" SQUARE CUTOUT AT BACK
OF LEG POSTS AND ENDS
OF FRAME SIDES

fig. 4

Surrounded by oriental rugs and Chinese vases, books on Colonial history and Colonial furniture, Stephen A. Tucker lives in a pretty little house in Narragansett, Rhode Island, up a dirt road from the Pettasquamscut River.

And in the workshop in his garden (chipmunks share the walks with him and woodpeckers tap happily at his giant oak), he fashions veneered jewelry chests. African mahogany, ivory, ebony, and holly go into his intricate designs. "If you're limited to working in a small way, you can get the most interesting effects in a box," Mr. Tucker says. "The Chinese knew this. So did Fabergé, the great Russian court jeweler, and all the fine silversmiths. And veneering isn't a costly craft," he adds. "You can get exotic woods at a fraction of the lumber price, and if people have old piano keys, the ivory in them is excellent for inlay. It cuts very easily with a little razor saw, and it gives a piece a certain flavor."

A slender, dark-haired bachelor, Mr. Tucker has been doing inlay as a part-time source of income for about twenty years. "If I were wholly dependent on it, I wouldn't derive the pleasure from it that I do," he explains. "It may take me two or three months to fill a commission. Fine. I'm not pressured. You mustn't be hurried if you're going to do veneering well."

When he is not in his barn workshop, where his father made furniture and his grandfather violins, or tending his effulgent garden of viburnum and tulips in spring, and phlox and roses in summer, or among the treasures in his house, Mr. Tucker is employed as a caretaker for the furniture and grounds of one of the handsomest houses in the neighboring town of Wakefield. "There I'm exposed to some of the choicest pieces in Rhode Island," he says, "and when you know what the best examples of furniture look like, it's a lot easier for you to make fine pieces yourself." If he is in his house as he talks, he will quickly bring forth a book about antique furniture, or Rhode Island history, or inlay, and point out his favorite designs.

He will explain the difference between intarsia, the method of using veneer that calls for cutting grooves in a solid piece of wood and inserting the veneer in the grooves, and marquetry, the style of veneering he does, in which the veneer is applied to the top of the wood. The visual results are the same — handsome rich-grained wood or wood and ivory designs.

·20·
THE ELEGANCE OF VENEER

And if he is sitting in the parlor as he talks, he is likely to point proudly to the peacock design on the wall behind the sofa and say, "That's an interesting grass cloth design that you're looking at. I got it from an old house that was being torn down. It probably dates from the eighteen nineties and was made in the Far East. It's grass applied to rice paper. Happily, I didn't have too much trouble getting it off. The dampness had released the adhesion between the grass and the paper, so I had to take care of that afterwards by applying new lining paper, but I was able to ease the paper itself off the wall with a knife. I'm always on the lookout for interesting things like that.

"I was driving in Providence one day when they were tearing down a public building, and I stopped and got out and went inside to see what the interior was like. There were some molded, glazed bouquets there made to look like terra cotta. Since I happened to be there at the right time, I got them and now they're in my garden."

Although he had done some woodworking with his father as a child, Mr. Tucker did his first serious cabinet work when he was asked to paint a rose medallion design from a piece of crockery on top of a set of glass-top tables. "I painted the tables themselves first and then the decoration. That was my first taste of decorating furniture. I went into marquetry afterwards."

Even though he has studied painting, Mr. Tucker says that ability as a painter is not necessary in his craft. "What it calls for is a sense of design."

Most of his customers, he says, are people who want a particular piece — most often a table — to fill a certain nook in a certain room. "But the people I deal with don't want something that's going to look new and out of place. Most of them have homes filled with antiques, so I find a picture of a chest or a table or whatever it is they need in an *Antiques* magazine or a book on antiques, and then I set to work."

For much of his larger veneered work, Mr. Tucker uses a base ("the carcass is what you call it") of waterproof lumbercore and chip board compressed into boards. "Chipboard is a waste product. It's sawdust, really, that's bound together with glue. The appearance is somewhat like oatmeal, but it's a stable composition. It's fine as a base for your veneer. You're almost doing a collage, you know, when you apply veneer."

For jewelry boxes and small veneered pieces, he uses a plywood carcass.

1. Materials Needed

For the top, 7″ x 12″ x ⅜″ plywood

For the sides, two pieces of 7″ x 9″ x ⅜″ plywood

For the back, 9″ x 11⅝″ x ¼″ plywood

For the bottom, 6¾″ x 11 7/16″ x ¼″ plywood

For the bracket feet, ⅜″ scrap plywood

For the drawer fronts, 1 7/16″ x 11 3/16″ x ½″ pine, 1½″ x 11 3/16″ x ½″, 2¼″ x 11 3/16″ x ½″, 2½″ x 11 3/16″ x ½″

For the drawer sides, 1 7/16″ x 6⅜″ x ¼″ plywood, 1½″ x 6⅜″ x ¼″, 2¼″ x 6⅜″ x ¼″, 2½″ x 6⅜″ x ¼″

For the drawer backs, 1 5/16″ x 10⅞″ x ⅛″ plywood, 1⅞″ x 10⅞″ x ⅛″, 2⅛″ x 10⅞″ x ⅛″, 2⅜″ x 10⅞″ x ⅛″

2. Construction

a. Cut the sides and top to measure.

b. Set the dado blade ¼″ wide x ⅛″ deep and make five cuts in the sides where the top, bottom, and drawers will be inserted. The first cut should be ¼″ from the top edge (Fig. 1); the second cut, 1 7/16″ below the first cut; the third cut, 1½″ below the second cut; the fourth cut, 2¼″ below the third cut; the fifth cut, 2½″ below the fourth cut.

c. Set the dado blade ¼″ wide x ¼″ deep and rip the side piece in two so that you have a left and a right side.

d. Cut the back and bottom to size.

e. Glue the back to the sides with Titebond Glue and reinforce with three ½″ x 18-gauge brads inserted from the outside in. There should be three brads in each side.

f. Glue the bottom to the sides and reinforce each side with three ½″ x 18-gauge brads.

g. With the dado blade set at ¼″ deep x ¼″ wide, rip two sides and the back of the top to accommodate the side pieces (Fig. 1). Glue and nail them in place using three ½″ x 18-gauge brads.

h. Cut the front drawer runners to size and glue them in place.

i. Cut the side drawer runners to size and glue them in place, but before the glue sets, make sure the chest is perfectly square. Use a tri-square for this. The chest is now ready to be veneered.

MAKING A VENEERED JEWELRY CHEST

3. Materials for veneer work, all of the same thickness

3 square feet of satinwood veneer

3 square feet of African mahogany veneer

1 square foot of madroña burl veneer

Two No. B 4 inlay border, 36" length

One No. B 81 inlay border, 36" length. All of these materials can be purchased from Constantine and Son at 2050 Eastchester Road in the Bronx, New York

Also necessary are Titebond Glue, masking tape, Contact Cement, ½" brads, a ½" brush, brush bath, jar of lacquer thinner, X-acto knife, X-acto razor saw, wooden roller, tri-square, and cutting board.

4. Veneering Process

a. On cutting board, cut one piece of satinwood 9½" x 4⅝" for the top panel. Draw center lines on the front and sides of the top piece of the chest. Draw center lines on the satinwood front and sides.

b. Measure in ½" on the center lines on the satinwood

and connect these points to form a diamond. Transfer this measurement to the mahogany veneer and cut out the mahogany diamond. When cutting all mahogany in this piece, put masking tape on the back of the veneer, between it and the cutting board, to prevent splits.

c. Frame the mahogany diamond with the No. B 81 inlay border, using masking tape to secure the pieces.

d. Center the diamond on the satinwood and mark its location with an X-acto knife.

fig. 1   *The sides of a jewelry chest cut to receive drawers. The top is ripped to accommodate the side pieces*
(Thomas D. Stevens)

Veneering equipment
(Thomas D. Stevens)

fig. 2 *The top of a veneered jewelry chest, showing the pattern*
(Thomas D. Stevens)

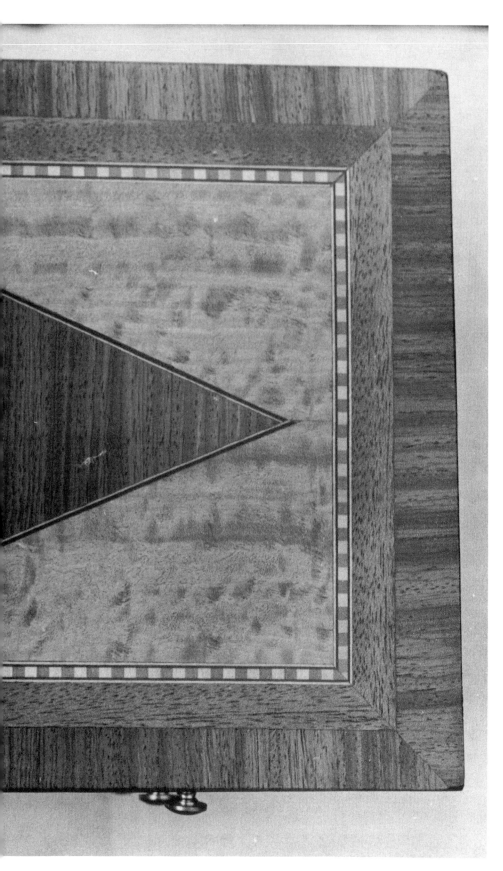

Remove the mahogany diamond and cut the satinwood diamond.

e. Insert the mahogany diamond and border and secure it with masking tape.

f. Brush Contact Cement on the marked chest top and satinwood panel and allow them to dry. Then place the panel on the chest top, using the center lines as guides. Roll with a wooden roller, working from the center to the outside edges to prevent trapping an air bubble. Either a rolling pin or a wallpaper roller will do as your implement.

g. Frame the panel with B4 inlay border (multicolored) using mitered corners. Glue as above (Fig. 2).

h. Frame the above panel with 7/16″ strips of mahogany, mitering the corners and gluing as above (Fig. 2).

i. Frame that panel with ¾″ mahogany strips with the grain of wood running the short way (see the outer panel in Fig. 2). This is called crossbanding. Miter the corners. Roll the edges with a wooden roller.

j. Now remove all masking tape from the surface. There will be an overhang of veneer on the edges. Do not trim at this time.

k. Cut one piece of satin-wood 6 3/16″ x 4⅜″ for one side. Frame it with No. B 4 inlay border, and tape it to the satinwood with masking tape. Frame this with ½″ mahogany strips, mitering the corners. Tape it to the inlay strip panel.

l. Cut one ¾″-wide strip of mahogany crossbanding (Fig. 3) for the bottom of the side piece. Miter the corners and tape it to the panel. Glue it to the side of the chest with crossbanding flush with the bottom.

m. Cut one ⅞″-wide piece of mahogany crossbanding, miter the corners, and fit it to the top of the side panel and the overhang of the top. Glue in place and trim any overhang flush with the side.

n. Cut two pieces of ¾″-wide mahogany crossbanding for the sides of the side design (Fig. 3). Cut to size. Miter the corners and glue. Now trim the sides.

o. Repeat the above procedure for both sides (ends) of the chest.

p. Cut one piece of ¾″-wide mahogany crossbanding and glue it flush with the bottom of the back (Do not miter). Fill in the remaining back space with mahogany veneer with the grain running horizontal.

q. Cut enough ½″-wide mahogany crossbanding to decorate the chest's front edge pieces (Fig. 4). Allow for ⅛″ overhang on each side. Glue in place.

r. Cut one piece of ⅜″-wide mahogany crossbanding for the top strip at the front of the chest. Do not miter the corners. Glue in place. Cut four pieces of ¼″-wide mahogany crossbanding for the rails. Glue.

s. Sand all the surfaces and corners with fine sandpaper. Give a wash coat of shellac thinned 50-50 with denatured alcohol. Let it dry one hour and sand lightly with No. 400 to 600 wet or dry finishing paper. This wash coat brings out the color of the wood and also keeps it clean for further finishing.

t. The molding for the front, sides, and back of the chest (Fig. 3) should be ⅜″-wide mahogany glued to ⅜″ x 1″ pine or plywood and cut to size. The corners should be mitered. Glue and nail the molding to the bottom of the chest with Titebond Glue and brads.

u. Cut four sets of bracket feet (Fig. 4) of ⅜″ plywood with mitered corners. Veneer the plywood with mahogany before sawing it out with a coping saw. Glue it in place with Titebond Glue.

fig. 3   *The side of a veneered jewelry chest, showing the pattern*
(Thomas D. Stevens)

5. Drawers

a. Cut the drawer fronts to size. Set the dado blade $1/4''$ x $3/8''$ and cut $1/4''$ in from the edge of the ends of the back side of each drawer front. Note that there is a left and right side to each drawer. At the bottom of the inside sides of the drawers, at what will be at right angles to the drawer bottom, run each side through the dado blade at a $1/8''$ x $1/8''$ setting so the back of the drawer will rest on the drawer bottom neatly.

b. Cut one piece of madroña burl $3''$ wide x $8''$ long. Then cut the $3''$ x $8''$ burl into four pieces, each one to the depth of a drawer, and center each piece (Fig. 4). The veneer design should run perfectly through all the drawers.

c. Glue the center burl panel in place on each drawer, following the method previously used of applying glue on the panel, then on the chest, and allowing it to dry before affixing.

d. Cut $8 1/8''$ x $8''$ satinwood into four pieces, each one to the depth of a drawer; then cut each in two, and glue them on each side of the center panel in the prescribed way (the grain should run across the chest as in Fig. 4). Roll with a wooden roller. Trim to the size of the drawer fronts, sand, and apply a wash coat of shellac.

e. Sand, dust, and give a wash shellac coat to the drawer sides, bottom, and back.

f. Glue the drawer bottom to the drawer front. Glue and nail the sides to the front back. Check to make sure the drawers are square before the glue dries. This is very important! If the drawers are glued up out of alignment, they will not slide properly.

g. Apply pastewood filler tinted a medium tan, and follow with a sealer coat of shellac. Sand, dust, and apply three coats of satinwood varnish.

h. Small brass knobs (Mr. Tucker buys his from the Period Furniture Hardware Company on Charles Street in Boston) may be used to advantage to decorate the drawer fronts. For inserting them, use a $1/8''$ drill bit. The pulls come with screws attached.

fig. 4　*The completed jewelry chest, showing bracket feet*
(Thomas D. Stevens)

Like a restaurateur or a gourmet cook, "I prefer fresh fish," Lawrence C. Irvine will say with a shake of his head to the fisherman who comes to his door in Winthrop, Maine, with a frozen brook trout or a largemouth bass lying stiff in a newspaper wrapping.

For Lawrence C. Irvine carves fish for fishermen who want to have a memento of their catch and eat it, too, and if his models arrive frozen "about all I can get is the length," he says sadly.

Mr. Irvine has been carving fish to order for twenty years, ever since he went to a Farmington, Maine, fair and saw carved fish that didn't look natural. "I've fished ever since I was a kid. I know practically every fish there is around here. I know all about the way animals and fish blend in with their surroundings, so I came home and made myself a fish. The first one didn't look too hot, but I hung it on the wall just the same. The next one looked a little bit better, and they've looked better right along. My wife used to laugh at me 'wasting my time fishing,' but she doesn't anymore," Mr. Irvine says as he takes off his red hunting cap

to set to work in his garage on a fish carving.

Lawrence Irvine is a machine operator in a plastics factory, but for three or four hours every night he's in his shop carving fish, "because if I weren't doing this, I'd be playing cards and losing money, or falling asleep watching TV. But this carving — I get a big kick out of it, and make money, too, and all it takes is a little elbow grease and some wood. It isn't expensive."

A good-natured man with a philosophical bent, Mr. Irvine remarks as he daubs a brook trout with house paint that "there are so many things a fellow can do today if he puts his mind down to them. It takes a little time, that's all, but a lot of these young fellows could do just what I'm doing and sell fish in gift shops and make a lot of money. [Irvine fish sell from $5 to $35.] All you need are some planks and some sandpaper and screws and house paint, a drill, a saw, and glue."

Mr. Irvine took a course in manual training in high school and once thought of carpentry as a trade, but Winthrop is a town of mills and factories, so he ended up working in them instead, in the woolen mill and the grain mill before he switched to the plastics factory.

He was born and brought up

· 21 ·

CATCH A FISH
AND CARVE IT

in Winthrop, in the days when it was less a suburb of Augusta than it is now, when partridge and woodcock and deer abounded, and when he wasn't fishing as a boy he was hunting. He still does a little hunting, with his Brittany spaniel, Rusty. "But every time you pick up a paper now you read some hunter's been shot, and that takes the pleasure out of it."

As he dries painted fish on an old wooden clothes dryer in his garage, or hangs them from the rafters, or draws a pattern for one on brown wrapping paper, he will point out some of the distinguishing characteristics of fish.

"When you're doing a smallmouth bass, for example, you've got to know that the upper lip stops under the eye whereas if the bass is a largemouth, the lip extends beyond the eye. And the largemouth is greener, and when they're swimming, if you look down, you'll see a black stripe on the side. A smallmouth doesn't have that."

Sport fishermen from all over the neighborhood bring Lawrence Irvine their fish to copy. "I lay out the fish, then measure it from the end of the mouth to the end of the gill. (A male, by the way, will always have a bigger head than a female — just like a tomcat.) Then I measure the width from the stomach to the back and the thickness looking from the back to the stomach. As I say, it's a lot better if I have the fresh-caught fish to measure, but I've done it from frozen ones. I've even done one when I was brought a picture of a little boy standing up with his fish as proud as proud could be. And there was one fish that a man brought down that had had a bite taken out of it by another fish. He wanted me to carve it just that way. The biggest one I've done was a twenty-two-pound striped bass. I'll tell you, I think I have it over the taxidermist, really, because when he does a fish, he still has to dry the skin after he's taken out all the insides. And then he has to paint it because it's lost all its color in the formaldehyde, and there's always the chance the skin may break even after that. But mine have no skin to break nor heads to crack. You have a copy of the fish you caught, and the real fish to eat."

1. Wipe the fish as dry as possible and lay it flat on a sheet of wrapping paper a little larger than the fish. Then take a No. 2 soft lead pencil, hold it straight up and down, and trace around the fish. If the fish is a little damp or wet, the imprint of the gill and eye will also appear on the paper.

2. Make sure that all the fins are extended when the fish is traced so that their exact location can be noted. Their position should be marked on the pattern (though they will be traced on other paper). This is important when you must put them back on the carved fish.

3. After tracing the fish, remove it from the paper and measure the length of the fins. Then remove the fish and trace the fins in the same manner as the fish. Also measure for the thickness of the fish.

4. After the paper is dry, put a piece of carbon paper under the tracing and place it on a white pine or basswood plank $1\frac{1}{2}''$ x $1\frac{5}{8}''$ thick (for a small fish). Then trace over the diagram to get the pattern on the board. Do not trace the fins at this time.

5. Saw the fish out of the board with a saber or band saw. If the fish is thicker than the wood you have used, trace its shape on a second board. Glue the boards together with diluted Weldwood Glue, and press them together with clamps for about twenty-four hours. Then screw them together from the back to the front with three flathead wood screws for which you have predrilled holes. If a fish is a truly fat one, Mr. Irvine says, it may even be necessary to put three planks together to get the required thickness. In this case, you would sandwich a $\frac{3}{4}''$-thick plank in the middle. A smaller fish, however, is much easier to make.

6. Shape the fish by placing it in a vise; saw the tail on a slant (as if the fish were lying on a table) one-third up the body. Then saw down both sides of the nose. After this, the fish can be better shaped with a knife or wood rasp. Finish up with sandpaper to make an oval body.

7. To make the fins, $3/16''$-thick white pine will be needed. When tracing them, make them $\frac{1}{2}''$ to $\frac{5}{8}''$ longer than they actually are so that they can project into the body of the fish. Saw them out as the fish was sawed. Sand. With utility knife and rat-tail file, cut grooves in the fins and in the tail. Sand.

8. Lay the carved fish back on the pattern to ascertain where the top and bottom fins should be located from the markings you have previously made on the pattern. With a $3/16''$ drill, drill a line of holes $\frac{1}{2}''$ deep from one end to the other of the area where the fin will be placed. After drilling the holes, lay the drill on its side and pull it forward, making a groove for the fins. The fins will be glued into these grooves and should fit tightly.

9. For any fins that go into the side of the fish, make rounded cuts in the appropriate place with a utility knife. On a brook trout (see Fig. 1 for those who do not wish to copy

CARVING A FISH

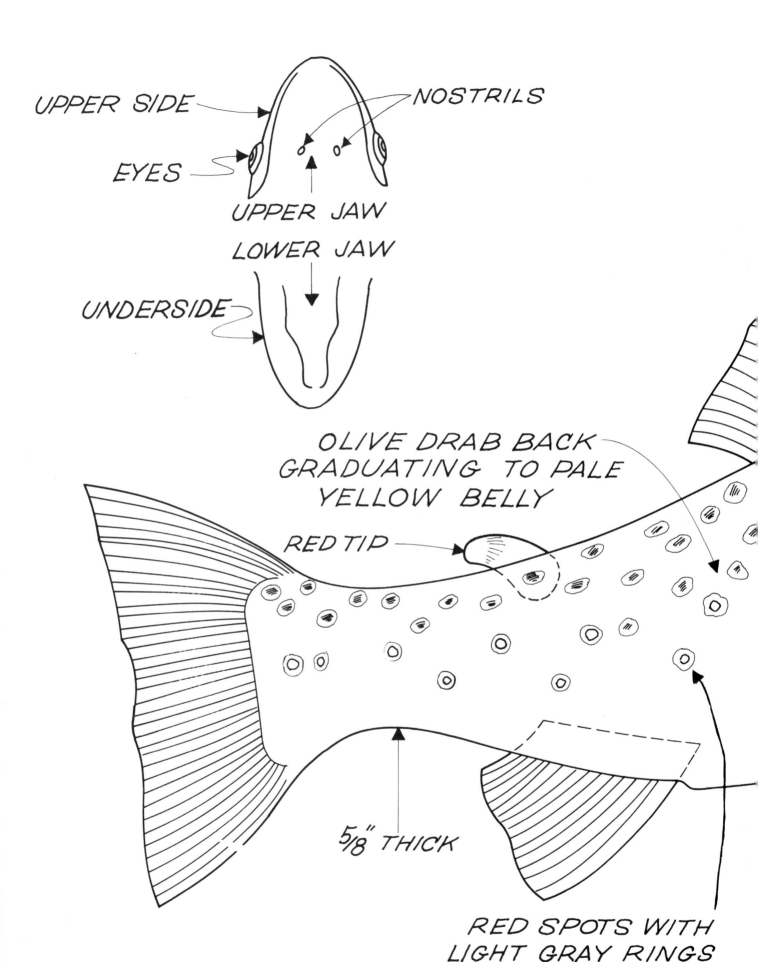

UPPER SIDE

NOSTRILS

EYES

UPPER JAW

LOWER JAW

UNDERSIDE

OLIVE DRAB BACK
GRADUATING TO PALE
YELLOW BELLY

RED TIP

5/8" THICK

RED SPOTS WITH
LIGHT GRAY RINGS

BROOK TROUT

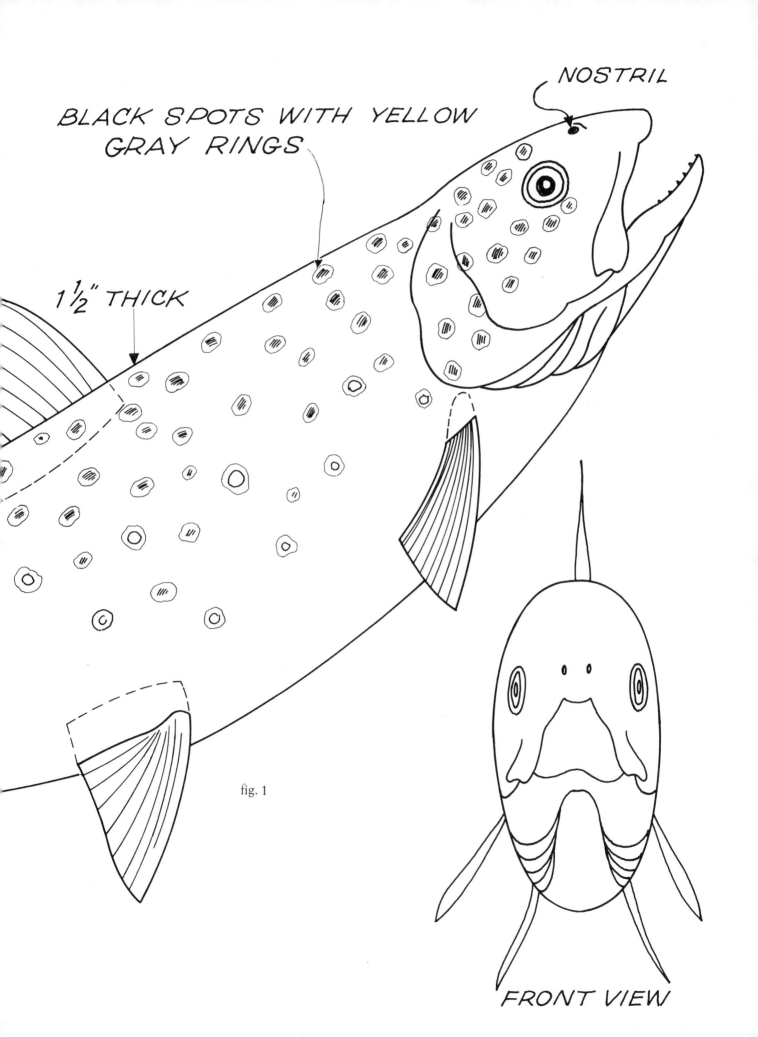

NOSTRIL

BLACK SPOTS WITH YELLOW
GRAY RINGS

1½" THICK

fig. 1

FRONT VIEW

Lawrence C. Irvine touches up one of his fish

their own fish), these should be set at a 45-degree angle. Coat the fins with glue and insert.

10. The eye is made from a wooden dowel of a size corresponding to the actual fish eye. Drill a hole of appropriate size to glue the eye in place.

11. The completed fish should be assembled and the plaque on which it is mounted prepared before you start any painting. For his plaques, Mr. Irvine uses ½" fir plywood cut into ovals of a size appropriate for framing the fish. His trout plaques are generally 2" to 2½" wider at the widest point than the fish and 3½" to 4" longer on each end.

12. Lay your fish on the plaque and make tiny pencil marks on it so you will be sure the fish is centered. Remove the fish and paint or varnish the plaque. (Mr. Irvine uses Zar varnish and borders his plaques with a brown edge.) Let the plaque dry.

13. Use wood putty to fill any holes in the fish and sand it smooth with fine sandpaper.

14. Paint your fish in appropriate colors, using outdoor house paint, but do not mix latex and oil-based paint. Some colors cannot be purchased but must be mixed in small amounts. When you apply paint, let one color or mixed color dry before applying another except when you wish them to blend. To mix, dab them with a piece of clean, soft cloth.

15. If the fish you are copying has scales, Mr. Irvine suggests that when you have finished painting with solid colors and they are dry, paint may be applied to an onion bag or wedding veil material or "nylon netting that you buy in any dry goods store," and it can be pressed down on the fish lightly, then removed. The resultant effect will be scalelike. Onion-bag marks are the right size for scales of bass, white perch, and yellow perch. Veil marks are right for smaller fish — brown and rainbow trout, togue, or lake salmon.

With all of his carving orders, Mr. Irvine has had little time to go fishing himself in recent years, but he's philosophical about that too. "They're not biting the way they used to, and if I can't catch them, I'd just as soon carve them."

Nobody could mistake John McLeod of Wilmington, Vermont, for a Yankee, for when he talks, it is with a soft Aberdeen burr. But he is a Vermonter by adoption, living on a high hill above a mountain village · of cozy wooden shops and houses. Outside his windows, the Haystack Ski Area glistens white with snow in winter three miles away.

He was en route to a job in Canada as a consultant engineer when his American-born wife proposed visiting for a bit in Vermont. Although it was the mud season then, when Vermont roads are an untidy black goo, John McLeod never made it to Canada. "I knew I wanted to be in Vermont."

And to stay in Vermont, he became a turner, established enough now after seven years of turning to have two assistants to help him in the preparation of his wooden objects. Of his wood supply, which includes twenty-three different varieties — rosewood, satinwood, holly, Brazilian imbuia, teak, India rose, zebra, African bubinga, purpleheart, afromosia, and maldao, among others — he says, "I probably have the biggest supply of exotic wood in Vermont."

It is stored in the cellar of his sparsely furnished house, fashioned by Mr. McLeod from a 150-year-old barn. Thick white sheepskin rugs are scattered on the floor; wide windows let the sun stream in from the hills. McLeod headquarters are shared with three Labrador dogs and four cats. And in the rooms along the hallway he stores his laminated salad bowls, long French rolling pins, mortars and pestles, nut bowls and carving platters, dinner plates, candlesticks, goblets, and breadboards, all turned of his rare woods, soaked to make the grain rise, sanded, and oiled until they gleam.

John McLeod is a practical craftsman.

"I suppose I could sit in a hut in the woods and hand-whittle my bowls, but that would be absolutely ludicrous. Obviously I don't like sitting in huts in the woods. I like to think up good designs and have the equipment to make them and produce them. If I'm going to make my living as a turner, I have to make more than one of a particular kind of object at a time and this requires machinery. If I could produce a magnificent article by hand, but because it took me so long to do it entirely by hand, I couldn't offer it at a price a customer could afford, it wouldn't be a viable article, would it? The craftsman who

· 22 ·

THE TURNING OF WOOD

isn't practical about his work will eventually leave the craft world without ever having fulfilled his potential in it," Mr. McLeod comments matter-of-factly as he sweeps a hand over his long red blond hair. And he adds that even though he uses a bench saw and a lathe in his work, both power tools, the lathe is "exactly the same principle as was used generations ago. When I was twelve, my father gave me treadle lathe and I suppose a purist today — who wasn't interested in production — could use it to turn bowls."

John McLeod did his first turning when he was nine, because he was continually losing the wooden pellets that he shot from his toy gun. His father, who had a metalworking lathe, got tired of buying pellets for his son, so he gave him lessons in operating the lathe and told him to make his own. "And when he got tired of having his kid touch his highly accurate machinery, he got me my treadle lathe. By the time I was nineteen, I was doing Jacobean turnery — candlesticks and things like that."

When John McLeod decided to abandon engineering for woodworking, and had made a batch of bowls with which he was satisfied, he packed them into a wicker basket and he and his wife set off for New York to try to find buyers.

"We gave ourselves three days in New York, and the last day it was snowing and blowing, and I was lugging this bloody great wicker basket everywhere with me. We went into Georg Jensen's, and we were told Miss Jensen was out to lunch, so we went across the street and established ourselves in a little deli with phones, and we kept calling from there to see if she'd come in yet. Finally, I couldn't stand it any longer so we walked up Fifty-second Street to Fifth Avenue, and there on the corner talking to a gentleman was a woman we recognized as Miss Jensen. So I stood and watched and waited, and finally I saw her go into the store. That was back in the days when Jensen's was on Fifth Avenue.

"We rushed into the store ourselves and told the clerk we were sure Miss Jensen was back from lunch, couldn't she get us in to see her? And we did get in, and I put bowls on top of her filing cabinets and lazy Susans on her desk, and she kept saying, 'I'll have a dozen of these and two dozen of those.'

"We walked out of the office and we were saying to each other, 'It's not true! It's not real!' Here we had a twelve-hundred-and-fifty-dollar order from Georg Jensen's!

"'Don't talk about it,' my wife whispered to me when we got outside the door. 'Wait till the window opens over there,' and she nodded toward Jensen's 'and someone shouts, "Fooled you!"'" But nobody did, and that same day we got a three-hundred-fifty-dollar order from B. Altman's department store. From the depths of despair, I'd achieved some success!

"We got back into the car and headed home. I had to borrow three hundred dollars to buy the wood to fill the orders we'd got, but that was seven years ago and I've been working ever since."

Mr. McLeod insists, however, that as important as talent in a craftsman is self-discipline. "You've got to go at it. Last Christmas I was working from seven in the morning until two in the morning and falling into bed with the wood chips. I like being my own master, but if I'm going to make a living from craft, I have to be a hard master. Too many people entering crafts don't accept that and so they soon have to leave. But I like what I'm doing so I work hard at it. My ego trip is a very simple one. What I do is good. It's as good as I can make it and that's all I need — no bulwarks of psychology to provide me with a raison d'être. There's always a challenge in doing something new."

Increasingly, over the years, Mr. McLeod has been experimenting with gluing different woods together in his designs and has managed to achieve effects that have been widely acclaimed. But gluing is a demanding procedure so he suggests the turning of a mortar and pestle to those who are familiar with turning but not yet accomplished in the art. He emphasizes that lathes can be dangerous machines and should only be used by those who have had proper instruction in them.

1. For the sake of the design, Mr. McLeod suggests that the wood of the pestle be of two kinds. "Use a light-colored wood like teak, maple, or cherry for the body of the pestle and a dark, hard wood like rosewood or ebony for your bearing surface." The wood should be kiln-dried.

2. To make the pestle, start with a 1¼"-square x 4½"-long piece of teak, maple, or cherry and a 1¼" square x 1¾"-long piece of dark, hard wood.

3. By making diagonal lines across the faces of both pieces, locate their centers. Drill holes at these two locations for a 3/16" white birch dowel. The holes should be 1/32" larger than the size of the dowel. The hole in the end of the long piece should be ⅜" deep. Be absolutely sure that the distance drilled into the long piece and short piece combined is greater than the length of the dowel to be used or the dowel will prevent the two ends of the pestle from coming into contact with each other (Fig. 1).

4. Sand the surfaces on the belt sander with a medium-grade belt where the holes have been drilled. When you have finished, the ends must be smooth and true so that they will fit together exactly all the way across each face.

5. Use a white glue like Titebond. Put the glue on the dowel you will use, in the holes, and on the faces of the two pieces, but first clean the surfaces of the wood to be glued with a solvent like wood alcohol or acetone. Fit the pieces together.

6. Clamp the pieces lengthwise in a vise, with a large C-clamp, or in a drill press.

Let them dry for an hour or so (Fig. 1). While they are drying, the mortar can be made.

7. For the mortar, you will need a wood like teak, maple, or cherry cut in a 4" x 5" block. Find its center on the end grain by means of diagonals (Fig. 2).

8. Screw the faceplate onto the end grain of the block which has been sanded square and true.

TURNING A MORTAR AND PESTLE

fig. 1   *Setting the pestle to dry in a vise*

9. Set the block between the centers on the lathe. Prepare to use a ¾″ turner's gouge on the outside of the block (Fig. 3). This is the right tool to use, for it "cuts instead of scrapes." You are now trying to achieve the perfect cylinder shape of the mortar.

10. "Turn the lathe at as fast a speed as is commensurate with your ability and experience," Mr. McLeod advises.

11. When you have formed a perfect cylinder, move the tool rest forward — closer to your work. Remember to stop the lathe at all times when moving the tool rest, Mr. McLeod emphasizes. Take ½″ skew chisel with a leading point for working against wood and feed the chisel in as if it were a pencil sharpener until the end of the tailstock is square across.

fig. 2 *Finding the center of the mortar block*

fig. 3 *Achieving the perfect cylinder shape for the mortar*

12. With the lathe turning, make pencil marks ⅝″ from the bottom of the mortar and another ⅝″ from that (Fig. 4).

13. Take a ½″ round-nosed scraping tool and cut a semicircular groove within the lines you have drawn. Always be sure that the tools you use with a lathe are sharp, Mr. McLeod advises.

14. Change the tool rest to the top of the mortar, and by using different sizes of round-nosed cutting tools start to remove the wood to make the interior cavity of the mortar. Leave plenty of wall thickness at the top.

15. Withdraw the tailstock and remove it from the lathe.

16. Readjust the tool rest across the front of the work and proceed to enlarge the cavity in the mortar (Fig. 5). If your work makes a vibrating sound, you are cutting the wood incorrectly. Back off. The cutting of the hollow should be done with even, sweeping strokes to insure that the interior of the mortar has a smooth, finished, curved appearance. Check the curve from time to time (be sure you stop the lathe first) to see if it is smooth inside.

17. In fashioning the mortar, take care to make the bottom of the cavity flat at the center so there isn't a single bump. The interior of the mortar should be about 2″ deep.

18. Slightly dish the top edge of the mortar to the inside with a skew chisel.

19. Remove the tool rest. Take medium sandpaper, and sand the mortar on the lathe with care. Again, take pains not to leave any bumps when sanding. Sand the outside also. To sand the groove at the pedestal base, roll the sandpaper into a tubular form.

20. Now use fine (No. 120) sandpaper and repeat the process. Be sure, so as not to destroy the design of the mortar, that you don't round the edges of the bottom groove or it will spoil the appearance of the piece. Lightly sand the top and bottom. By the time you are through, you should be using No. 180 sandpaper.

fig. 4   *Making pencil guidelines on the mortar*

fig. 5   *Enlarging the cavity of the mortar*

21. Remove your work from the lathe.

22. Plug the holes made by the faceplate screws. Use Elmer's glue and insert the dowels to fit. Sand the bottom and the edges of the mortar.

23. Now Mr. McLeod uses an old cabinet-maker's trick and soaks the mortar to let the grain rise, then dries it before sanding with 220 sandpaper. Wetting it in this way assures that the wood will stay smooth despite use.

24. When the pestle pieces that have been glued together are sufficiently dried, put a drive center into the lathe. Find the center of the wood by marking diagonals and mount the pestle on the lathe between the drive center and the tailstock. Place the teak end of the pestle in the drive center and the other end against the tailstock.

25. Use a ½" gouge to fashion the pestle and start to pare it down into the cylinder.

26. Mark it twice to show the ends, and taper your work to the top of the pestle to form the finished shape. The diameter of the pestle may be as you desire, but it should not be unduly small.

27. With the aid of a ½" chisel and a scraping tool, form a round end at the base of the pestle.

28. Make a shallow parting tool cut where you wish the top of the pestle to be, but do not make it very much longer than 5¼" overall.

29. Draw lines ½" down from the top of the pestle. Using a ¼" round-nosed tool, cut a groove on the pestle to match the groove on the mortar.

30. Sand your work smooth on the lathe with No. 120 sandpaper.

31. Soak, dry, and sand it with No. 220 sandpaper. Coat both the mortar and the pestle with Mazola. Be sure not to sand too much after soaking, for if you do, you will defeat the purpose of having made the top grain rise.

In the red shop behind Lauriston Vinal's house in Jefferson, Maine, there is always a good, hot fire going in winter in the square black stove. It was just that kind of stove, Mr. Vinal remembers, that he stood by to keep warm when he was a boy starting school in Jefferson sixty-nine years ago.

It roars when it's filled up with wood, and there's a homely quality about it. Harold Orff from across the road is likely to be there, leaning back in the green-slatted garden chair and talking a little about the weather, but not very much because he isn't a talkative man. A retired woodsman, he's a first-rate assistant at bending ox-bows though. And after school, Mr. Orff's grandsons, when they've had a snack at Bond's General Store, may come to ask Mr. Vinal if he has any chores he'd like done. Graham Hall, the blacksmith, will stop with an order of oxbow pins, rings, and staples for the yokes, or John McDonald from the farm up the road will perch on a box under the rack of ox yokes and offer advice about oxen and how to deal with them.

Mr. Vinal used to be a "kind of a gentleman farmer," as he puts it, and he worked for the registry of motor vehicles for twenty-nine years, but nineteen years ago he began making oxbows and yokes (he calls them "yoks" as Maine men are likely to do).

"We're kind of a queer bunch here," he says, adjusting his green work cap. "We say 'yok' and we say 'popal' for poplar. I guess we do it because it's quicker. We have a great way of clipping things Down East. You 'calate' to do something here. You don't cal-culate to."

Lauriston Vinal, who is tall and lanky and not stooped a bit by his years, savors words and books — especially books about Maine — at the end of a day of yoke-making. And he recounts with relish the stories he reads. A favorite is about the rock monument that was hauled to the center of Jefferson, just in front of the church, by twenty-two pairs of oxen, when the village cele-brated its centennial in 1907. "And they had a washtub full of rum for the drivers," he adds with a chuckle.

A man with an inclination to laughter, he also chuckles about the day he ran out of any "sticks" of wood to make oxbows and he and two friends, ages eighty-three and seventy-four, set off to the woods after good young elm trees growing near a bog. "The elm's

· 23 ·

A MARKET IN OX YOKES

got to have straight grain for bows," he explains, "and it should have grown quick. That kind's easiest to find near a brook. You want wood that will bend, but won't break. It's like the difference between an old man and a boy. A boy is more limber — so's a young tree."

He and his wood-chopping companions were hardly young, nor were they limber, and he speculates about what passers-by must have thought of them sawing and splitting and lugging. He likes it better when friends call up and offer him a tree. "If it's no good, I burn it up as firewood. But I don't tell them that, of course, or it would spoil their courage."

Mr. Vinal had thought on and off for years about making yokes. "There was an old fellow in town who could do it — he would do all the blacksmithing and everything that's part of it. He wanted me to learn how from him, but I was too lazy. Then when he died nine years ago, he left me his stove to do the steaming with — you have to steam the bows into a U shape, you know," Mr. Vinal explains, stretching his long legs out and resting his feet on top of a box, "and I started in. I only got five dollars apiece for those first yokes — I even sold one man sixty-four of them at four dollars apiece. Now I sell them for twenty-five to sixty dollars. Sometimes I paint them and sometimes I don't. If I do, it's dump-cart blue, that nice bright blue they always used to paint carts with.

"One day a fellow came in. I had one painted yoke and one unpainted one. I said the painted one was ten dollars and the other five dollars. He said he'd take the painted one, so I painted the other after he'd gone and raised the price on that to ten dollars, and I've pretty much been painting them ever since. He taught me something, that fellow did."

Today, Mr. Vinal's customers come from as far away as Illinois and from all parts of New England. Although there are other ox-yoke makers in New England, they are few, and antiques dealers often seek the old yokes he has collected and repaired.

"If any genuine old ox man saw some of them, he'd laugh at them," Mr. Vinal says, and smiles a half smile. "But I've sold a lot of those old yokes. People who come from out of state to fairs and see the oxen pulling with them like to buy them."

Although well-seasoned elm ("it needs about six months of seasoning — your yoke will crack otherwise") is Mr. Vinal's favorite yoke wood, when it is hard to find he will use either yellow birch or poplar. His bows, if he can't find elm, are of white oak. In areas where shagbark hickory grows, it is likely to be used, too, for bows. It is best to fell the trees for yokes in the fall because the sap is out of them then. For bows, the wood should be cut in the spring when the sap is in so the wood will bend more easily.

It is important to know the size of the ox to be fitted when you are fashioning a yoke, Mr. Vinal points out, and when it is completed, it must be "tried on." The bow of the yoke must go between the animal's shoulder bone and neck, and the bow must fit well enough so the ox will not wiggle its neck inside it. Neither should it press on the points of his shoulder bones and hurt him when he pulls a load.

"And then sometimes you have one ox that's stouter than the other — he's more ambitious, like some people," Mr. Vinal says. "When that's the case, or when one's just a little smaller than the other ox, you move the ring that goes in the middle of the yoke over a little to one side. The lazy ox, or the small one, gets the longer leverage. And then there's a slide yoke that works sort of like a curtain rod. Some oxen crowd each other; others pull off. If an ox tends to pull off, a slide yoke is designed to make him walk up straight, and it's good, too, for going in the woods because it slides together if the trees are close together so the oxen can get through.

"Of course," Mr. Vinal continues, rising and stretching his long frame, taking off his glasses, and rubbing his gray green eyes, "don't many people work oxen now. They have them mostly for fun. If you want to haul lumber today, a tractor's superior, but time was when pulling lumber sleds around here was a big job for oxen."

On a shelf above his hardware, Mr. Vinal has a parade of table-sized models of ox-drawn logging sleds, ox-drawn snowplows, an ox-shoeing rig, dumpcarts, oxcarts, and hayricks. When the wood is no good for yokes and bows, or he simply doesn't feel up to making things that big, he whittles his models from pine wood and sells them to gift shops or interested visitors. And he relates, as he shows them off, how their full-sized originals worked.

"Take the snowplow," he says, and pulls it off its shelf. "When there was a storm and the roads had to be plowed, the people in the section that needed the plow would hitch their oxen onto the snowplow or roller that tramped down the snow as the plow went by their door. And then they'd drive the plow up to the next house where they would hitch on their oxen, and then on to the next house. Why they might end up with twelve or fifteen pair of oxen to break out a road!

"I'd like to get some metal oxen to hitch onto these things I've made," Mr. Vinal murmurs, admiring his handiwork. "They'd really make the models look real. Down in Nova Scotia they have a place where they cast them."

On the subject of full-sized ox yokes, however, and how to make them, he had the following to offer.

MAKING AN OX YOKE AND OXBOWS FOR A CALF

1. Select a good stick of elm. Take about 5' off the butt end of the tree. Set the butt end of the piece on the ground and split it from the top. Split it with wedges and a maul. Then quarter it. For the bows, the sticks should be about 8" across at the small end and should also come from the butt of the tree. Since the butt of a tree is larger at the bottom and grows smaller as it reaches the top, bow sticks are not the same diameter for their whole length when you cut them.

2. On a bench saw, if you are making 5"-in-diameter (calf-sized) bows, trim the sticks down to nearly 1" in diameter. In length, they should be 36".

3. Next, Mr. Vinal shaves sticks down with a drawknife on a shaving horse. ("I use the kind they used to use to make barrel hoops. My grandfather used to do that. He made barrels and hauled them to Rockland — that's on the coast about twenty-five miles from here, and it's where they made the lime for plaster in the old days. Years ago, all our houses were plastered. In Rockland, they'd fill up the barrels with lime and put them aboard boats and ship them to where they were needed. Of course, it was mighty dangerous if the lime got afire or got water on it. Get a little water on unslaked lime and it heats like fury, but you can't slake it till you're ready to use it. You have to build a first-rate barrel to carry lime in — as watertight as you can make it.")

4. When the sticks have been shaved down (if no shaving horse is available, this can be done with a woodworking vise) Mr. Vinal slides the sticks through his gauge to check the diameter (Fig. 1). A bow that is 5" across should be made of wood 1" thick at the ends and 1" thick in the middle. Bows can be tapered on the shaving horse so that they are thinner in the center and therefore more bendable. Mr. Vinal, however, does not taper them.

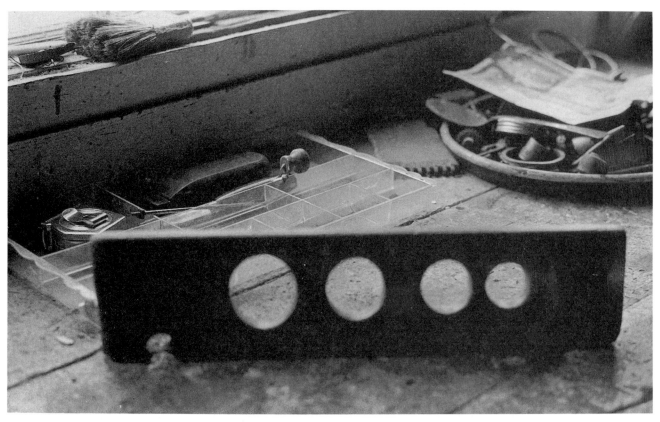

fig. 1 *The gauge for checking the diameter of oxbows*

fig. 2 *The oblong pine box for steaming the oxbows*

5. Bow sticks must then be steamed about one hour until they are pliable. Mr. Vinal does this in an oblong pine box, 45″ long x 8″ across x 8″ deep, with a large hole in the bottom (Fig. 2, 3). This is set on an old-fashioned wash boiler. Inside, Mr. Vinal makes racks of white birch dowels that go across the steam box and on which rest the sticks to be steamed. He puts 2″ of water in the boiler, and the steam from it rises up into the steam-box, softening the wood for the bows. "Get a good hot fire going underneath," he advises. "Maple makes a good one." Mr. Vinal attaches his steam box to the ceiling by means of chains which keep it from tipping over. It does rest directly on the steam kettle, however. (Another method is used by James Kelso of Middletown, Connecticut, another bow-maker. He simply uses "absolutely green wood, kept wet until I'm ready for it. As soon as it's split, I lay it down on the floor and throw water over it to keep it damp at all times.")

fig. 3 *The interior of the oxbow steamer has racks of white birch dowels*

fig. 4   *An oxbow bending form*

6. Meanwhile, prepare your bending apparatus. For Mr. Vinal this consists of a wide plank about 2″ thick on which he lays the bow while it is being bent and eight to ten sturdy elm pegs 1″ thick and 8″ long to hold the bent bow. In the center of his bending frame form, Mr. Vinal bolts a 2″-thick piece of pine shaped as shown in Fig. 4. This should be the size of the bow you are making (5″ across for a calf bow).

7. Bend the steamed bow around the center form. Bend a band of iron ⅛″ thick around the bow and wedge it into place inside the pegs. Two people are needed for this job. Leave the bow on the rack about two weeks.

8. During the two weeks the bows are being bent, Mr. Vinal makes his yokes. For the yoke to go with 5″ bows, you will need 52″ of 4″ x 5″ elm wood, yellow birch, or poplar. The actual length of wood you will need is 40″, but if you go to a lumber yard, ask for a longer piece in case the ends of the timber crack.

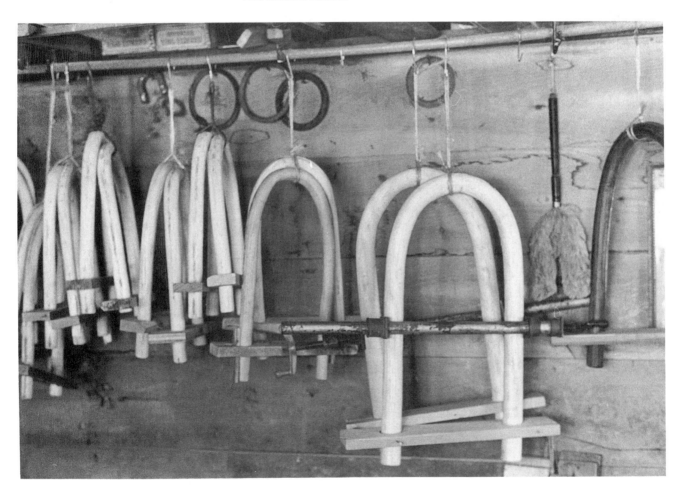

A shed full of oxbows

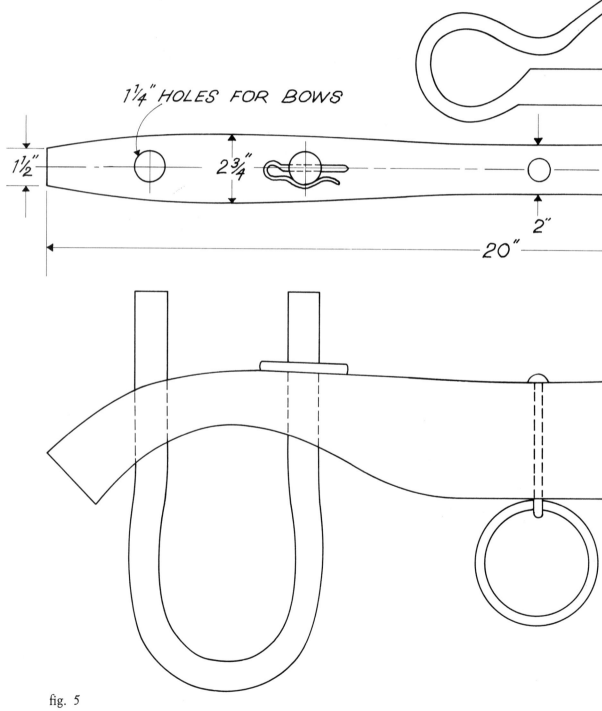

1¼" HOLES FOR BOWS

1½"

2¾"

2"

20"

fig. 5

9. Lay your pattern (Fig. 5) on the wood. Trace around it with a soft pencil, but while the board is still uncut drill four holes 1¼″ in diameter where the bows will be fitted into place (note the position of the holes on the pattern). In drilling, be sure the drill goes straight through. The holes must not be at an angle. It may be, after the holes have been drilled and you try to insert the bows into them, that you will see that the holes must be enlarged. Mr. Vinal does this by heating a long piece of iron, red hot on one end, in his forge and burning out the holes until they are the right size. A reamer could also be used.

10. Now use a skill saw to cut out the rough shape of the yoke. Then finish with a cooper's adz or a band saw. The band saw is easier and does a somewhat better job, according to Mr. Vinal.

11. Drill holes for the ⅜″ iron bow pins in one end of each bow where it protrudes through the back of the yoke. It does not matter which end the bow pin is in.

12. Ask a blacksmith to bend two steel bow pins (Fig. 5) for you and insert them into the holes in the bows to hold the bows in place. About 3″ of bow should protrude through the back of the yoke. Also ask the blacksmith to make a ring 4″ to 6″ in diameter so that you can hook a chain onto your yoke for pulling. You will also need an iron staple to hitch the ring to the yoke.

13. When the bows, bow pins, and ring are all in place, finish the bows with linseed oil or any wood refinisher you choose. Paint or finish your yoke as you choose.

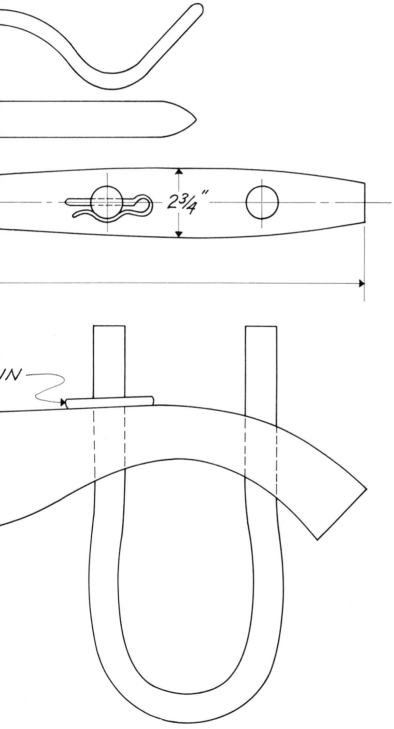

SCALE: ¼″ = 1″

Edward Boggis did his first carving when he was in the Coast Guard in World War II, working in a detraining center for dogs. He was on duty in the sick bay one day and noticed a knothole in a wall, peered through it, and discovered a stand of birch trees outside. The knothole just framed the clump of birch.

"So I drew the trees on a piece of wood and then there were odds and ends of tools in the shed, so I carved it," he remembers.

Today, in what was once a wheelwright's shed in Ascutney, Vermont, just across the Connecticut River from his home in Claremont, New Hampshire, Mr. Boggis carves cigar-store Indians. The American Tobacco Company buys them, as does the sporting goods store of Abercrombie & Fitch. As soon as one is sold, he hauls another white pine or basswood log in from a pile he keeps outside, lays it flat on the floor, marks off the head, shoulders, navel, and crotch; takes his chain saw and makes his first heavy cuts, and then with an adz and two-inch-wide chisels and a carving mallet begins to fashion a new Indian.

Sometimes he carves Indian chiefs with crossed arms. Sometimes his Indians have tobacco leaves around their necks and waists as decoration. Sometimes they clutch knives, and sometimes they bear bundles of cigars and boxes of snuff, or clubs of scrub birch root.

"What's so satisfying — and so mysterious — is being able to make something out of nothing," Mr. Boggis says. "You have just a tree trunk to begin with, and then you end up with something you want." Even after twenty-nine years of carving, Ed Boggis is a little incredulous about his success. A native of Nashua, New Hampshire, he was interested enough in drawing animals as a boy to apply for a job at Benson's Animal Farm in nearby Hudson, but in his high school years the Second World War started and he joined the Coast Guard's Canine Corps. After the war, he logged for a while; then he entered the Pennsylvania Institute of Criminology in Philadelphia, where he specialized in fingerprinting and photography, and after that he went to work for the fingerprinting department at the Vermont State Correctional Institute in Windsor. Like his Indians, Ed Boggis towers. He is six feet, three inches tall, and weighs 235 pounds. "So I always was the first one in a cell," he remembers.

• 24 •

CARVING IS A SATISFYING CRAFT

When he was a prison worker, he also began to teach woodcarving to the inmates. He admits it was a worry to be among prisoners handling knives and gouges, but he adds that rarely were they used in any prison escapades. For the last few years of his employment at the prison (he resigned in 1973), he spent much of his time trying to obtain an outlet for the prisoners' carvings. "That was what they needed. Just after I left, I'm happy to say, they got it. They've a shop now just below the warden's office."

Ed Boggis doesn't know what inspired him to start carving Indians. "The first Indian things I did were when I was logging and I'd use dead pine branches to carve heads from. They were just little heads — about five inches or so that I'd carve when we stopped to have dinner at the noon hour." Then, when he was working at the prison, he did his first full-sized Indian.

"I went to the Rutland Fair with the prisoners once and I took that first seven-foot Indian along, even though it wasn't quite finished. A man from Lake Lucerne, New York, saw it, and he said, 'Make me two more.' Then he said, 'I'd like half a dozen more.' He was just about to retire and he got really interested in my Indians. He's been selling them all over the country ever since. The American Tobacco Company in New York even has one — eight feet, one inch tall."

As he chips at giant logs with his gouges, dislodges his Siamese cat from her resting place on a cigar-store Indian's torso, or ruffles the ears of the police dog that keeps him company in his shop, Ed Boggis willingly tells what he knows about carving, interlacing his directions now and then with stories about some of his favorite creations.

"I carved a six-foot gorilla once and left it near the night watchman's desk at the prison," he recounts with a chuckle. "And when he came to wind the clock, there was this gorilla standing there. I traded that one, along with a three-foot Indian, for an Evinrude motor and a Sport Craft boat. I'd read an ad in a magazine that said some fellow in Wall, Mississippi, had an airport and he wanted carved figures to decorate it, so I put the Indian and the gorilla in my station wagon and I drove to Wall."

Mr. Boggis tries to carve his Indians as nearly as possible like the cigar-store Indians of the past. He reads extensively about them and will recite such historical facts as their being most important in folk art from the 1850s into the 1880s.

"A good many of the people making them in those days were ship's figurehead carvers from around New York City. When tobacco became more prominent, and shipping started to fail, they began making Indians as display signs from the pine logs of the Erie Basin."

The cigar-store Indians at the Shelburne Museum in Shelburne, Vermont, have served as an inspiration for him, too, and as a source of information on repairing the cracks that are likely to develop in the wood as it dries.

"Of course these Indians take an awful beating outside, cracking and swelling in the weather. At Shelburne, they tacked pieces of zinc over the cracks when they were repairing them. What I do is cut a wedge-shaped piece of wood and tap it into the crack — though not too hard (Fig. 1). If you pound your piece in, the pressure will cause more cracking if the wood swells a little. Basswood cracks easier than pine, I think. Sometimes I've seen it crack almost in half.

"The other method I use, besides the wedges, especially if I have a good carving I don't want to spoil, is to use wax to repair the crack. Then, when the wood starts to swell, the crack will close and the wax squeeze out. It gives a little leeway."

Still another method of dealing with potential cracking is used by Willard Shepard, the carver at Connecticut's Mystic Seaport. He laminates his large carvings — makes them of seasoned planks or boards, screws and glues them together to the thickness he desires, and then carves them. "You simply can't season a whole tree trunk properly — it's too thick, as far as I'm concerned," he says.

But most Indians of the past were carved from the whole log, more or less following the same method Mr. Boggis uses today.

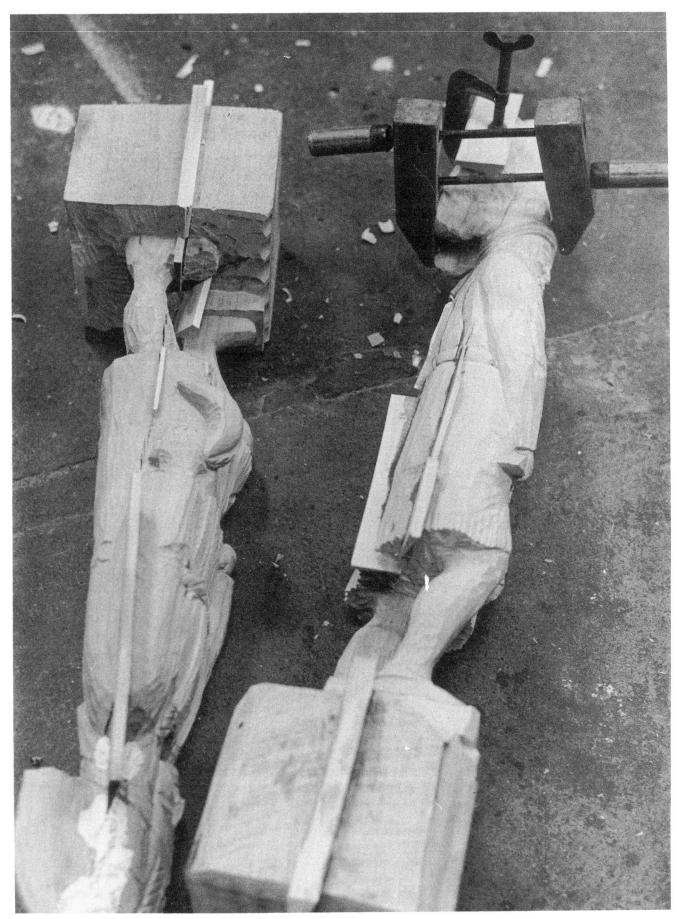

fig. 1   *Filling the cracks in a carving*

CARVING A CIGAR STORE INDIAN

1. Debark a white pine or basswood log, 6′ to 8′ long, using a hatchet and a cant hook used in lumbering, or a hardwood stick, to open the bark. Basswood is extremely slippery, "like a greased pole," according to Mr. Boggis, "but the bark will come off very easily." Let the wood set for two or three weeks in a dry place till the surface dries out, or, in the case of pine, until the pitch has set.

2. Take the debarked log. Lay it flat on the floor and try to locate its center. ("You can have a problem with that because a log is round," Mr. Boggis says, "but what I do is find the center of the top and bottom by measuring the diameter at the top and bottom, and with a straightedge or chalk line I draw a line the length of the log. Once I get this center line for the Indian's body, then I figure out that a person is seven and a half or eight heads tall, and I mark the body off into sections with chalk or colored pencil." To make an effective-looking Indian, Mr. Boggis emphasizes, the head should be somewhat larger than it would be on an actual man.

3. Once you have decided

fig. 2

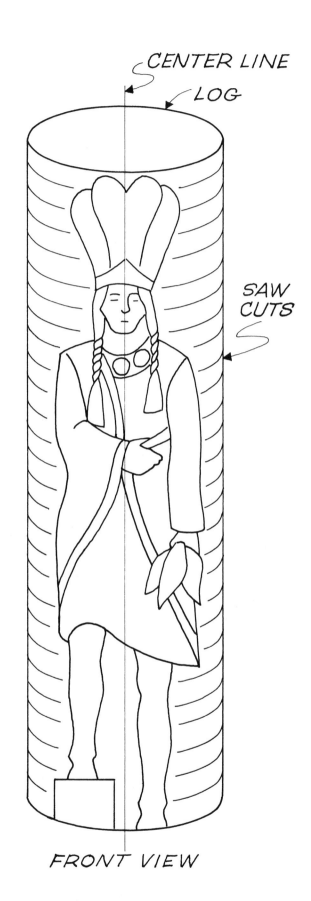

FRONT VIEW

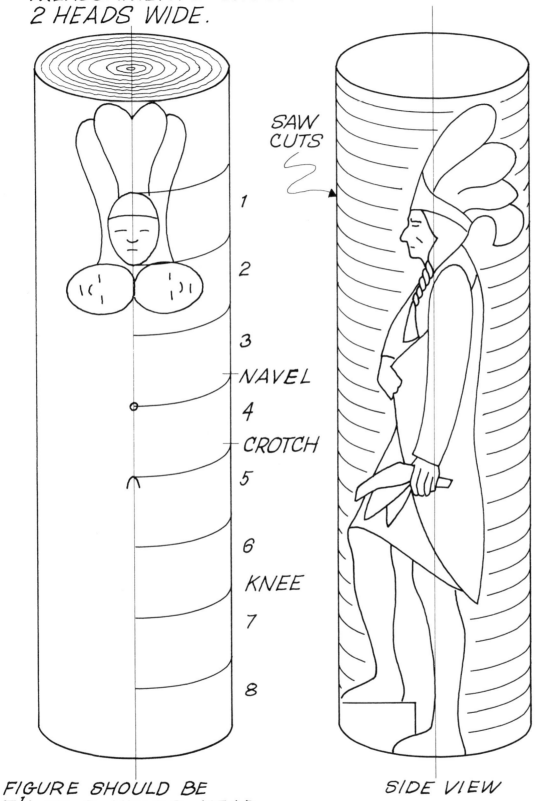

HEAD USED FOR
MEASURMENTS-SHOULDERS
2 HEADS WIDE.

SAW
CUTS

1

2

3

NAVEL

4

CROTCH

5

6

KNEE

7

8

FIGURE SHOULD BE
7½ TO 8 HEADS: HEAD
SHOULD START ABOUT
11" BELOW TOP OF LOG
TO ALLOW FOR HEADDRESS

SIDE VIEW

what your head size will be it is used as the measurement for the other segments of the body. From the chin to the nipples the distance will be the length of one head. From the nipples to the navel will be the length of one more head. It is one more head length from the navel to the crotch. On the legs, Mr. Boggis estimates, the distance from the crotch to the base of the knee is about two heads, and from the base of the knee to the foot is slightly less than two heads' length. The width of the Indian at the shoulder is two heads across. The elbows should be slightly above the navel, and the hands should hang halfway between the crotch and the knees (Fig. 2).

4. With a saw (this is where Mr. Boggis uses a chain saw), make the notches marking the neck, shoulders, waist, etc. Then with an adz and large chisels, begin carving (Fig. 3). The tools Mr. Boggis uses principally in his work are three or four No. 11 gouges, a No. 12 V-gouge, a No. 8, two or three No. 3 gouges, and a carving knife purchased from Woodcraft Supply Corporation in Woburn, Massachusetts. Before the front rough carving is too far along, stand the figure erect and examine it.

"If you don't, you can easily find that one shoulder is higher than the other, or one eye is. You have to stand the figure upright to even everything off," Mr. Boggis says. "And don't forget and cut the front too deep to begin with because you still have the sides and back to do." He estimates that in this initial carving stage, none of his front cuts is deeper than 4".

5. When the front of the Indian has been roughly carved in this way from top to bottom and is standing upright, draw a side-view pattern and a back pattern on it (Fig. 2). Start to rough-carve the sides and back.

fig. 3   *Starting to carve*

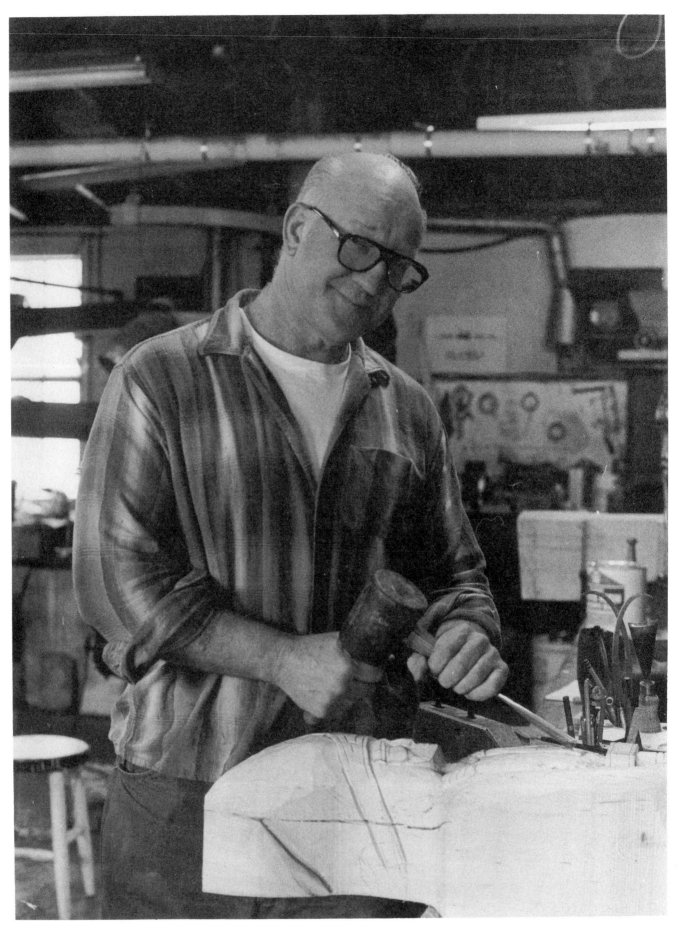

fig. 4   Ed Boggis doing the fine carving

"But be careful not to take a lot off the back to start out with because if I have problems later on finishing up the front, I can carve in deeper and correct them if I haven't taken too much off the back."

6. When the entire piece is rough-carved, lay it flat again (Mr. Boggis puts his Indian on sawhorses at this point so that he does not have to bend over to the floor to work on it). Work the entire front, back, and sides at this point, but not the fine lines in the face.

7. Let your Indian set in a dry place about six months. The piece will crack in a number of places. Fill these by sawing long strips on a bevel, fitting into the cracks and gluing. Recarve these areas, then shellac and paint. For skin tone, Mr. Boggis uses two coats of orange shellac, letting it dry between applications. Then he paints the Indian's robes with indoor-outdoor-based oil enamel, in whatever colors are appropriate to his costume. One coat, he says, is generally adequate.

8. Do the fine carving (Fig. 4).

"After that dries, I put on burnt-umber antiquing. I buy the paste and mix it with linseed oil and turpentine until it's the color I want. It should be about the thickness of light cream too. Then, after I put it all on, I wipe it all off. How much antiquing you do depends on how long you let it set before wiping it off with a cotton cloth. The longer it sets, the less you can wipe off, of course, and the darker it becomes."

9. When the antiquing has dried for about three days, spray with clear enamel. An antiqued surface without the enamel coating tends to pick up dust.

10. Some of Mr. Boggis' Indians have the unfinished end of the log they are made from flattened on the bottom as their base. For others, he saws a flat or a tapered separate base. For a 6' Indian, cut a tapered base about 12" high, 17" across the top, and 21" at the bottom.

11. Attach the base to the Indian's feet, using two 2"-long screws, but make sure that they are not screwed too close to the ends of the toes or the toes will crack. A simpler base is made from a 2" plank, 16" square, glued to the Indian's feet with Resorcinol waterproof glue or Elmer's plastic resin cascamite glue. Even if strong glue is used, be sure that several 20-penny spikes are driven into his feet through the base.

Two cigar store Indians

Another northern New England carver — sometimes of cigar-store Indians but more often of smaller objects — lives and works a half-day's journey away in Rutland, Vermont. Twenty-eight-year-old Duncan Hannah did his first carving before he was six, for his father, Pat Hannah, was a carver whose chunky little figures decorated many a New England corner cupboard.

"You pretty well learn to carve when your father is doing it all the time. You pick up little wood chips and start playing with them. When I was seven, my father was putting some of my carvings on the bargain table at fairs and things. I'd take scraps of wood and make little boxes with sliding doors and sell them for twenty-five cents apiece," Duncan Hannah recalls while he carves the same little men — Scotsmen in kilts, Shriners, golfers, fishermen, seamen — that his father carved a generation ago.

"People would ask my father how he ever got started as a carver," Mr. Hannah recalls, "and he'd be quite facetious about it and say his mother was frightened by a woodpecker, but actually it was a hobby that developed in the Depression."

As far as young Duncan Hannah is concerned, he took to carving when his friends were competing for after-school jobs as dishwashers. "It was a lot easier to carve than to work for someone else. If you're involved in a craft like carving, you can call your own shots. You have more control over your own destiny than you do when you work for someone else. It's all up to you. If you succeed, it's your success."

Even though he knew that carving would be his livelihood, Duncan Hannah went to the University of Vermont to study economics. "I was hoping it would help me in the business aspects of my work." After graduation, he married a Rutland girl, set her to painting his carvings on their honeymoon, and thereby established a team.

"It was kind of a working honeymoon," pert, dark-haired Marilyn Hannah remembers good-humoredly. "His mother had always done the painting for his father's figures, so I guessed I could do Duncan's."

In the workshop off the kitchen of their yellow Victorian house, while wood chips crackle in a potbelly stove and watermelon plants grow in the window ("I don't really expect to get many

Duncan and Marilyn Hannah with their mantelpiece carvings

watermelons in Vermont, but all I need is one for the benefit of my skeptical friends," Duncan Hannah says with a grin), he and his wife carve and paint and drink tea for refreshment. "His always has an ice cube in it because he's impatient," his wife explains. "We're tea drinkers by descent, I guess. His father came from Canada and his mother from England. My mother was born in Ireland."

The Hannahs' workday is ten to twelve hours long: five to six hours are spent carving and another five or six in painting, answering requests for orders, and in taking care of the affairs that are part of running your own small business. "But at least we don't have to get up by an alarm clock — they're my nemesis," Duncan Hannah says.

"We have the freedom not to have to pay attention to an alarm clock, doing this kind of work," Marilyn Hannah adds, "but if we don't get up when we should, we have to make up for it later because we have orders that have to be filled. Too many young people who think about crafts nowadays figure they're just an easy way to make money, but they're not. You have to remember, in a recession, the gift market is always one of the first to go."

Duncan Hannah's favorite material for carving is basswood. "It has a straight, true grain and it doesn't split easily. The trouble with it is that it tends to be spongy when you get down to fine detail. Cherry and walnut, being harder, aren't that way. The one thing you can do to make it better for detail carving is to burnish it with a piece of mother-of-pearl. That compresses the wood a little," he explains.

Most of Mr. Hannah's figures are 1¾" x 2" x 6". Here are his carving directions.

CARVING A LITTLE MATEY

1. Draw the design of the matey figure or any other simple figure you would like to carve on paper the same size as the wood to be carved. If you draw directly on the wood, and have nothing to follow on paper, you will be removing your directional marks as you cut. When you draw your figure, have the head comprise about one fifth of the total piece. This is larger, proportionately, than the head is to the body, but otherwise there will be no room for details of the face. "And that's the eye-catcher," Duncan Hannah says. "That's where most people look." The torso and head should make up about the top half of your figure and the legs the bottom half.

2. Trace your drawing on the wood (Fig. 5) and bandsaw it into a rough shape. Mark with a pencil those parts of the body that will remain the highest parts of the figure — the parts from which you will carve away wood. These are likely to be jutting elbows, bumps to suggest knees, the nose, and a paunch. "Start carving at the elbows since they stick out," Mr. Hannah says, "but plan all your cutting maneuvers before you begin them (Fig. 6). Remember, once you've cut something away, you can't put it back again." Mr. Hannah uses a Frost sheath or hunting knife with a laminated blade — soft steel outside and hard inside — that bends with the wood, but if this is not available, he suggests a slender blade knife, 3" long. He has gotten them from Woodcraft in Woburn, Massachusetts. Slender hunting knives are the best of that type. "Be sure, whatever kind of knife you get, to cut notches in the handle," he advises, "to make sure it won't slip, and take as much paint off the handle as you can for the same reason."

fig. 5   *Carving steps in a matey figure*
(Thomas D. Stevens)

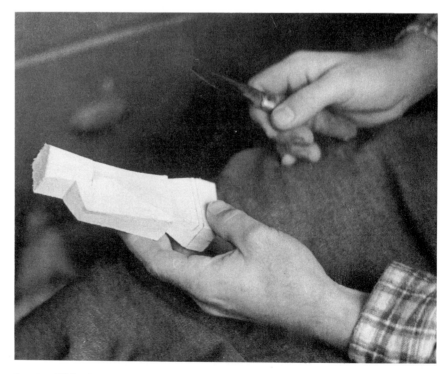

fig. 6   *Chipping away*

3. Have on hand, as well, for convenience though not of necessity, a short-handled round chisel (one that fits your hand) for carving coat buttons and a V-chisel for separating planes under the arms, around the rim of a hat, etc.

4. Once you begin carving, be sure to redraw the pattern marks that you remove. "Eyeball your work," Mr. Hannah says, "and balance one shoulder against the other; keep the arms and hands the same size. Don't turn the figure's head too far in one direction or the other unless you also turn the body in that direction. Once I saw a carving of a man that had a fine head and fine feet, but the head was going one way and the feet the other way. Your whole figure has to be done with an eye to all of it."

5. If your figure has flowers on its hat, or a cigar in its mouth, carve these and glue them in place with Elmer's Glue-All.

6. When the carving is complete, finish it with boiled linseed oil, wax or varnish, or paint. Always apply light colors before dark. The first color the Hannahs apply is the face color. For this, they use ground oils diluted to a stain with linseed oil or paint thinner. (Whenever they are using a yellowish shade they use oils.) As soon as they are applied, buff them off with cheesecloth or an old sheet. Rub hard to get a good sheen. You may, as you are rubbing, have to apply more oil. For shades other than yellows, the Hannahs use water-based acrylics. These are not buffed.

After a while, Mr. Hannah says, a carver should be able to do portrait figures as well as stock ones. From time to time he does, as his father always did.

"Some of these native Vermonters, you can find a lot of interesting things about them," Duncan Hannah comments. "There was this old guy, Hiram, who walked past our house every day when I was a kid. There was a slouch to his walk and on his old hat it said, 'Wayne's Food Store.' As he was walking by one day, my father invited him in and carved him while they conversed. Hiram couldn't believe it when my father handed him the carving. He thought it was just a friendly chat. Hiram's a figure I carve now too.

"A lot of people have a desire in their leisure time to draw or carve the human figure, and if they do a little studying of carvings, and try to duplicate them, they can have a lot of fun. Anybody who knows how to keep knives sharp and how to use them can carve wood," Duncan Hannah says.

In the summer of 1973, a tall, blond young man from Greenville, New Hampshire, showed up at the forested Manouane Indian Reserve, 100 miles north of Montreal, Canada. He and two friends arrived on the bush pilot's four-seater that occasionally brings visitors. He had seen a film about an elderly Manouan canoe-builder and wished to talk to him.

The American was twenty-four-year-old Henri Vaillancourt, whose carpenter grandfather moved from French Canada to New Hampshire. Ever since he was a small boy, Henri Vaillancourt has been fascinated by Indians and Indian craftsmanship. He has taught himself to tan skins, to make snowshoes and paddles, and when he was fourteen, he made his first canoe.

"I'm very persistent," he says simply. "If it's something I'm interested in, I never give up."

And that persistence is paying off. Today, he is a full-time canoe-maker, building canoes only on order and selling them at prices from $700 to $900 apiece. Because he insists on quality workmanship, peeling the bark for his own canoes, cutting down the trees for their ribs and planks and digging his own roots for binding them, he limits himself to producing six canoes a year. But they are his means of support.

It was in search of more and better knowledge of canoe-building that he went to the Manouane Reserve. "At first, I think they thought I was some dude from the city," he recalls a year later as he squats in the side yard at his parents' yellow and black frame house in Greenville and shapes birchbark for a canoe, "and the canoe-builder spoke only Indian, but he had a son-in-law who was my age and could translate for us, and after a while, we were able to exchange ideas even without him, by demonstration, since we were both canoe-builders."

For a year, before he took up canoe-building as an occupation, Henri Vaillancourt studied forestry at the University of New Hampshire. He enjoyed it but not so much as he does working at his own craft. "I must admit I've learned everything the hard way — that first canoe was built from a vague magazine article, and I learned how to tan from a book, and to make snowshoes on my own."

The snowshoes that he fashions in winter, when the snow is in mounds outside the workshop

• 25 •

BIRCHBARK CANOES
MADE INDIAN FASHION

that his grandfather built, are Ojibway and Cree in style. Both are tribes of the Great Lakes area.

The hides he has tanned include deer, moose, and bear, and visitors stopping to talk to him on a cold day will find they are soon offered an animal skin to wrap themselves in. "But tanning is just something I do for my own needs, not for other people," he remarks.

The canoe that he makes is Malecite. "They're Indians of the Algonquin linguistic stock, like the Penobscots and the Passamaquoddy of Maine. They live around New Brunswick and Quebec, and in Maine. I think there's the best workmanship in Malecite canoes. There's better design than in most others. Some Indians in the extreme north make canoes that look like patchwork quilts, for example, because the birches up there are so small, but the Malecite canoe isn't like that. I like its looks."

Birchbark canoes, Mr. Vaillancourt maintains, not only are useful because they are lightweight for north country portages (they were used primarily by Great Lakes and Northeastern Indians), "but a well-made one can be tougher than canvas. I can show you birchbark canoes as much as thirty years old, and they're still in usable condition, though I'll admit that's something of an exception."

Fingering the edge of a bark skin, Mr. Vaillancourt describes birchbark as "probably one of the weirdest substances in the world. It has a grain that runs around the tree. If the grain ran lengthwise, it would be likely to split when you were stretching it out. And it has a certain elasticity, and it absorbs next to no water."

Summer is the season when Henri Vaillancourt does most of his canoe-making, because it is in late June and July that birchbark is easiest to peel from the tree. That also is the time when he can work best out-of-doors, shaping the bark on the earth bed he has prepared for canoe-building.

"It's a totally different world working from wood that you have split from a tree yourself than it is when you work with sawed wood. Split wood has a certain life and spring to it. I can tell the difference between it and sawed wood with my eyes closed."

Mr. Vaillancourt talks solemnly and earnestly of his work and the satisfactions of it. The only modern material that he uses in his canoes is roofing tar for caulking the seams because it is less affected by temperature than pitch is.

Pitch has to be tempered according to the season, Mr. Vaillancourt explains. For summer application, it should be hard. If you are using it in cold weather, you must add more animal fat to soften it and make it less likely to crack. "I don't use much natural pitch at all unless people really want it, but if they do, I get it from white pine or spruce. With spruce, you strip off a length of bark a year or so ahead and scrape the pitch away from the wound any time in the year from then on. For pine pitch, I go wherever lumbermen are cutting pine and scrape the pitch from the stumps with a putty knife.

Then I put it in a burlap bag — the Indians always used cedar-bark bags — and I stick the bag in boiling water. The pitch will come out and the impurities stay in the bag. I boil it for several days, and it will settle at the bottom of the water. Then I melt it or chip it out of the bottom of the can I have boiled it in, and when I am ready to use it, melt it to a syrup consistency over a low flame."

More to Henri Vaillancourt's liking is going in search of the birchbark for a canoe skin, white cedar for the framework, and ash or maple for the thwarts.

Much of his birchbark comes from New Hampshire. Ordinarily, he locates good trees in advance of going to get them. "My memory of where trees are is pretty good when it comes to fine birch."

White birch is the only one that is good for canoe-building, Mr. Vaillancourt emphasizes. "Yellow would be impossible. Other woods that the Indians used to use are spruce, elm, and cedar, and sometimes hickory, but all of them are much coarser than white birch."

In general, one birch provides only enough bark for one canoe, though on occasion, Mr. Vaillancourt has found a tree with bark enough for two.

A bark canoe, according to Mr. Vaillancourt, differs from any other boat in its construction because the outer skin is stretched and shaped first and then the framework is put inside it. He describes it as "almost like an inverted barrel process. You have temporary ribs that hold in the planking. When you start out, the bark is puckered and wrinkled."

Making a canoe takes Mr. Vaillancourt about three weeks to a month. He warns that, for the beginner, canoe-making will take a good deal longer.

1. Tools and Materials Needed

a. The single most important tool in bark-canoe building is the crooked knife. It consists of a straight blade 4″ to 6″ long, the end of which is curved upward on the flat of the blade. This blade is fitted to a wooden handle that has some form of upward projection at the end opposite the blade. The back of the blade is flat and is beveled only on its top face. When using this knife, draw it toward yourself. Grasp it fingers up, with your thumb resting on the upward projection. In other words, use it in the manner of a one-handed drawknife. Hold the wood being worked in your other hand. Generally, the flat part of the blade is used for shaving narrow surfaces and the curved portion for wider areas. With this tool (Fig. 1), used in conjunction with an ax for splitting and removing large quantities of wood, you can make the entire framework of a canoe.

b. An awl is needed to sew the bark, and this is generally made from a small three-cornered file, sharpened and ground down to remove the roughness. The blade should be approximately 3/16″ thick and is fastened firmly into a wooden or antler handle (Fig. 1).

c. The first material requisite in making a birchbark canoe is suitable bark. The bark should be smooth, not less than 1/16″ thick (⅛″ is ideal), and tough. The section of trunk to be peeled must be straight in order to remove a piece of bark in one piece. The bark would split during removal from a tree that curves. Sample the tree by cutting a piece of bark 2′ or 3′ above the ground. Test it for toughness and pliability. If the bark splits along the grain very easily when it is bent, reject it. Bark that has a tendency to separate into layers is also of poor quality.

MAKING A BIRCHBARK CANOE

fig. 1 *Materials for canoe building*

fig. 2   *Prying the bark from a birch tree*
(Richard Nash)

When you find a good tree, make an incision with a knife, lengthwise, on the trunk. Pry one edge of the bark from the wood with the knife (Fig. 2). If you peel the bark in June or July, it will come off very easily, Mr. Vaillancourt re-emphasizes. But at other times of the year the bark sticks tightly to the tree. To facilitate removal at these times, a 9″ or 10″ square of thick birchbark is beveled thin along one edge and inserted between the bark and the trunk. By working this tool back and forth, you separate the bark from the tree along the whole length of the cut. You must remove the bark evenly along this cut and not lift more of it in one spot than another at a time. There is a tendency for the bark to stick more toward the middle of the cut than toward the ends. Regardless of the difficulty in the middle, you must still pry the same amount of bark loose there as you do at the ends as you progress, for any unevenness here can cause the sheet to split along the grain.

If the sheet of bark is too long, you need a ladder or support while you work on the tree. An alternative is to fell the tree, as long as you are careful not to let it fall against another tree or a rock that might damage the bark. Then proceed.

When the sheet is off, roll it lengthwise across the grain so that the width of the bark becomes the length of the roll. Then tie it tightly in several places, making it a convenient roll for storage and also preventing the bark from curling.

d. The woodwork of a bark canoe is almost always made from the Northern white cedar. Select a tree for your canoe for straightness of grain and freedom from knots. If the furrows in the bark spiral around the trunk, the grain will be similarly twisted. A straight-grained tree is marked by straight furrows in its bark.

For the gunwales, you need a good section of log slightly longer than the canoe you plan to make. For the planking, the pieces should be half the length of the canoe. For the ribs, you should have pieces at least 5′ long. Tree trunks a foot or more thick are ideal.

Split the cedar you plan to use in halves with an ax, wooden wedges, and a maul. Pound the ax into the end of the log with blows from the maul. Further divide the trunk with the wedges. Then split it into quarters and eighths depending on the size of the log and the size of the pieces needed (Fig. 3). Split these sections again, into gunwales, ribs, and planking.

Be sure to split away the middle portions of the log with a froe and to discard them as they are always rotten or knotty. You will find that the trunk is easiest to split if you divide it as closely in half as possible. This halving process and continued cutting produces progressively thinner pieces, and when they are thin enough to bend, the split can be controlled to a greater extent. If one side of the split becomes stronger and thicker than the other, bend it toward the thinner side to encourage the split in that direction. By this technique, and with some practice, you can very accurately and evenly split pieces as thin as ⅛″ into planking.

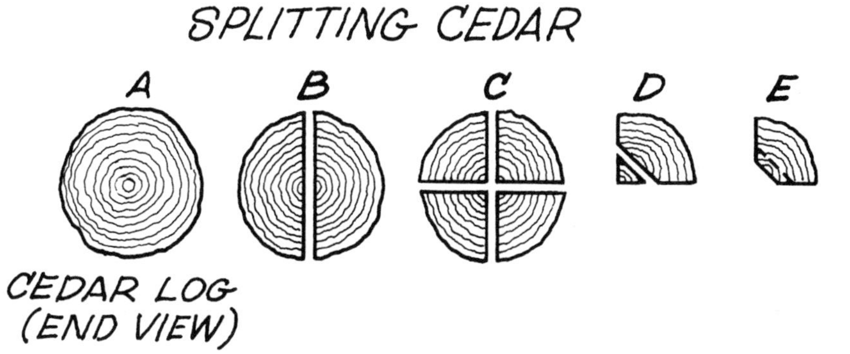

SPLITTING CEDAR

A   B   C   D   E

CEDAR LOG
(END VIEW)

fig. 3

e. For sewing the bark canoe, roots of white, black, and red spruce, along with cedar, tamarack, and various pines are best. The roots you use depend to some extent upon those available in your area. Good roots, however, are characterized by a fairly constant diameter, freedom from side roots, and a certain toughness and pliability. Dig roots up with the hands. Generally, they lie very close to the surface of the earth. An ideal length of root for canoe work is 8' to 10' with a diameter of $\frac{1}{2}''$ or so, although roots as short as 5' with a diameter either somewhat thinner or thicker than $\frac{1}{2}''$ will do.

Peel the root bark by scraping the roots with a dull knife, and split them in the same way as you did the cedar, but use a knife and your hands. Roots $\frac{1}{4}''$ or so thick are split in two parts, but larger ones should be quartered, with the middle portion of each quarter being split away. Use only the outer part of the root. Scrape and thin this section further by drawing the root under a dull knife held stationary against a pad on the worker's leg.

For lashing the gunwales, split the root strands to a flat, thin thong approximately $\frac{1}{4}''$ wide. Roll this root material into bundles, bind it, and allow it to dry. When needed, soak it for a time in water so that it regains its pliability.

f. The pitch for sealing the seams of a canoe is generally the gum of white or black spruce or pine. When you have obtained the pitch from the wound in a tree, melt it to liquid consistency and strain it through burlap to rid it of its impurities. Test it for pliability by dipping a thin strip of birchbark into it and then into cold water. Then bend the piece of bark, and if the pitch cracks, add animal fat. If the pitch is flexible, be sure it is not too tacky. If it is, boil it some more to harden further. This is the way the pitch is tempered. In colder weather, you will have to add more grease to obtain a more pliant pitch.

2. Assembly

a. The inwales are the first part of a bark canoe to be assembled. These consist of two cedar battens $1\frac{1}{8}''$ wide, $1\frac{1}{4}''$ deep, and 16" long. Taper the ends to $\frac{3}{4}'' \times \frac{3}{4}''$. Mortise the gunwales to receive five thwarts (Fig. 4). Cut the first mortises in the exact center of each gunwale. All mortises

should be 2" long x $\frac{1}{4}''$ wide and go through the entire thickness of the gunwale. After you have cut the first set, cut another set at a distance of 3' each way from the center and the last set 29" from these.

b. Make the thwarts from maple or birch. The center one should be 31" long x 2" x $\frac{1}{4}''$ at the ends. The thwart gradually narrows from the ends, but it thickens to about 1" x 1" in the center (Fig. 5).

The first set of thwarts from the center are shaped like the very first set, but they should be 24" long. The last set should be 2" x $\frac{1}{4}''$ thick at the ends and from there widen to 3" x $\frac{1}{2}''$ in the center. Their length should be $13\frac{3}{4}''$.

Fit the ends of the thwarts to the mortises which are held by a small wooden peg driven through the inwale and thwart end (Fig. 4). Fasten the ends of the gunwales to a small triangular cedar block held by a peg and a root lashing. Bevel off the lower outboard corner of the gunwales about $\frac{3}{4}''$ to receive the heads of the ribs later on (Fig. 4).

CROSS-SECTION OF GUNWALE

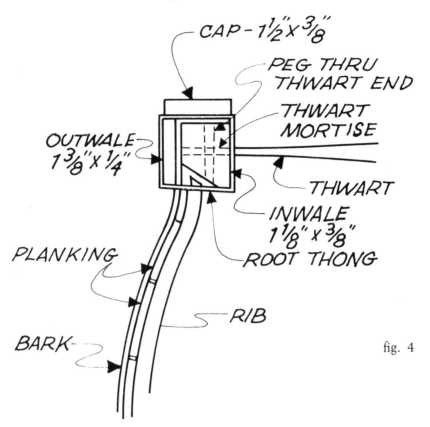

CAP - $1\frac{1}{2}'' \times \frac{3}{8}''$

PEG THRU THWART END

THWART MORTISE

OUTWALE $1\frac{3}{8}'' \times \frac{1}{4}''$

THWART

INWALE $1\frac{1}{8}'' \times \frac{3}{8}''$

ROOT THONG

PLANKING

RIB

BARK

fig. 4

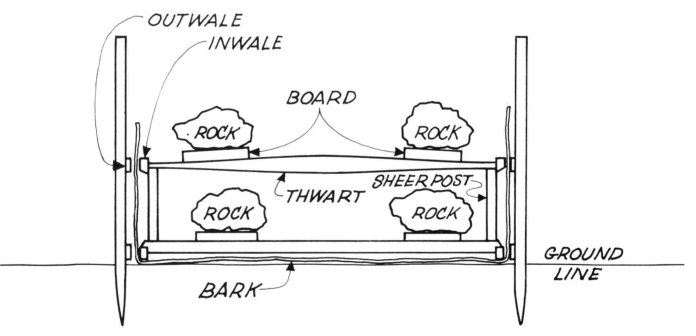

OUTWALE

INWALE

BOARD

ROCK

ROCK

ROCK

THWART

SHEER POST

ROCK

GROUND LINE

BARK

fig. 5

fig. 6   *Gunwale frame*

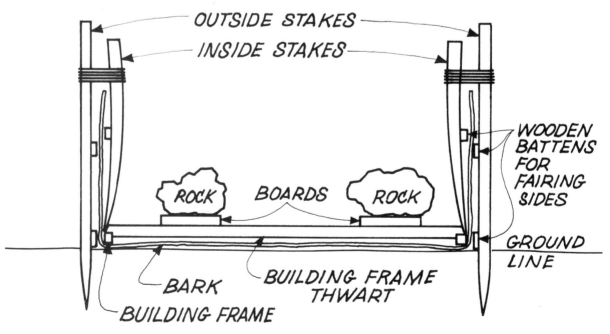

fig. 7

c. Make a building frame exactly the same shape as the gunwale frame (Fig. 6), but spread it apart by temporary thwarts which are not mortised into it but are notched to fit over the longitudinal end and held by a lashing of root material (Fig. 7).

d. Prepare a building bed by raking a spot of firm ground absolutely smooth and level. Place the building frame on it, and hold it with a few rocks. Stretch a string along the center line of the frame and extend it beyond the line at each end about 18″. Hold the string firmly in place at either end by two stakes. Along both sides of the frame, pound 15 pairs of stakes into the ground. Make these stakes from straight spruce saplings 2″ thick and 3′ long.

Put one stake at each thwart end, and also one in between (Fig. 7). Set another pair at the ends of the frame, and evenly space two pairs beyond each frame end.

Set the stakes in the ground vertically about ¾″ from the frame. After they have been accurately set, pull them up carefully and lay them near their holes. Then take the frame up and lay it aside.

e. On the bed, unroll, inner surface down, a sheet of bark of sufficient length and width for the canoe. Then center the frame carefully on the bark, holding it down with heavy rocks put on boards laid across the thwarts (Fig. 7).

f. Starting near the center thwart, make slits at 1″ intervals in the bark that is projected beyond the width of the frame. These slits permit you to fold the bark around the frame in an upright position so that it won't buckle. The last 5′ or so near the ends of the canoe do not need to be slit because at this point you can turn the bark around the frame without breaking it.

g. Now pound the stakes back into their holes, thereby forcing the bark upward. Then place a long, thin wooden batten near the base line of the canoe on the outside of the bark, but on the inside of the stakes, to distribute the pressure evenly (Fig. 7). Place two similar battens near the

top edge of the bark to even the sides. The battens and the bark are held rigidly in place with inside stakes 1″ x 1″ thick x 30″ long (Fig. 7). Bevel their bottom ends and insert them between the outside of the building frame and the bark on the inside of the canoe. Tie the top end of each inside stake to the outside stake.

h. With the sides secured, trim the gores so that their edges are flush. This requires cutting a narrow V-shaped section at each gore.

i. The gunwale frame can now be brought in and positioned over the building frame. Set posts on the building frame to stand under each thwart end in the gunwale frame. These posts set the gradual sweep of the canoe from bow to stern and are, of course, shorter in the middle of the canoe than at the ends. The center ones are 8″ long; the next two pairs each way from the center are 8½″ long; the last pair are 13″ long. The gunwale frame is held securely on the posts by rocks placed on boards across the thwarts (Fig. 5).

j. Now bring the outwales in. These, made of cedar, are 18" long x ⅜" thick x 1¼" deep along most of their length. The ends should be tapered in depth to about ½". Bevel the lower inboard corner of the outwale by about 3/16" (Fig. 4).

k. Place the outwales on the outside of the bark even with the inwales (Fig. 5). Remove the two longitudinal battens holding the top edge of the bark and remove the inside stakes. With ¼" ash or maple pegs set every 6" or so, fasten the outwale securely to the inwale. The bark is thus clamped between the outwale and inwale and the excess bark protruding above the gunwales can be trimmed off.

l. Now lash the gunwales in groups with roots, with each lashing about 2" long (Fig. 8), leaving a space of about the same distance in between the lashings for the installation of ribs later on. For lashing, use the three-cornered awl to punch holes in the bark just below the outwales. Sharpen one end of the root and thread it through the hole from the outside. The other end of the root should be held securely under the first few turns of the lashing. Generally, make two turns of the bark through one hole to avoid weakening it with too many closely spaced holes.

m. In doing the lashing, leave nine spaces between the lashings that are between the middle and first thwarts, eight between the first and last thwart, and seven between that and the end of the gunwales. Place a lashing at each thwart and pass through three or four holes bored in the thwart itself (Fig. 9).

n. When the canoe is completely lashed (Fig. 10), lift it from the bed after you have removed the rocks and pulled out the stakes. Then dismantle the building frame by cutting the lashing of its thwarts and removing it from the canoe. Sweep out and clean the canoe interior.

o. Now it is time to pitch the canoe thoroughly on the inside. Do this by smearing the heated gum to a width of 3" or 4" over the vertical gore slits and any other splits or small holes in the bark. Similarly smear a strip of cloth or thin bark with pitch and paste it over each seam.

fig. 8

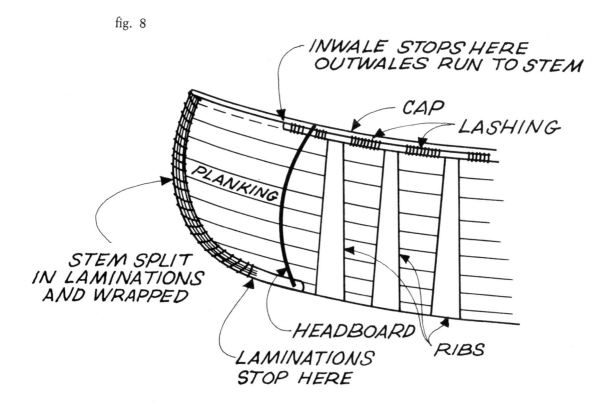

INWALE STOPS HERE
OUTWALES RUN TO STEM
CAP
LASHING
PLANKING
STEM SPLIT
IN LAMINATIONS
AND WRAPPED
HEADBOARD
LAMINATIONS
STOP HERE
RIBS

fig. 9   *A canoe showing the lashing through the thwarts
and partial planking*
(Richard Nash)

fig. 10 *The canoe lashed and ready to remove from its building
bed and stake enclosure*
(Richard Nash)

p. Make the stems for the canoe from a piece of cedar approximately 3' long x 1½" wide x ½" thick, with one of its narrow edges sharpened. Bend this piece edgewise into the canoe by means of laminations split with a knife (Fig. 11). Leave the heel of the stem solid. Using hot water, bend the stem to the desired profile and wrap the laminations tightly with cedar or basswood bark to hold the shape. Cut a notch in the solid part of the stem at the bottom.

q. Place the stems between the bark at the ends with the top end projecting somewhat above the outwales and between the outwales where they come together at the ends. Hold the stem in place temporarily by putting a few small pegs through the stem and the bark. Cut the bark parallel with the stem approximately 1" from its outboard edge. Make several clothespinlike clamps from two flat sticks lashed together and place these clamps over the bark and stems to hold them more firmly together.

r. The planking for the canoe is made in 9' lengths, ⅛" thick and from 1½" to 2½" wide. Taper the center plank to about ½" at one end. Lay this plank so that its narrow end underlaps the stem about 1". It, and all other planks, will extend to the middle of the canoe. Then the end of the plank that is at the middle should be thinned for about 5" of its length where the planks coming from the other end overlap (Fig. 9). Hold the planking temporarily in place with ribs made from small saplings. The ends of these ribs, as well as those of the permanent ribs you will make later on, are caught in the bevel of the inwale (Fig. 4). With the bottom part of the rib slanted toward the middle of the canoe, drive the rib forward with blows from a mallet or hammer. This stretches the bark cover and gives it the required shape.

s. When you have installed the planking in half of the canoe, the permanent ribs can be placed. Make these from cedar in 5 lengths for the middle portion of the canoe and somewhat shorter toward the ends. They are 2¾" wide and ⅜" thick in most of the canoe, but the last few toward the ends should be about 2" wide and 5/16" thick.

Mark the width of the building frame on each rib according to its position in the finished canoe. With a curved piece of wood that has the curve desired for the bilge, bend the ribs in pairs after thoroughly boiling to soften them. Starting at the middle thwart, place one rib on either side of it and so on toward the end of the canoe.

To hold the ribs in position after they are bent, tie their ends, somewhat in the fashion of a bow, and set them aside to dry.

The first rib you should install is the last one at the end of the canoe. Place the rib in its position inside the canoe and make a mark on it slightly higher than the top of the gunwale. Trim the excess length at the end and bevel the cut on the inside. Taper the rib in width to 1½" at the end. The

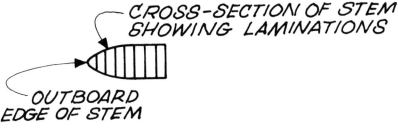

CROSS-SECTION OF STEM
SHOWING LAMINATIONS

OUTBOARD
EDGE OF STEM

fig. 11

fig. 12   *Driving the ribs*
(Richard Nash)

rib ends are caught in the bevel of the inwale and the bottom part of the rib should be slanted toward the middle of the canoe (Fig. 12). Then drive the rib forward with a mallet. Between the mallet and the rib place a small piece of wood to receive the mallet blows directly and thus prevent damage to the rib. Pound each rib in only partway before you install the next rib. Each rib in half the canoe is thus driven in a little at a time over a period of several days, and this gradually stretches the bark cover to shape. Pour hot water over the bark to make it more flexible during this rib-insertion period and to reduce the danger of splitting it. If a rib drives too hard, shorten it a little.

When one half of the canoe has been so treated, do the same with the other half, overlapping the planking of the first half as mentioned earlier.

t. With the ribs installed, sew the stems permanently in place with a simple spiral stitch, passing the strands through the bark and the stem (Fig. 13). But first, trim the bark flush with the edge of the stem. Begin sewing at the bottom and progress to the top of the stem.

fig. 13   *Stitching the stem*

Fold a piece of birchbark over the inwale ends and extend it toward the stem. Since the inwales are shorter than the outwales, the open space that is left is adequately covered by the bark deck.

u. Install a bulkhead-type board in the ends of the canoe to strengthen and support them. The board should be ¼" thick and shaped to fit the cross-section of the canoe at that point. Notch the bottom of the board (Fig. 14) to fit over the notch in the base of the stem. The top part fits over the inwales where they come together at the ends and a small, narrow projection comes up between them.

Peg a strip of cedar over the outwale and inwale tops to act as a guard to the sewing (Fig. 8). This strip, called a cap, should be as long as the outwales and ¼" thick x 1½" wide. Taper the ends in width to about ½".

Before you install the headboard, stuff the dead space between it and the stem with shavings to give added stiffness at that point.

v. Finally, pitch the canoe thoroughly on the outside after you have melted the pitch to a syrup consistency. Smear the hot pitch over all the cuts and holes and press with a wet thumb or finger into the seam before the pitch cools and hardens. Fig. 15 shows a completed canoe.

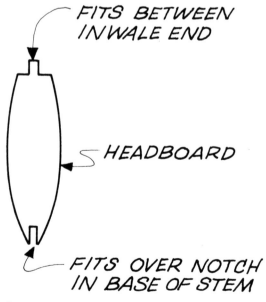

FITS BETWEEN INWALE END

HEADBOARD

FITS OVER NOTCH IN BASE OF STEM

fig. 14

fig. 15 *A completed Vaillancourt canoe*
(Richard Nash)

The eye of the traveler along old Route 1 in Nobleboro Village, Maine, is caught on a windy day by the gyrations of miniature wooden men and birds that wave their arms and flap their wings in the yard of Wilson Hutchins.

There are spotted white cows being vigorously milked, too, as the wind turns a propeller. Two dogs toss dolls between them when a good breeze blows; a woodsman saws a log.

"Why, I can make anything under the sun, out of wood or out of iron," the broad-shouldered, hefty creator of this menagerie announces matter-of-factly when he has been found out in the clutter and noise of his machine shop.

"I've made grandmother clocks and sold them all around. I've made four-seat lawn swings as well as those sailor boys who wave their arms when the wind blows. I've made weathervanes that stay right out in the hurricane winds and work and the wind doesn't bother them a bit either. I've made hydraulic bodies and trailers and snowplows and a wind machine that used to pump water and run a water wheel. I had a nice little lighthouse outside for a while with a big fan on it to turn in the wind. I didn't want to sell that one, but a fellow came along and he was so persistent and liked it so much I said, 'Take it.'

"I'm sixty-nine going on seventy. I've done enough work in my life to kill three men. What makes me mad is that now I'm too damn old to do anything! I'd like to turn out more work than I do, but I just can't."

In his lifetime, Mr. Hutchins has done a myriad of things — built and plowed roads, cut ice, lumbered, worked on the railroad, wired houses, and spent forty years as an automobile mechanic. Today, though, he spends most of his time with wood. He still likes designing a weathervane of metal from time to time, but it's less of a chore working with wood. "You don't have to have all those torches and that sort of business.

"I don't know why I make all these things," Mr. Hutchins says, and scratches his head. "I just simply started making one or two of them for myself — wind machines and such — because I like them. Then people saw them and said, 'Make more,' so I made more and more and more."

Now, not only in the Hutchins' yard is there a magical display of whirligigs, but the rafters of the garage beneath his house are crowded with them.

· 26 ·

WIND MACHINES
OF COMIC CHARACTER

"Do you like my house?" Mr. Hutchins is inclined to ask. "It used to be a filling station, and you wouldn't think so, would you? I moved it here myself and built a house around it. I used to live on the other road here, but I got burned out in thirty-nine. When we moved in here all we had was one room and the grass growing up through the floor." And he offers a tour of the house, with his wife, Eleanor, nodding approval. "Now look out there at my birdhouses. I'm a jack-of-all-trades."

"Tell about the snow clearing," Mrs. Hutchins likes to interject, launching her husband in a recollection of the great storm of February fifteenth — "It was back in the fifties, and I plowed snow for four days and four nights and never went to bed at all. It blew something terrible that day!"

Wilson Hutchins will sit down at the table in his pink and gray kitchen, push aside the bowl of artificial fruit, scratch the rhinestone-collared neck of his wife's poodle, Peter, and nostalgically tell about that adventure.

"It was my job to plow in Damariscotta. It began snowing about ten o'clock at night. When I started out, there was only two inches of snow on the roads. I never put on heavy clothing or anything. I thought I'd be coming right back home. But it wasn't long before you couldn't see a thing. I struck a ledge and went down over a bank — truck — plow — the whole damn thing. I walked back to town to find help. You wouldn't have known, as you walked along, that I'd been there with a snowplow at all, it had filled up so fast.

"Those were pretty different times from these times. Why, sometimes the snow was up over my head. Nowadays, we just don't have snow anymore. As a matter of fact, I just sold my plow," he says, quitting the dog and the kitchen table to head for the breadbox after a chunk of his wife's chocolate cake.

"You get hungry on a job like that," he says.

"You get hungry on a lot of the jobs I've been on," he continues. "I used to put up four thousand tons of ice a winter and haul it as much as twenty-six miles to Damariscotta. I had my own special ice saw that would saw ice just as fast as you could cut it. Of course, you don't cut ice unless it's twenty or more inches thick. You saw down about ten inches, and where you've made seams, you take a chisel and tap the joints full of snow. You have to caulk the seams that way as you go or the ice'll freeze up again, you see. Then, finally, you hand-saw the cuts and break up great islands of ice. Pemaquid Pond was where I did my ice-cutting. But you don't have ice like that around anymore. Wish we did. It was fun cutting it.

"I'll tell you something else I used to do," Mr. Hutchins says, cake in hand. "I used to haul wood, and — here's an experience — when I was eighteen years old — January twenty-eighth, nineteen eighteen, was the date — I got a bullet through me on a hauling expedition.

"I always liked to hunt, you see — nothing so good as a rabbit stew, is there — so I had my gun with me in case we saw any game. It was a forty-forty rifle and somehow it went off and went right through my lungs. We were hauling a mile into the woods and were three and a half miles from the nearest doctor, and when I got to him he looked at me and said, 'He'll be dead in a few minutes.' I said to myself, 'You ain't dead yet, you son of a gun. I breathed through that bullet hole for three days, but, as you can see, I survived.

"That was more than my brother did. He was a fireman on the railroad and he was killed in that wreck in Ottawa — a head-on collision — in nineteen eighteen. You know, just before he left he took a little cucumber on a vine and put it in a bottle with salt and water and for years it kept green. He mixed the salt and the water until it could float a potato or an egg and then he put the cucumber in it. I still have it, and it's pretty interesting." Mr. Hutchins rises to bring down a Mason jar with a pale giant cucumber in it from a kitchen cupboard.

But with the cake and reminiscences ended, he is ready to tell more about whirligigs and pull out the patterns in his garage. "Though I've had trouble with some of them — the mice chewed them," he says. White pine is what he suggests using for a wind machine.

MAKING A WHIRLIGIG

1. Using Figs. 1 and 2 as patterns, cut with a table saw:

   a. Cow's body from ¾" pine

   b. Cow's legs from ⅜" pine

   c. Piece between cow's legs from ¾" pine

   d. Man from ⅜" pine

   e. Man's stool from ¼" plywood

   f. Flat base for whirligig from ¾" pine

   g. Square wood base into which whirligig shaft fits from 1¾" square piece of pine, 3" long

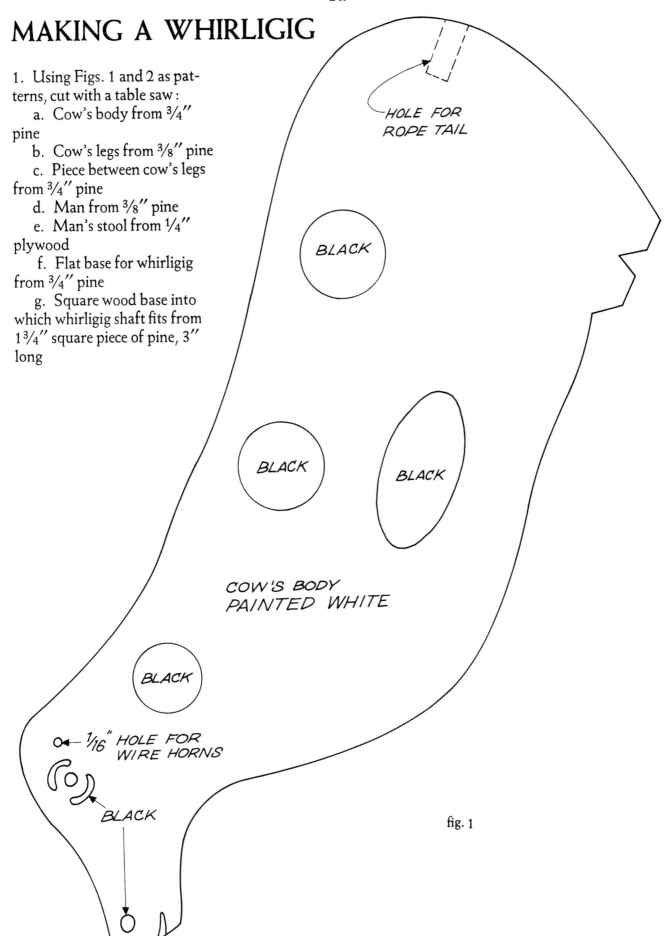

HOLE FOR ROPE TAIL

BLACK

BLACK

BLACK

COW'S BODY
PAINTED WHITE

BLACK

¹⁄₁₆" HOLE FOR WIRE HORNS

BLACK

fig. 1

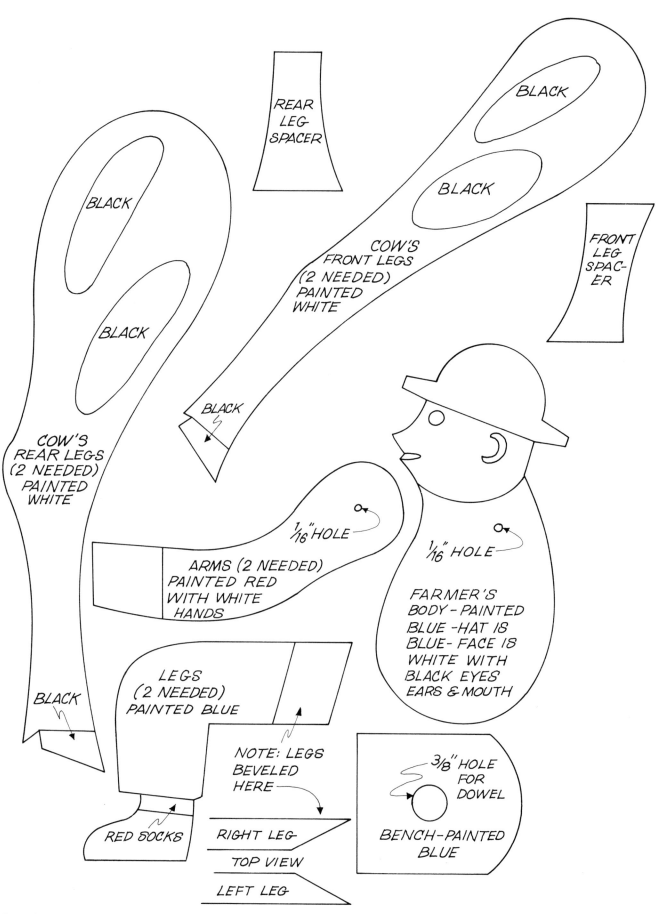

REAR LEG SPACER

BLACK

BLACK

COW'S FRONT LEGS (2 NEEDED) PAINTED WHITE

BLACK

FRONT LEG SPAC-ER

BLACK

BLACK

COW'S REAR LEGS (2 NEEDED) PAINTED WHITE

1/16" HOLE

1/16" HOLE

ARMS (2 NEEDED) PAINTED RED WITH WHITE HANDS

FARMER'S BODY - PAINTED BLUE - HAT IS BLUE - FACE IS WHITE WITH BLACK EYES EARS & MOUTH

BLACK

LEGS (2 NEEDED) PAINTED BLUE

NOTE: LEGS BEVELED HERE

3/8" HOLE FOR DOWEL

BENCH - PAINTED BLUE

RED SOCKS

RIGHT LEG

TOP VIEW

LEFT LEG

fig. 2

h. Propeller blades from ¼" masonite

i. Rudder from ¼" marine plywood

2. To simplify fitting the pieces of the cow together, prepare a board with a shelf for the cow's legs to rest on (Fig. 3). Lay the cow's body on it, positioning the legs on one side of the cow. Nail them to the body with 1" No. 18 nails. Turn the cow over. Repeat the process on the other side, making sure the nails don't hit each other. "Be sure to drill the holes for the nails first," says Mr. Hutchins, "or you'll split the wood to hell."

3. Drill holes in the bottoms of the legs on one side and through the block of wood positioned between the cow's legs to allow for fastening in place with 1" No. 18 nails. Turn the cow over. Repeat on the opposite side.

4. Drill holes for the horns and insert a piece of soft telephone wire (obtained from old lines that are taken down). The wire should be approximately 3" long.

5. Nail the cow to the flat stand by inserting two wire brads from the tops of the spacers between the cow's legs, going into the stand. Reinforce with a 1½" No. 6 screw inserted from underneath the flat stand (Fig. 4).

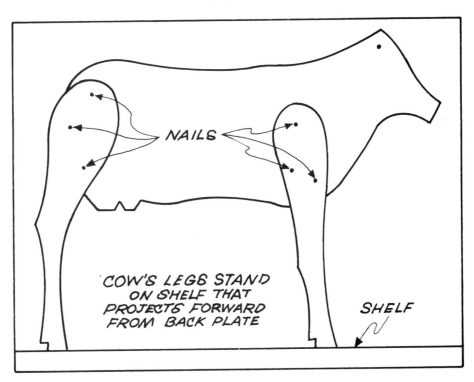

fig. 3

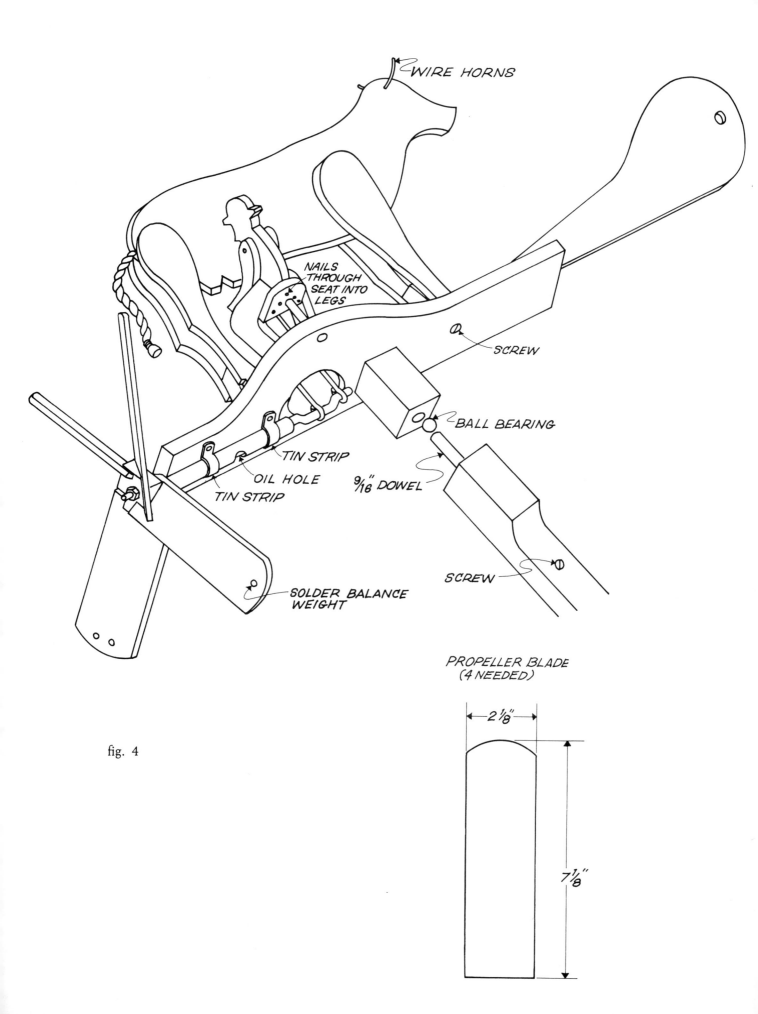

WIRE HORNS

NAILS
THROUGH
SEAT INTO
LEGS

SCREW

BALL BEARING

TIN STRIP

OIL HOLE

9/16" DOWEL

TIN STRIP

SCREW

SOLDER BALANCE
WEIGHT

fig. 4

PROPELLER BLADE
(4 NEEDED)

2 1/8"

7 1/8"

6. Nail the man's body together, using two ¾″ No. 18 nails to attach each leg to the body after drilling holes for the nails. To attach the arms, drill a hole to insert ⅛″ of sawed-off tubing. Do not fasten the arms too closely to the body, for they must move freely to milk the cow. To hold the tubing in place, use 1½″ No. 6 copper nails. On one side, it will be held by the nail head; on the other, snip off the nail and rivet it off (Fig. 5).

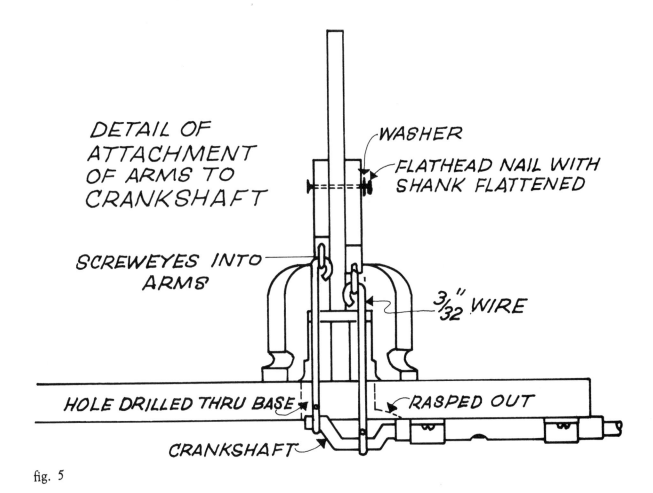

DETAIL OF ATTACHMENT OF ARMS TO CRANKSHAFT

WASHER

FLATHEAD NAIL WITH SHANK FLATTENED

SCREWEYES INTO ARMS

3/32″ WIRE

HOLE DRILLED THRU BASE

RASPED OUT

CRANKSHAFT

fig. 5

fig. 6

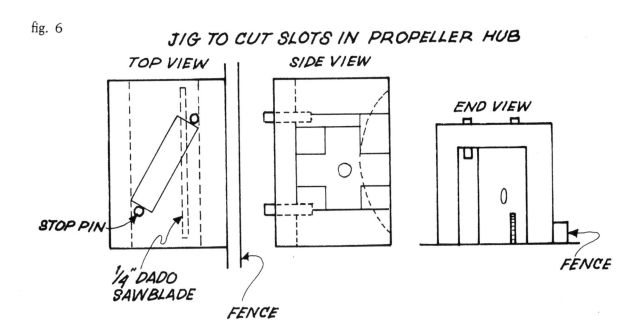

JIG TO CUT SLOTS IN PROPELLER HUB

TOP VIEW

SIDE VIEW

END VIEW

STOP PIN

¼″ DADO SAWBLADE

FENCE

FENCE

7. To attach the man to his seat, use six ¾″ No. 18 nails (Fig. 4). Also drill a hole through the seat and into the base of the man for a ⅜″ dowel. There should be a corresponding hole for the dowel in the flat base piece. Drive in the dowel. Reinforce it with a 1″ No. 18 nail from the back of the base piece.

8. With a 9/16″ drill, drill into the square base (pedestal) for a ½″ dowel. Attach the square wood base with four No. 6 screw nails, inserted from the top of the flat base.

9. Screw the two screw eyes into the bottoms of the man's hands. (Drill holes for the screw eyes). With pliers, attach the telephone wire to them (Fig. 5).

10. With an acetylene torch, bend one end of a ¼″ rod to the shape of the crankshaft (Fig. 5). With a round file, make slight indentations around the rod to attach the opposite ends of the telephone wires from those connected with the man's hands. In the other end of the rod, there should be a ¼″ die used to thread the end for the propeller. Turn the threads down 1½″ from the end.

11. Bend two 1½″-long, ¾″-wide galvanized tin strips (Fig. 4) to go around the ⅜″ tube into which the steel crankshaft is to be placed. Later, these will be soldered to the shaft and screwed into the flat base piece. (Rods and tubing are available from Peter Frasse in Cambridge, Massachusetts, according to Mr. Hutchins.)

12. With a ½″ dado saw, cut the base into which the propeller blades will be fitted. A block of wood 2″ x 2″ will do. Drill a ¼″ hole in its center (Figs. 6, 7).

13. Put waterproof Ambroid glue into the dado cuts and slide in the propeller blades. Nail them in place with ¾″ No. 18 nails (Fig. 7).

14. Balance the propeller by screwing it into a wooden frame that, in turn, is screwed into a vise. Be sure it can spin freely, however, when you touch it. Hold one pair of blades even across the middle of the frame. Let go. If one blade sinks below the other, it is the heavier. Counterbalance this weight by drilling a hole in the lighter blade and inserting a little lead solder. Test again. If the other blade is still heavier, drill a second hole and add more solder. Continue until each pair of blades is evenly balanced. Then attach the propeller to the steel rod that will link it to the flat base of the whirligig. Hold it in place on both sides with a washer and nut (Fig. 4).

15. Insert the shaft into the tube to go under the flat base piece. Solder and screw galvanized tin supports to the underside of the flat base with ⅝″ No. 5 screws (Fig. 4). Attach the telephone wires in the man's hand to the filed-off surfaces of the rod, squeezing them into place with pliers.

Wilson Hutchins with his whirligig of a man sawing wood

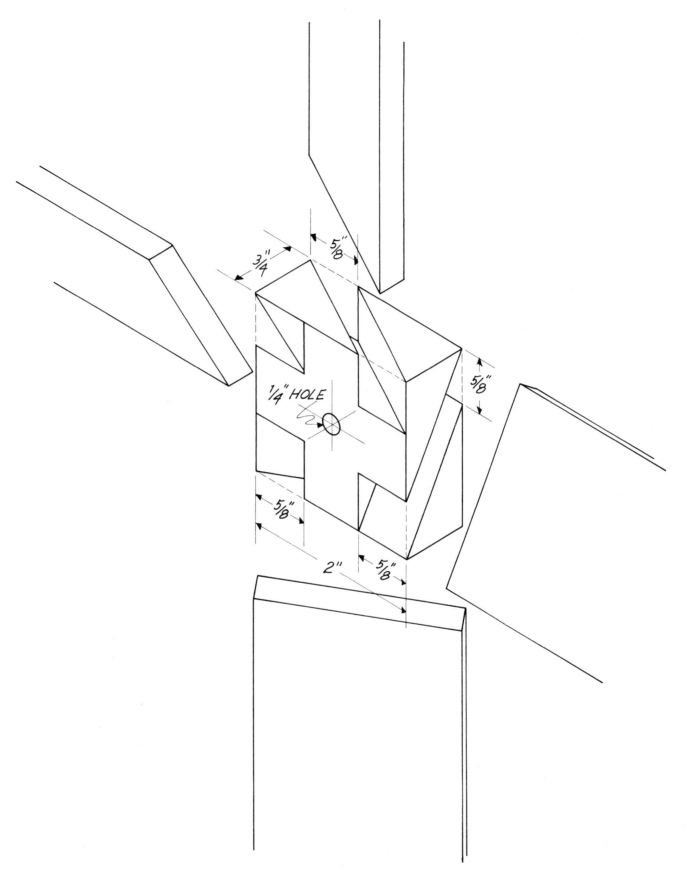

fig. 7

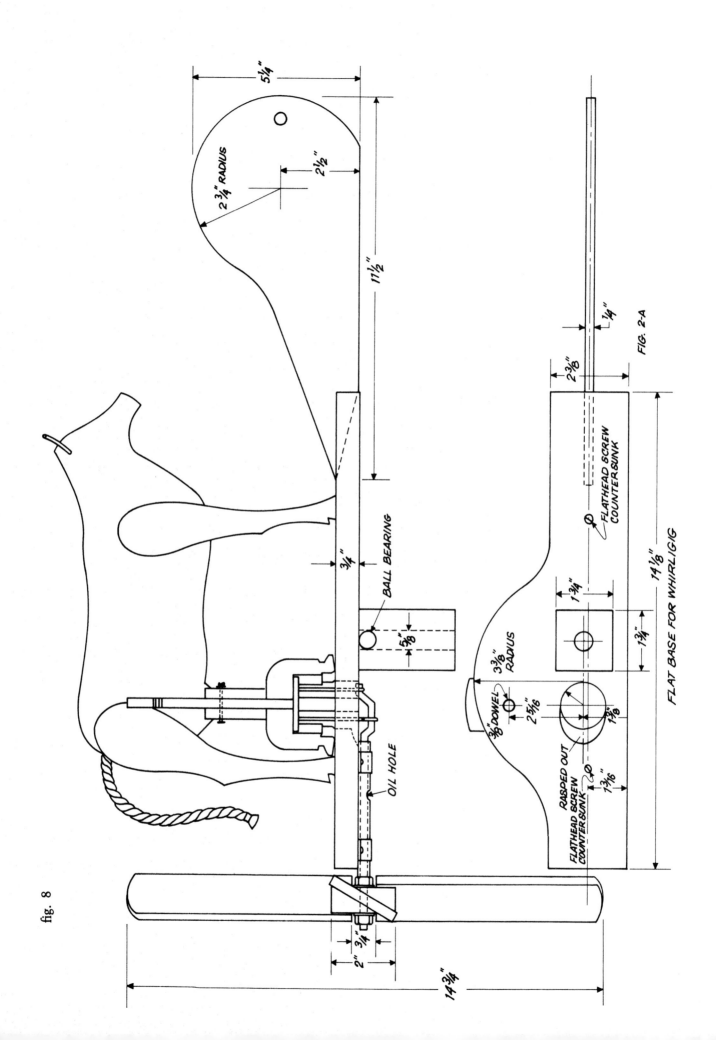

fig. 8

5¼"

2 ¾" RADIUS

2½"

11½"

2⅜"

¼"

FIG. 2-A

FLATHEAD SCREW
COUNTERSUNK

3¾"

1¾"

14⅛"

FLAT BASE FOR WHIRLIGIG

3⅜" RADIUS

2⁵⁄₁₆"

1⅛"

⅜" DOWEL

RASPED OUT

FLATHEAD SCREW
COUNTERSUNK

1¾₁₆"

BALL BEARING

¾"

⅝"

OIL HOLE

2" ¾"

14¾"

16. Fit the ¼″ plywood rudder into the back of the flat base piece (Fig. 8). Fasten it in place with two 1″ No. 8 finish nails, but do not drive them all the way in in case you wish to replace the rudder later (plywood warps) or remove it if the whirligig is to be transported.

17. After the whirligig is assembled "paint" all its raw edges of plywood and all its surfaces (faces and edges) of masonite with a waterproof glue. This prevents absorption of moisture. When the glue dries, paint the whirligig with ordinary outdoor house paint, colorfully and simply.

18. Drill a hole 1″ deep to insert the cow's tail — a rope painted black. Nail it in place with a 1″ No. 18 nail.

19. Drill a hole all the way through the length of the square pedestal for a ½″ dowel (Fig. 9). Be sure that it is perpendicular. If you like, you can put a ⅜″ ball bearing into the hole before the dowel to facilitate spinning in the wind.

SUPPORT POST

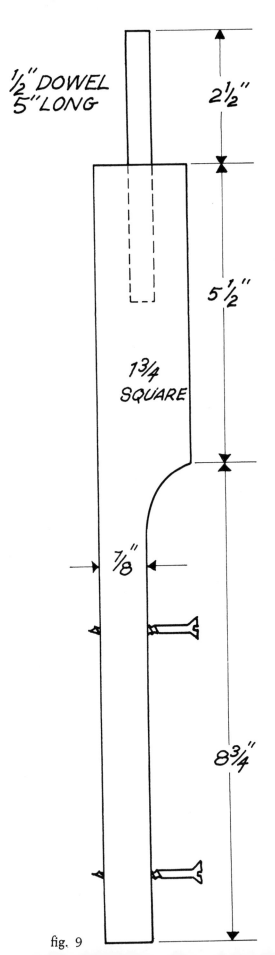

½″ DOWEL 5″ LONG

2½″

5½″

1¾ SQUARE

⅞″

8¾″

fig. 9

■ Since it was necessary to limit the number of craftsmen featured, in detail, in this book, the following directory of traditional artisans judged notable by their colleagues, but not discussed in the preceding pages, is offered.

Decorative Bird Carvers: W. J. McChesney of Edgartown, Massachusetts; Arnold Melbye of South Yarmouth, Massachusetts; Ted Mullikin of Old Saybrook, Connecticut; Harry Ross of South Paris, Maine; Robert and Virginia Warfield of Jaffrey, New Hampshire; and John A. Franco of Assonet, Massachusetts

Birdhouse Builder: Maurice Paré of Plainfield, Connecticut

Jigsaw Puzzle Artists: Peter Green of Wiscasset, Maine, and Steve Richardson of Stave Puzzles in Norwich, Vermont

Boat Builders: Malcolm Brewer of Camden, Maine; George Hodgdon of East Boothbay, Maine; and Bud McIntosh of Dover, New Hampshire

Doll Makers: Noreen Huff of Clinton, Maine

Dollhouse Builders: Warren Kimble of Brandon, Vermont; Martin and Kit Sagendorf of Fairfield, Connecticut; and Charles Mead, Oak Bluffs, Massachusetts

Toy Makers: Hank and Carol Glass of Wolcott, Vermont, and Donn Springer of Durham, New Hampshire

Pitchfork Makers: Timothy Gastler, Steve Levine and David Sawyer of Quaker City, New Hampshire

Decoy Carvers: Rolf Coykendall of Weston, Vermont; Charles Murphy of the Sneak Box in Concord, Massachusetts; and Gerald Smith of Marblehead, Massachusetts

Miniature Furniture Makers: Hank Miller of Granville, Massachusetts, and Gus and Alice Schwerdtfeger of Poland Springs, Maine, specializing in Shaker furniture; Mell Prescott (Mrs. Blake Prescott) of Warrenville, Connecticut; and Betty Valentine of Manchester, Connecticut

Fish Carvers: Don and Peter Thompson of Weeks Mills, New Sharon, Maine

Turners: Alan Stirt of Jeffersonville, Vermont

Carvers (primarily of quarterboards, trailboards, figureheads, and signs): David J. Holmes of Plymouth, Maine; Charles Savage of Northeast Harbor, Maine; Paul White of East Sandwich, Massachusetts; and Douglas P. Amidon of Sandwich, Massachusetts

Wind Machine Designers: Daryl Mann of Harpswell, Maine

appendix